Globalizing Care

Feminist Theory and Politics

Virginia Held and Alison Jaggar, *Series Editors*

Globalizing Care: Ethics, Feminist Theory, and International Relations, Fiona Robinson

The Power of Feminist Theory, Amy Allen

The Feminist Standpoint Revisited and Other Essays, Nancy C.M. Hartsock

Feminists Rethink the Self, edited by Diana Tietjens Meyers

Revisioning the Political: Feminist Reconstructions of Traditional Concepts in Western Political Theory, edited by Nancy J. Hirschmann and Christine Di Stephano

Care, Autonomy, and Justice: Feminism and the Ethic of Care, Grace Clement

A Mind of One's Own: Feminist Essays on Reason and Objectivity, edited by Louise M. Antony and Charlotte Witt

Globalizing Care

Ethics, Feminist Theory, and International Relations

Fiona Robinson

Carleton University

Westview Press
A Member of the Perseus Books Group

Feminist Theory and Politics

Published in 1999 in the United States of America by Westview Press, 5500 Central Avenue, Boulder, Colorado 80301-2877, and in the United Kingdom by Westview Press, 12 Hid's Copse Road, Cumnor Hill, Oxford OX2 9JJ

Library of Congress Cataloging-in-Publication Data
Robinson, Fiona.
Globalizing care : ethics, feminist theory, and international relations / Fiona Robinson.
p. cm. — (Feminist theory and politics)
Includes bibliographical references and index.
ISBN 0-8133-3356-3 (hc). — ISBN 0-8133-3357-1 (pbk)
1. International relations—Moral and ethical aspects.
2. Feminist theory. I. Title. II. Series.
JZ1253.2.R63 1999
327.1′01—dc21 98-41072
CIP

The paper used in this publication meets the requirements of the American National Standard for Permanence of Paper for Printed Library Materials Z39.48-1984.

10 9 8 7 6 5 4 3 2 1

Contents

Acknowledgements

This book would not have been possible without the support and advice of a number of people. Geoffrey Hawthorn supervised my doctoral research at the University of Cambridge, where these ideas first took shape. His vast knowledge and patient good nature will always be an inspiration to me. All of my former colleagues at the University of Sussex deserve my thanks for providing me with both lasting friendship and a stimulating intellectual community over the past four years. Michael Nicholson read an early draft of chapter 1, and John Maclean read and commented on an early draft of chapter 6. Conversations with Marc Williams and Christien van den Anker helped me to clarify my arguments. Virginia Held and Alison Jaggar provided me with useful comments on the finished manuscript.

I would like to thank Sue Miller for all her efforts, and her encouragement, during the book's earliest stages. Cathy Murphy, Sarah Warner, and Lisa Wigutoff at Westview Press have been helpful, efficient, and understanding at all stages of the project. Cindy Buck was a most thorough and careful copyeditor.

Perhaps most of all, however, I am grateful to my family. My parents ensured that all possible opportunities for learning were available to me, and they encouraged me, unselfishly, in all my endeavours. My husband, Derek Taylor, has provided me with invaluable support over years of study and writing.

Parts of this book have appeared previously in other publications. An earlier version of chapter 1 appeared as 'Globalising Care: Ethics, Feminist Theory and International Relations', *Alternatives: Social Transformation and Humane Governance* 22, no. 1, January-March 1997, © 1997 by Lynne Rienner Publishers. An earlier version of chapter 7 appeared as 'Beyond Rights and Duties: Building Attachments and Focusing Moral Attention on World Poverty', in Paris Yeros and Sarah Owen, eds., *Poverty in World Politics: Whose Global Era?* London: Macmillan, (forthcoming), © Millenium Publishing Group, and is reprinted with the permission of the publisher. Sections from chapters 1 and 4 have appeared previously in 'The Limits of a Rights-based Approach to International Ethics' in Tony Evans, ed., *Human Rights Fifty Years On: A Reappraisal*. Manchester: Manchester University Press, and New York: St. Martin's Press, 1998.

Fiona Robinson

1

Introduction: Rethinking International Ethics

It is possible to encapsulate all the several normative questions in the one central question: 'What in general is a good reason for action by or with regard to states?'

Mervyn Frost, *Ethics and International Relations*, 1996 (p. 79)

We act rightly 'when the time comes' not out of strength of will but out of the quality of our usual attachments and the kind of energy and discernment which we have available. And to this the whole activity of our consciousness is relevant.

Iris Murdoch, *Existentialists and Mystics*, 1997 (p. 357)

This book presents a critical analysis of both commonplace assumptions and dominant modes of reasoning about ethics in international relations and attempts to work towards a new understanding of the nature and purposes of moral enquiry in the context of global social relations. I start from the general assumption that ethics is not distinct from, but embedded in, both the practices and the theories of international relations. Moreover, I assume that those practices and theories are themselves mutually constituting. 'Ethics' and 'international relations' cannot be regarded as the opposition of 'ought' and 'is'; the way that we live and organize ourselves can be understood only through reference to the historically developed and evolving ideas and beliefs that we hold—ideas and beliefs which have value and thus reflect our ideas about morality.

These starting points might be regarded by many as counterintuitive. Commonsense reasoning seems to tell us that ethics plays no part in the ruthless business of international politics. Moreover, until recently, most theorists of international relations have sought, not without some considerable degree of success, to distance the discipline from moral considerations and ethical reasoning through the development of increasingly scientific theories and methodologies. In spite of this, however, the development of orthodox international relations theory has relied heavily on claims regarding knowledge, truth, and the nature of existence that are inherent in and intimately linked to the dominant traditions in Western moral theory. This influence is evident in the 'new normative theory' in international relations, much of which remains narrow in its modes of moral reasoning and use of moral concepts and is preoccupied with questions regarding the justification of moral action—of the 'rightness' or 'wrongness' of moral claims based on their epistemological status. The aim of this book is to broaden the scope of our thinking about ethics in the context of global social relations, first, through a critique of the 'leading traditions' in international ethics, and second, through an exploration of the ways in which certain strands of feminist moral philosophy may offer us an alternative perspective from which to view ethics in international relations. This single aim, then, serves a dual purpose in that it addresses and seeks to broaden and enrich not one but two academic debates.

First, it seeks to expand the debate on 'normative theory' in international relations by bringing in the important contributions from feminist moral theory—contributions which are noticeably absent from the debate. One of the key objectives of this book, then, is to demonstrate that a feminist ethics—and particularly, ideas surrounding what is widely known as the 'ethics of care'—can offer insights regarding the nature of morality, moral motivation, and moral relations which could move the debate in international relations theory beyond its currently narrow frontiers.

The arguments of this book also address the literature on and debates surrounding feminist ethics, and specifically the common criticism of the ethics of care that it is personal and parochial and therefore 'unable to address large-scale social or global problems', and that its focus on 'attention to intimates and proximate strangers can lead to neglecting those who are further away'.[1] I argue that it is indeed the case that an 'orthodox' reading of care ethics may be an untenable basis on which to construct an approach to moral relations for the contemporary global context. What is required, instead, is what I call a 'critical ethics of care', which is characterized by a relational ontology—that is, it starts from the premise that people live in and perceive the world within social relationships; moreover, this approach recognizes that these relationships are both a source of moral motivation and moral responsiveness and a basis for the construction and expression of power and knowledge. The moral values of an approach to international ethics based on care, then, are centred on the maintenance and promotion of good personal and social relations among concrete persons, both within and across existing communities. These values, I argue, are relevant not only to small-scale or existing personal attachments but to all levels of social relations and, thus, to international or global relations.

Ethics and International Relations

It has been argued by Steve Smith that we are experiencing a resurgence of normative theory in IR.[2] Indeed, he made this claim in 1992 in a review of a new book by Chris Brown called *International Relations Theory: New Normative Approaches*.[3] Brown gave readers an introduction to normative theory in IR, which he described as

> that body of work which addresses the moral dimension of international relations and the wider questions of meaning and interpretation generated by the discipline. At its most basic it addresses the ethical nature of the relations between communities/states, whether in the context of the old agenda, which focused on violence and war, or the new(er) agenda, which mixes these traditional concerns with the modern demand for international distributive justice.

This was in contrast to empirical theory, which Brown described as 'descriptive, explanatory and predictive, attempting to provide an accurate account of how the world works'.[4] Six years earlier, Mervyn Frost's book, *Towards a Normative Theory of International Relations*—which was rewritten and republished in 1996—argued that normative problems in IR are those that require of us that *we make judgements about what ought to be done*. Normative questions, he claimed, are not answered by pointing to the way things are in the world.[5]

I would argue, however, that while such a conceptualization of normative theory has been both important and useful in highlighting and reviving the debates in ethics and political philosophy which have been ignored by, despite being crucial to, IR theory, the strict delineation of what counts as normative theory could also be seen as harmful and restricting. Much of what is currently described as ethics in international relations is characterized by, first, ethical arguments which are primarily justificatory in nature, and second, the use of a limited number of moral concepts in building those arguments: specifically, rights, obligations or duties, contracts, fairness, reciprocity, autonomy, and justice. When I say that the arguments are justificatory, I mean that they focus on constructing principles which can be applied to situations to find reasons which justify the taking of action; as Frost says, all the normative questions in IR can be encapsulated in one central question: 'What in general is a good reason for action by or with regard to states?'[6] These arguments are concerned with the epistemological status of moral judgements—the construction of principles to determine right and wrong. Because the moral concepts described earlier are limited in number, the modes of moral reasoning used are, in general, deontological-liberal or liberal-contractualist in nature.

This, I argue, has led to the creation of a body of work which is highly abstract, formalized, and often conservative. Far from challenging the status quo in IR theory, this sort of normative theory can reinforce it. As Roger Spegele has argued, the rise of positivist-empiricist epistemology in contemporary IR theory is inextricably bound up with a certain type of ethics, which is characterized by five features, namely, that moral reasoning is obligational, universal, impartial, prescriptive, and rational. This kind of ethics poses no threat to the leading positivist-empiricist idea that science is the realm of observation and ethics is the realm of 'the normative'; understood in this way, he argues, it is not hard to understand why positivist empiricists have been attracted to neo-Kantian noncognitivism.[7]

Both the *epistemology*—concerning the nature and status of knowledge—and the *ontology*—concerning the nature and status of being or existence—of the dominant liberal traditions in Western moral and political theory resonate strongly in the so-called settled norms of international relations.[8] As has been suggested, this is rarely the way that the relationship between international relations and ethics is understood. Because versions of Kantianism and neo-Kantianism are (mistakenly) taken 'exclusively to define what an argument in ethics must be', the universalism of such theories is usually understood to be at odds with the apparent denial of universalism evident in the most basic premises of realism.[9] But as Rob Walker has observed, the ethical universalism of Kant and the 'realist submission to a Weberian power politics' in international relations are 'merely the twin offsprings of modernity'.[10] Thus, while we tend to concentrate on the chasm between 'justice' or 'the good' as the lofty aim of ethics and 'order' or 'stability' as the more immanent aspiration of international relations theory, these turn out to be, on closer inspection, two sides of the same coin rather than an intractable opposition.

Moreover, while we may contrast the universalism embodied in Kantian deontological ethics with the apparently 'amoral communitarianism' of realist theory, and while international relations theorists, especially in the United States, tend to make much of the liberal/realist controversy in international relations, these popular oppositions again belie the degree to which all prevailing IR theory has been heavily influenced by the same broad traditions of ethical and political thought: specifically, by the ideas embodied in Enlightenment rationalism, liberalism, and contractarianism. Indeed, in spite of the differences between realist and liberal accounts of international relations, both perspectives share ideas about autonomy and agency—the stress on explaining the behaviour of separate and typically self-interested units of action.[11] It is because they emerge historically out of the same tradition of thought that these two 'most popular' theoretical perspectives overlap and reinforce each other by speaking to common concerns and issues.[12]

Indeed, it is no accident that, as David Mapel and Terry Nardin note in the concluding chapter of their book *Traditions of International Ethics*, 'most of the traditions discussed in this book employ the idea or at least the language of rights'.[13] They do so because virtually all of the traditions represent, broadly speaking, a *single* tradition—one which emphasizes rights and other liberal values such as non-interference, autonomy, self-determination, fairness, reciprocity, and rationality. Certainly, while we can isolate and distinguish among the various traditions of ethical thought in international relations—classical and contemporary realism, natural law, Kant's global rationalism, utilitarianism, contractarianism, liberalism, and rights-based ethics—the tendency to isolate these as 'competing' traditions serves, naturally, to obscure their similarities and common historical and intellectual foundations.

Moreover, although Mapel and Nardin frame the debate in international ethics in terms of the conflict between 'rule-oriented' and 'consequence-oriented' traditions, the emerging consensus is that the more salient opposition is between 'universalist' or 'cosmopolitan' ethics and 'particularist' or 'communitarian' approaches. This dichotomy is used by Brown[14] and Linklater[15] to explore the historical development from the rationalism of Kant to the historicist romanticism of Herder and Hegel. This latter tradition is thought to be based on appeals to Aristotelian virtue, local communities, and republican conceptions of citizenship—thus, to a more organic notion of community rather than to the individualistic, deontological conception of individuals co-operating for the sake of mutual gain. Certainly, these two 'traditions' represent contrasting views of the nature of persons, and of ideas such as liberty and community. But here again, the differences between these approaches are often overstated; communitarianism retains a broadly liberal agenda, so that these two positions are competing only over the question of the source of moral value and hence the *scope* of our moral community(ies), rather than articulating radically different views regarding the nature of moral relations. Moreover, as shown in chapter 4, the particularist ethical starting point of communitarianism, its tendency to draw moral boundaries around established political communities (nation-states), and its association within international relations theory with theories of nationalism and even realism, have meant that most attempts to articulate a theory of *international* or *global* ethics have, for obvious reasons, rejected communitarianism and resorted, via either Kant or Marx (and occasionally both), to some form of cosmopolitanism.[16] As I argue at length in chapter 4, the cosmopolitan/communitarian debate is a limited, often misunderstood, and increasingly irrelevant debate between two equally untenable positions; the result is not only an impoverished conceptual debate on international ethics but limits on the search for real, useful answers to pressing questions about what motivates people to identify with and care for one another.[17]

If we recognize the extent to which the defining principles of the orthodox neo-realist and neo-liberal theories in international relations—autonomy, sovereignty, reciprocity—are historically constituted through the dominant traditions of Western moral and political philosophy, we will also recognize that ethics must not be seen as something separate from international relations but as something which is inherent in both the relations themselves and our dynamic and socially constructed understandings of them. The theory of international relations as an academic discipline cannot be separated from those ideas in moral and political philosophy from which it has evolved. But more than this, if we truly reject the assumptions of positivism and the rigid separation of politics and ethics, then we must reject the deontological distinction between 'normative judgements', on the one hand, and 'the way things are in the world' on the other. Indeed, we must begin to think about a different kind of ethics—'a less rule-bound phenomenology'[18] that is contextual and situated, that starts from our experience of the world, and that focuses on real, particular individuals whose lives find meaning only within webs of personal and social relationships. It is to this task that the remainder of this book is devoted.

Outline of the Book

Chapter 2 explores the central questions and controversies surrounding the ethics of care and approaches the idea of care in the global context. It examines three contentious debates surrounding the ethics of care: first, the 'gendering' of ethics and, specifically, the alleged 'essentialism' and practical 'antifeminism' of care (some critics argue that identifying a woman's morality is not only false and exclusive but can support and uphold the structures that have subordinated women); second, the debate between 'justice thinking' and 'care thinking', and the contention that only a combination of these two types of moral thinking can provide an adequate approach to ethics; and third, and most important, the alleged parochialism of care. Finally, this chapter sketches a picture of a critical ethics of care that seeks to combine the strengths of care ethics with an attention to structural and normative inequalities in the global system.

Chapter 3 sets out in more detail the argument for a feminist international ethics based on the idea of a critical ethics of care. It discusses the nature and purpose of feminist theory and, specifically, feminist ethics. I argue that an ethics of care shares with pragmatism and other philosophical critiques of deontological ethics a scepticism regarding ethical *theory*, favouring instead an approach which pays close attention to particulars in our efforts to understand the nature of moral and other social relations. Thus, this feminist international ethics does not resemble an ethical *theory* but rather a kind of moral phenomenology, which explores the sociopolitical conditions, the moral and psychological dispositions, the personal and social relations, and the individual and institutional strategies which may work towards overcoming exclusion and promoting care and focused moral attention on a global scale.

Chapter 4 explores the dominant traditions in international ethics. First, it examines what I see to be strong links—in terms of both ontology and value advocacy—between liberal contractarianism and rights-based ethics, on the one hand, and mainstream modernist approaches in international relations theory on the other. I argue that shared assumptions about the primacy of values such as autonomy, independence, non-interference/non-intervention, self-determination, reciprocity, fairness, and rights have led to liberal ethics representing the 'acceptable voice of morality' in international relations. This, I argue, has resulted in the creation of a global 'culture of neglect' through a systematic devaluing of notions of interdependence, relatedness, and positive involvement in the lives of distant others. This chapter also examines the cosmopolitan/communitarian debate in international relations theory, arguing that the portrayal of these perspectives as antithetical is overstated and based on a confusion, and that neither picture offers a plausible or meaningful position from which to understand moral relations in the contemporary global context.

Chapter 5 looks more closely at the ways in which a critical ethics of care might be situated in the contemporary world. I argue that, in the current era of globalization, the nature of time, space, and social relations is changing and our assumptions about identity and community in the world are in question. It is suggested that the commonplace assumption that a 'globalizing' world is 'one which demands an account of ethical possibility that begins with the priority of people as people' is fundamentally flawed, in that it regards this priority as a precondition for both moral relations and moral enquiry.[19] What characterizes the contemporary global order is not ethical convergence, unity, or a sense of seamless 'humanity', but rather the persistence and sometimes the exacerbation of structures and processes of exclusion, marginalization, and domination. While it is certainly the case that the nature of individual identities and patterns of relationships across borders is changing rapidly, we must be wary of universalizing solutions in a world which is still fundamentally characterized by difference.

Chapter 6 argues that an adequate approach to morality in the contemporary world must respond to the patterns of exclusion discussed in chapter 5. The first section of the chapter explores arguments from critical theory and postmodernism, which offer some of the more promising responses in international relations theory to the problem of social exclusion on a global scale. I argue in favour of a social-relations approach to difference and exclusion; this approach draws upon the strengths of critical theory but argues that the current world order demands an interpersonal, relational morality which focuses on the real contexts of relationships among particular persons. Such an approach recognizes that patterns of exclusion on a global scale are systematic and structural, and that an adequate global ethics must address these patterns through the adoption of an appropriate ontology, based on relationships, and epistemology, based on the social construction of knowledge.

Finally, chapter 7 explores a critical ethics of care in the sociopolitical and economic contexts of international relations. I explore the notion of ethical 'issues' in international relations and the preoccupation with the problem of sovereignty and intervention. Through an analysis of ethical approaches to humanitarian intervention and the wider problem of poverty in a North-South context, this chapter demonstrates the ways in which a critical ethics of care casts a new light on the moral nature of, and appropriate moral responses to, global social and political relations. This chapter does *not* argue that 'a more caring world' is one in which global poverty and human suffering will be eradicated. Rather, it suggests that the ways in which we confront the profound moral questions arising from these issues will be radically and irretrievably altered when we renounce our principled moral theories of obligation in favour of a vision of ethics which recognizes the moral incompleteness, and the profound contextual inappropriateness, of an ethics which seeks to uphold impartiality by maintaining a depersonalized, distancing attitude towards others.

Notes

1. Alison M. Jaggar, 'Caring as a Feminist Practice of Moral Reason', in Virginia Held and Alison Jaggar, ed., *Justice and Care: Essential Readings in Feminist Ethics*, Boulder, CO: Westview Press, 1995, pp. 194–196.

2. Steve Smith, 'The Forty Years' Detour: The Resurgence of Normative Theory in International Relations', *Millennium: Journal of International Studies* 21, no. 3, 1992: 489–508.

3. Chris Brown, *International Relations Theory: New Normative Approaches*, Hemel Hempstead: Harvester Wheatsheaf, 1992.

4. Ibid., pp. 2–3. It should be noted that Brown uses this distinction primarily for analytical purposes, and that he acknowledges the risks involved in making such a distinction. He reminds us that 'a very great deal of what is traded in international relations as non-normative theory is steeped in normative assumptions' (p. 3), but he insists that 'normative is a term that is so widely used now to

describe the broad area in question that it is futile to try to resist (p. 4). Thus, although the book is not primarily concerned with this question, Brown does explicitly resist the idea that normative theory is some kind of cordoned-off area separate from the rest of the discipline of international relations (p. 4).

5. Mervyn Frost, *Ethics in International Relations: A Constitutive Theory,* Cambridge: Cambridge University Press, 1996.

6. Ibid., p. 79.

7. Roger Spegele, *Political Realism and International Theory,* Cambridge: Cambridge University Press, 1996, p. 192.

8. I have taken the term 'settled norms' from Frost, *Ethics and International Relations,* pp. 105–112.

9. Geoffrey Hawthorn, *Enlightenment and Despair: A History of Social Theory,* 2nd ed., Cambridge: Cambridge University Press, 1987, p. 262.

10. R. B. J. Walker, *Inside/Outside: International Relations as Political Theory,* Cambridge: Cambridge University Press, 1993, p. 156.

11. Robert Keohane, 'International Liberalism Reconsidered', in John Dunn, ed., *The Economic Limits to Modern Politics,* Cambridge: Cambridge University Press, 1992, p. 174.

12. Charles R. Kegley, Jr., 'The Neoliberal Challenge to Realist Theories of World Politics: An Introduction', in Charles R. Kegley, Jr., ed., *Controversies in International Relations Theory: Realism and the Neoliberal Challenge,* New York: St. Martin's Press, 1995, p. 26.

13. David R. Mapel and Terry Nardin, 'Convergence and Divergence in International Ethics', in Terry Nardin and David R. Mapel, eds., *Traditions of International Ethics,* Cambridge: Cambridge University Press, 1992, p. 311.

14. Brown, *International Relations Theory,* pp. 52–81.

15. Andrew Linklater, *Men and Citizens in the Theory of International Relations,* London: Macmillan, 1990.

16. Onora O'Neill uses the example of Michael Walzer's work to demonstrate the inability of communitarianism to address questions of international ethics. She claims that because Walzer holds that the largest sphere of justice is the political community, rights and duties do not and cannot go beyond borders. A commitment to community is a commitment to the historical boundaries of political communities, whatever these happen to be and whatever injustices their constitution and their preservation cost. Thus, O'Neill claims that when boundaries are taken wholly seriously, international justice is not just played down but 'wiped off the ethical map'. See Onora O'Neill, 'Justice, Gender, and International Boundaries', in Robin Attfield and Barry Wilkins, eds., *International Justice and the Third World,* London: Routledge, 1992, p. 56.

17. See Fiona Robinson, 'Rethinking Ethics in an Era of Globalisation', Sussex Papers in International Relations, no. 2, Brighton: University of Sussex, 1996.

18. I take this phrase from Judith Shklar, *The Faces of Injustice,* New Haven, CT: Yale University Press, 1990, p. 28.

19. Walker, *Inside/Outside,* p. 76.

2

The Ethics of Care

This chapter explores the increasingly prolific work in moral and political philosophy which has challenged the traditional focus on the autonomous, abstract, rational agent and on 'justice' as the first virtue of society. Specifically, it examines the work of feminist theorists who have developed what is now widely known as 'the ethics of care'. This literature has its origins in the work of moral and social psychologists such as Nancy Chodorow and, most notably, Carol Gilligan, who famously argued that many girls and women tend to interpret moral problems differently from the way boys and men tend to interpret them. Feminist theorists who developed these initial insights have argued that a morality of caring sees persons as interdependent rather than independent individuals, and that ethics should address issues of caring and empathy and relationships between people rather than only or primarily the rational decisions of autonomous moral agents.[1]

So influential has this work been among feminists that it is tempting to take the phrases 'ethics of care' and 'feminist ethics' as synonymous. However, as Susan Hekman points out, 'even a cursory examination of the literature on feminist ethics reveals that there is no single "feminist moral theory"'. Thus, while it is clear that 'discussions of the ethic of care, and of the "different" moral voice of women, have been an important force in feminist ethics in the last decade', it would be incorrect to suggest that all or even most feminist moral theorists wholeheartedly embrace the ethics of care, or indeed to suggest that they categorically reject the notions of autonomy, justice, rights, and duties embodied in 'traditional' moral theory.[2] Moreover, it would also be wrong to suggest that it is only feminists who have rejected the central assumptions of traditional Kantianism or utilitarianism; although their arguments certainly differ in many important ways from those embodied in the ethics of care, many moral philosophers who argue in favour of 'alternative' or untraditional approaches to ethics are clearly sympathetic to both the concerns and the ethical starting points articulated by many feminist moral theorists.[3]

With this aim in mind, this chapter explores in some detail the emergence of the idea of an ethics of care and traces the development of this alternative understanding of morality and moral relations. It addresses three central controversies surrounding care: first, the debate over the alleged 'essentialism' of much theorizing about care, which embraces the question of whether there can be such a thing as a morality of and for women; second, the debate between 'justice' and 'care', which addresses the alleged incommensurability of the two perspectives and asks whether an adequate moral theory must, or indeed can, include elements from both; and third, whether 'care' describes what is essentially a personal moral response in that it relies on relationships between particular individuals and ignores the wider moral implications of social structures and institutions, which may be largely responsible for exclusion and suffering. Related to this last question, of course, is the question which is of central importance to this book: whether care ethics is intrinsically parochial and thus ignores (or is ill-equipped to address) questions of moral relations among distant strangers in the global context.

An analysis of these questions demonstrates that, far from being three separate debates, they are very closely related. Indeed, these debates have arisen among both the critics and the advocates of care owing to fear, or skepticism, about the ability of 'care' to act as a starting point for moral reasoning and to deal effectively with a broad range of moral dilemmas. I argue, however, that all three of these questions arise only when care is understood in a particular way. If care ethics is understood solely as a 'corrective' to universalistic, impartialist theories, or simply as a 'useful addition' to our moral vocabulary, then it will always retain its image as a 'private', 'personal' morality which is antithetical to justice and most relevant to women as mothers and, more generally, occupiers of the private sphere of the household and the family. This chapter illustrates that care can transcend these apparent limitations when it is understood not simply as a narrow psychological disposition, or a 'moral theory', but as a value and a practice which informs our daily lives, with the capacity to transform our understanding of both morality and politics and, ultimately, of the relationship between them.

Morality and Psychology

The philosophers of deontological ethics—from Kant to G. E. Moore—have been staunch in their condemnation of the 'naturalistic fallacy'—the conflation of the way human beings *ought* to behave with the way they actually *do* behave. As a result, ethics as a philosophical field has remained, for some time, almost totally severed from psychology and sociology. Although psychologists like Jean Piaget and Lawrence Kohlberg have done interesting crossover work in moral psychology, their contributions have been largely consigned to the margins of 'mainstream' psychology and have received rather cool responses from mainstream moral philosophers.[4] It could be argued, however, that cognitive and developmental psychologists have recently become increasingly interested in moral reasoning, and that, likewise, moral philosophers have come to recognize the importance of psychology in their own work.[5]

For example, Lawrence Blum's *Moral Perception and Particularity* represents his 'continuing effort to help bring moral psychology into more direct contact with contemporary moral theory'. He argues that owing to moral philosophers' focus on rational principle, impartiality, and universality and on rules and codes in ethics, the importance of the psychological dimension of moral life has been masked, implicitly denied, or at least neglected. Drawing on the work of Iris Murdoch, Blum explores what he calls the psychic capacities involved in moral agency and moral responsiveness—emotion, perception, imagination, motivation, and judgement.[6] Murdoch herself, ever critical of 'English' or 'Oxford' philosophy, has argued that a working 'philosophical psychology' is required, even if only to connect the language of modern psychology with the language of virtue: 'We need a moral philosophy which can speak significantly of Freud and Marx, and out of which aesthetic and political views can be generated. We need a moral philosophy in which the concept of love, so rarely mentioned now by philosophers, can once again be made central'.[7]

This movement towards an examination of the psychology of moral agency is evident in the work of many feminist developmental psychologists and social theorists, who have relied on both empirical psychology and psychological theory in the development of new understandings of the nature of morality and moral motivation. Of these, perhaps the most important for the development of the ethics of care is Carol Gilligan, whose work was partly a response to that of her former colleague, the psychologist Lawrence Kohlberg. In the development of her own ideas and theories, Gilligan was influenced by Nancy Chodorow, whose work has focused on psychoanalysis and the sociology of gender.

In *The Reproduction of Mothering,* Chodorow analyzes the way women's mothering is reproduced across generations. She argues that the contemporary reproduction of mothering occurs through social, structurally induced psychological processes. Specifically, she suggests that the needs and capacities of mothering in girls are built into and grow out of the mother-daughter relationship itself. By contrast, women as mothers (and men as not-mothers) produce sons whose nurturant capacities and needs have been systematically curtailed and repressed. This process, she argues, prepares men for their less affective family role and for primary participation in the impersonal extrafamilial world of work and public life. Thus, Chodorow offers an explanation not only for the reproduction of mothering but for the contrasting moral-psychological 'starting points' of men and women: 'The sexual and familial division of labor in which women mother and are more involved in interpersonal, affective relationships than men produces in daughters and sons a division of psychological capacities which leads them to reproduce this sexual and familial division of labor'.[8]

Chodorow cites two contributions to feminist theory as having influenced her work. First is the 'sex-gender system'—'a set of arrangements by which the biological raw material of human sex and procreation is shaped by . . . social intervention'. This system is analytically separate from the dominant mode of production in any society, but the two must be seen as 'empirically and structurally intertwined'.[9] The second construction extends the first by suggesting that one can distinguish analytically in all societies between domestic and public aspects of social organization. Because mothers and children form the core of domestic organization, men find a primary social location in the public sphere. The public sphere, unlike the private, defines its institutions according to normative/social, rather than 'natural', criteria. Society is thus defined as masculine, and this gives men the power to create and enforce institutions of social and political control—including those which control sexual reproduction.[10]

Even at this early stage in her argument, it is clear that Chodorow does not limit it to narrow, psychological concerns. Hers is a critical analysis of the institutional and normative social arrangements which perpetuate the hierarchical, structural differentiation of domestic and public spheres. It is within this context that she seeks to explain why women, rather than men, are 'mothers'. Rejecting 'arguments from nature', Chodorow relies on psychoanalytic theory to demonstrate how the family division of labour in which women mother gives socially and historically specific meaning to gender itself. Specifically, she uses object-relations theory to show how women grow up to have generalized relational capacities and needs, and how women and men create the kinds of interpersonal relationships which make it likely that women will remain in the domestic sphere—in the sphere of reproduction—and, in turn, mother the next generation.[11]

Not surprisingly, there has been much criticism of object-relations theory, both as a psychoanalytic theory and as the basis for ascribing different moral voices to different genders. As Lois McNay notes, while many feminists have found in Chodorow's theory a cogent account of the psychic differences between men and women, it nevertheless has problematic foundations in ahistorical and essentialist assumptions. Lacanian theorists have criticized the object-relations theorists' over-stable conception of the subject, arguing that the unconscious must be recognized as a source of discontinuous and chaotic drives which render the ego a perpetually unstable phenomenon. By claiming that certain kinds of identifications are primary, object-relations theorists make the relational life of the infant primary over psychic development itself, conflating the psyche with the ego and relegating the unconscious to a less significant role.[12]

Feminist anthropologists, moreover, criticize the extent to which object-relations theorists give the role of the mother as nurturer a central place in their ahistorical, acultural definition of women. Thus, the theory is accused of focusing on Western societies—where the notions of 'woman' and 'mother' overlap—and ignoring the link in particular cultures between the category of woman and certain attributes of motherhood such as maternal love, nurturance, fertility, and so on. It has been argued that despite its claim to value heterogeneity, mothering theory does not develop the methodological tools to deal with difference related to class, ethnic, and other cultural variants.[13]

When exploring the link between feminist ethics and object-relations theory, it is also important to address the more general dangers in linking morality to psychology. In spite of the importance of bringing psychology into moral and political philosophy, we must be vigilant in ensuring that the advances made by an exploration of morality which considers qualities such as perception and motivation does not retreat too far into the relatively narrow frontiers of human cognition, leaving behind the human suffering and inequality of the social and political world. On the other hand, while traditional moral theorists may claim that the greatest danger of linking ethics to psychology lies in the conflation of what 'is' with what 'ought to be', it could be argued that this is not a problem but rather a step towards the solution. Thinking about morality must start from experience of the way that people actually behave, and it must explore how that behaviour is socially constructed, asking how attitudes and practices manifest themselves at the level of social relations. If an exploration of the psychological capacities involved in perception of and responsiveness to moral situations can help us in constructing such a view of ethics, then its contribution ought to be taken seriously.

Gilligan and the 'Different Voice'

While important in its own right, Nancy Chodorow's work is now well known for its influence on Carol Gilligan and her research. It was in 1982 that the first edition of Gilligan's book, *In a Different Voice,* was published. Between that time and 1993, when the second edition was published, it would not be an exaggeration to claim that the book influenced the entire direction of Anglo-American moral philosophy. Whether to support it, develop it, or condemn it, a wide range of moral philosophers began to address the challenge posed by care ethics to traditional Kantian or utilitarian moral reasoning. Today, five years after the publication of the second edition, the debate continues.

In a Different Voice is the result of empirical research in developmental psychology. Gilligan tells her readers of how her subjects spoke about themselves, about morality, and about their judgements and responses to a variety of 'moral dilemmas'. She claims to have heard a distinction in these 'voices'—two ways of speaking about moral problems, two modes of describing the relationships between other and self. In recording these different voices, Gilligan posits that the disparity between women's experience and the representation of human development, rather than signifying a problem in women's development, may in fact signify a problem in the representation—'a limitation in the conception of human condition, an omission of certain truths about life'.[14]

Specifically, Gilligan challenges the model of moral development put forward by Lawrence Kohlberg—a six-stage, three-level progression from an egocentric understanding of fairness based on individual need (stages one and two) to a conception of fairness anchored in the shared conventions of societal agreement (stages three and four), and finally to a principled understanding of fairness that rests on the free-standing logic of equality and reciprocity (stages five and six). Moral maturity, according to Kohlberg, results when the subject has reached an understanding of morality as a principled conception of justice.[15] Gilligan challenges this model using empirical and interpretive analysis of girls' and women's responses to a series of moral dilemmas. She argues that the 'different voice' of girls and women does not signify that women simply stop at an 'inferior stage' of moral development but rather that the voices of women represent a different but equal moral orientation which is morally valuable. For example, Gilligan describes how 'Amy', a young female subject, saw the particular moral dilemma not as 'a math problem with humans' but as 'a narrative of relationships that extends over time'; she describes Amy's view of 'a world comprised of relationships rather than of people standing alone, a world that coheres through human connection rather than through systems of rules'.[16] This 'different voice', Gilligan argues, is a sign not of developmental failure but of the failure of moral philosophy and developmental psychology to understand, or even explore, the experiences, feelings, and perceptions of women.

Since the first edition of *In a Different Voice* was published, there has been a substantial amount of research, primarily by feminist moral and political philosophers, around the idea of care and the ways in which it can help us to explain, understand, and ultimately transform the nature of moral, political, and social relations. Here I refer to the excellent work of Annette Baier and Marilyn Friedman, who have broadened the debate to include analysis of the ideas of trust (Baier) and friendship (Friedman); the writings of Virginia Held on care and noncontractual society; and Joan Tronto's 'political argument for an ethic of care'.[17] Even those philosophers who have remained sceptical about this kind of ethics, such as Susan James, Alison Jaggar, and Susan Moller Okin, have recognized its importance as a critique of liberalism and, specifically, its importance to debates regarding citizenship and justice.[18]

Lawrence Blum has argued that Carol Gilligan's body of work in moral developmental psychology is of the first importance for moral philosophy in terms of the questions it raises. If there is a 'different voice'—a coherent set of moral concerns distinct both from the objective and the subjective, the impersonal and the purely personal—then moral theory needs to give some place to these concerns.[19] Blum's work also reminds us that in Gilligan's arguments one can detect a clear resonance of the ideas of Iris Murdoch—the novelist, dramatist, critic, and philosopher who was writing about ethics more than twenty years before Gilligan. As early as the 1950s Murdoch criticized 'Oxford' philosophy, which exalted freedom, right, will, power, and judgement and focused exclusively on 'right action' and the principles and rules which allow us to make moral choices. Against this, Murdoch argued in favour of a moral philosophy which helps us learn how to focus our attention on others whom we can recognize as 'real'; she argued that human beings are naturally 'attached', and that it is the development, purification, and reorientation of those attachments which must be the task of morals. Morality is not just about action, she argued, but can be about learning how to wait, be patient, trust, and listen.[20]

Similarities between Gilligan's arguments and Murdoch's philosophy demonstrate that the ethics of care may be located in the context of a wider critique of Kantian and neo-Kantian ethics. Seyla Benhabib has observed that the widespread recognition and controversy surrounding Gilligan's work arose not only because it reflected the coming of age of women's scholarship within the paradigms of normal science; equally significant was that the kinds of questions which Gilligan was asking of the Kohlbergian paradigm were also being asked of universalist neo-Kantian moral philosophies by a growing and influential number of critics, including communitarians, neo-Aristotelians, and even neo-Hegelians. Thus, she argues, there is a remarkable convergence between the Gilligan-type feminist critique of Kantian universalism and the objections raised by these other thinkers.[21]

That said, it is clear that Gilligan's work has been regarded as so significant not just because it represents an alternative approach to ethics, but because of its specifically feminist orientation. Susan Hekman has suggested that what Gilligan proposes is an alternative framework in which women's 'stories' are interpreted as genuine moral statements. If we interpret relationship, care, and connection as integral to human life and development, then we will interpret women's stories as genuinely moral narratives, distinct from, but every bit as moral as, those based on abstract principles.[22]

As suggested earlier, however, the ethics of care has not been unanimously accepted by all feminists. Indeed, Gilligan's work has received both praise and criticism from feminist and nonfeminist moral philosophers and political theorists. As Hekman notes,

> [Gilligan's work] has been hailed both as the harbinger of a new moral theory and as the final blow to the exhausted masculinist tradition of moral philosophy. It has also been condemned as methodologically unsound, theoretically confused, and even antifeminist. Gilligan's critics and defenders have cast her, respectively, as either villain or savior in the ongoing intellectual debate of the 1980s and 1990s.[23]

One of the most common interpretations of Gilligan's research—rather than of the idea of an ethic of care as such—is that she makes strictly empirical claims and argues that it is a statistically provable fact that men and women have different moral voices. Defined as an empirical claim, Gilligan's thesis is dismissed by critics who argue that her research lacks objectivity and is not adequately supported by evidence. Gilligan herself, however, states unequivocally that her point is interpretive rather than empirical; indeed, as Hekman argues, these empiricist criticisms may persist because Gilligan's theory not only threatens to displace traditional moral theory but also challenges the foundations of empiricist, objective social science. Claiming that Gilligan's work is factually inaccurate, she points out, is one way of dismissing its radical implications.[24]

In addition to this criticism of Gilligan's methodology and her specific empirical and interpretive findings, the idea of an ethic of care itself, and the ambiguities and potential dangers contained within it, has also begun to be criticized. This criticism has been directed at the literature on feminist ethics which has sought to define and advance Gilligan's initial claims. For example, negative criticism of Gilligan's research came, unsurprisingly, from Kohlberg himself, and from the moral and political theorists who sought to defend their 'justice' perspective against Gilligan's claims. Kohlberg's response to Gilligan's feminist challenge was to resort to a reaffirmation of moral boundaries along extremely traditional lines: he suggested that the moral values identified (by Gilligan) with women are associated with the private sphere, with the world of family and friends. Thus, the ethics of the public sphere—the ethics of justice—remains intact. Read in this way, care becomes not a new way of thinking about the nature of morality, but something outside of the sphere of morality altogether. As Habermas has claimed, comparisons between what Gilligan discusses and morality amount to 'a category mistake'.[25]

The social and political implications of Gilligan's work have also been addressed by liberal moral and political philosophers. In his book *Justice as Impartiality,* Brian Barry interprets the ethics of care as an invitation to dispense with morality and replace it with nepotism, favouritism, and injustice. Characterizing caring as a determination to advance at any cost to principle the interests of those to whom we are closely related, Barry fears that children who grow up in such an atmosphere are 'liable to become monsters'. He concludes that a caring society would unavoidably be one in which 'women would have to be excluded from all public responsibilities [because] it would be impossible to trust them to carry out public duties conscientiously'.

> It would have to be concluded that women were incapable of practising first-order impartiality in cases where that is required by holding some public office. Thus, the many leading Western political philosophers who have held precisely this view of women would have got the last laugh.[26]

While it could be argued that Barry's criticisms demonstrate a fundamental misunderstanding of the ethics of care, his conclusion that a society based on caring might reinforce structures and norms which oppress and exclude women must be taken seriously, not least because it is one which is shared by many other philosophers, including a number of feminists.

Arguing from a Kantian perspective, Onora O'Neill argues that feminist critics of the liberal perspective can end up endorsing rather than challenging social and economic structures that marginalize women and confine them to a private sphere. Separatism at the level of ethical theory, she argues, 'can march with acceptance of the powers and traditions that be'. Like Barry, she predicts that such a philosophy would reinforce stereotypes and confine women to the private sphere:

> A stress on caring and relationships to the exclusion of abstract justice may endorse relegation to the nursery and the kitchen, to purdah and to poverty. In rejecting 'abstract liberalism', such feminists converge with traditions that have excluded women from economic and public life. An appeal to 'women's experience', 'women's traditions' and 'women's discourse' does not escape but rather echoes ways in which women have been marginalized or oppressed.[27]

Even feminist theorists, such as Joan Tronto and Sarah Lucia Hoagland, have voiced fears about the 'essentialism' of care ethics and the identification of care as 'women's morality'. Tronto, for example, argues that 'the view that morality is gendered reinforces a number of existing moral boundaries and mitigates against change in our conceptions of politics, of morality and of gender roles'.[28] Hoagland refers to care ethics as an 'ethics of dependence', which is 'often explored within the framework of mothering in which the idea of dependency can be explored and is often romanticized'.[29]

While these concerns over the essentialism of care ethics must be taken seriously, I would argue that it is only a narrow, 'orthodox' ethics of care—the view of care as essentially a morality for women, belonging in the private sphere and valorizing 'dependence' over 'independence'—to which these criticisms actually apply. Indeed, as suggested in subsequent chapters, care ethics can provide the basis for an international ethics only if it is supported by other critical-relational approaches—in social and legal theory, and critical and feminist political economy—which problematize the structures of inclusion and exclusion which exist in the context of global social relations.

In the following three sections, I address three central areas of criticism in turn; first, the idea that care may be specifically a *women's* morality; second, the notion that care and justice are distinct moral orientations; and finally, the claim that care is a personal, private, and hence parochial morality which is ill equipped to address wider social and political concerns.

Gendering Ethics?

In her influential and controversial book *Maternal Thinking*, Sara Ruddick argues that the practice of mothering—which includes, among other activities, protecting, nurturing, and training—gives rise to specific metaphysical attitudes, cognitive capacities, and conceptions of virtue. Among these virtues, Ruddick identifies attentive, clear-sighted love, but also the ability to wait and the ability to trust and be trustworthy. Maternal action, she argues, is prompted by the ability to act, and when it is most successful, it gives way to the action it informs.[30] However, according to Ruddick, maternal thinking is not only relevant to the 'private sphere' of the family and home but also has a public, and indeed a political, significance. The political importance of maternal thinking, then, is that it provides 'an engaged and visionary standpoint from which to criticize the destructiveness of war and begin to invent peace'. Thus, maternal thinking and practices are important resources for developing peace politics.[31]

In support of her argument, Ruddick cites Nancy Harstock's Marxist notion of a privileged political and epistemological 'standpoint'—'an engaged vision of the world opposed and superior to dominant ways of thinking' which is shared by those who also share socially and political significant characteristics. Thus, Ruddick describes the feminist standpoint as a superior vision produced by the political conditions and distinctive work of women. This, she argues, provides not only the epistemological and political base for maternal thinking but the critical power: 'by looking and acting from a feminist standpoint, dominant ways of thinking . . . were revealed to be as abstract and destructive as I suspected'.[32]

'Standpoint' feminists argue that their perspective accounts for the achievements of feminist theory because it is a politically engaged approach which starts from the perspective of the social experience of the subjugated sex/gender. But the idea of a distinctly feminine standpoint from which we can arrive at a less partial, less distorted understanding of social relations is contested by other feminists. For some, the idea of a feminist standpoint appears still too firmly rooted in distinctively masculine modes of being in the world. To argue for an authentic feminist standpoint is to put forward yet another falsely universalizing project. Moreover, although it is clear that standpoint feminism seeks to identify the common aspects of women's social experience cross-culturally, it has been suggested by postmodern and cultural feminists that it cannot be presumed that there are commonalities to be detected in all women's social experience or worldviews. Thus, the critique of standpoint feminism concludes that no particular women's experience can uniquely generate groundings for the visions and politics that will emancipate all women from gender hierarchy.[33]

This debate has important implications for the ethics of care. Gilligan herself has been interpreted as a standpoint feminist, insofar as the alternative way of thinking about morality and moral relations which she advocates is linked to a distinctly 'women's' way of knowing. Moreover, both Ruddick and Gilligan have been accused of an implicit essentialism which, in discussing women's roles in mothering and caretaking, fails to make a clear distinction between what is naturally—physiologically and psychologically—feminine and what is a socially constructed account of gender roles and characteristics. Linda Nicholson, for example, has argued that the lack of an historical account in Gilligan's work leads to the tendency of her analysis to ignore factors such as class, race, and historical changes as variables. She argues that Gilligan's map of women's moral development—from initial selfishness to a position which integrates the needs of both self and other—can be explained within the historical context of a highly individualistic modern Western society. In such a society, she argues, female children are encouraged to abandon selfishness in conjunction with their socialization in becoming 'feminine'. This has been particularly true, she points out, for white, middle-class girls, for whom the ideal of femininity has been more directly influential in shaping behaviour than it has been for many black, poor, and non-Western women.[34] Similarly, Lawrence Blum has suggested that it is a deficiency of most of the literature on the morality of care that it does not explore the constituents of individual identity which would need to be taken into account in true caring towards a particular individual. More specifically, he claims that insufficient attention has been paid to the cultural/ethnic/religious dimension of identity.[35]

As well as pointing out the limitations of basing a moral orientation on gender alone, many advocates of a caring approach to morality have explicitly rejected the gendering of care ethics. Susan Moller Okin argues that, to the extent that findings about women's moral development are interpreted to mean that women are more attached than men to particular others and less able to be impartial or to universalize in their moral thinking, they seem not only to misread the data but to reinforce the negative stereotyping of women that has been employed to exclude them from political rights and positions of authority.[36]

In defending her argument against such criticism, Gilligan has pointed out that the title of her book is *In a Different Voice,* not *In a* Woman's *Voice,* and that she explains in her introduction that this voice is identified not by gender but by theme. Although she does note the association of this voice with women, she cautions the reader that 'this association is not absolute, and that the contrasts between male and female voices are presented here to highlight a distinction between two modes of thought and to focus a problem of interpretation rather than to represent a generalization about either sex'. Thus, she claims, the care perspective in her rendition is neither biologically determined nor unique to women.[37]

Despite her advocacy of care as a value and practice which can inform social and political life, Joan Tronto has argued that, in its original formulation, the ethic of care did not disturb the basically exclusive logic of Kohlberg's theory. There is no victory, she suggests, in the admission that caring deserves to be seen as a part of moral theory as long as it is kept in its place, especially in the household or in 'relationships'.[38] An ostensibly 'feminine' approach to caring, she argues, cannot serve as a starting point for a broader questioning of the proper role of caring in society. If the feminine is constructed as the antithesis of the masculine, then the construction of women as tied to the more particular activity of caring for others stands in opposition to the more public and social concerns of men. The 'attentiveness' which characterizes caring could then be seen as a survival mechanism for women who are dealing with oppressive conditions—a way of anticipating the wishes of one's superior. Thus, a feminine approach to caring bears the burden of accepting traditional gender divisions in a society that devalues what women do. From this perspective, she argues, caring will always be a corrective to morality, an 'extra' aspect of life, neither suggesting nor requiring a fundamental rethinking of moral categories.[39] Tronto distinguishes a 'feminist' approach from the 'feminine' approach described earlier. Her vision of a feminist approach to caring, in contrast, needs to begin by broadening our understanding of what caring for others means, both in terms of the moral questions it raises and in terms of the need to restructure broader social and political institutions if caring for others is to be made a more central part of the everyday lives of everyone in society.[40] It is precisely such an approach, informed by this vision of a *political* theory of care, that must provide the starting point for thinking about the ethics of care in the context of international relations.

Clearly, the importance of the ethics of care, and its transformatory potential, does not, and indeed must not, rest on its association with women. While it is crucial to avoid undermining its feminist origins and orientation, the ethics of care is significant because it represents an alternative view of ethics which is relevant beyond the role of women within the family or even within local or national societies. Indeed, the transformatory potential of an ethics of care extends beyond the personal to the political and, ultimately, to the global context of social life. Marilyn Friedman argues that the different-voice hypothesis has a significance for moral psychology and moral philosophy which would survive the demise of the gender difference hypothesis. She insists, convincingly, that at least part of its significance lies in how it reveals the lopsided obsession of contemporary theories of morality with universal and impartial conceptions of justice and rights and the relative disregard for particular, interpersonal relationships based on partiality and affective ties.[41]

The Care-Justice Debate

There has been extensive discussion of the question of whether care and justice do indeed represent two distinct types of moral thinking, and of whether care, on its own, can adequately address all types of moral situations or whether what is required is an approach to ethics that includes and integrates both care and justice thinking. Thus, as well as debates among feminists about the tenability of a 'feminist standpoint' and, indeed, a 'feminine' or 'feminist' ethics, Gilligan's work has led to another debate about care and justice—specifically, whether these in fact denote two contrasting approaches to morality, or whether they articulate differences not in ethical position but in emphasis of one against the other of two types of moral duties.[42]

Marilyn Friedman has argued that the care-justice dichotomy is rationally implausible and that the two concepts are conceptually compatible; this argument, in turn, creates the empirical possibility that the two moral concerns are intermingled in practice. She sees this point as integral to the argument against the 'gendering' of these moral outlooks: 'That the genders do not, in reality, divide along those moral lines is made possible, though not inevitable, by the conceptual limitations of both a concept of care dissociated from considerations of justice and a concept of justice dissociated from considerations of care'.[43]

While not seeking to dispose of the different-voice hypothesis, Friedman argues that there are ways in which justice pertains to close personal relationships. A personal relationship, she claims, is a miniature social system which provides valued mutual intimacy, support, and concern. Justice sets a constraint on such relationships by calling for an appropriate sharing, among the participants, of the benefits and burdens which constitute their relationship.

Susan Moller Okin has also criticized the alleged dichotomy between justice and care—and between impartiality and universalizability, on the one hand, and the recognition of otherness and difference on the other. Illustrating this claim through an analysis of Rawls's *Theory of Justice*, Okin argues that an understanding of Rawls's theory must include a recognition that, in order to develop the sense of justice required of people if a well-ordered society is to have any hope of being achieved or, once achieved, preserved, human beings must be nurtured and socialized in an environment that best develops these capacities in them.[44] Rawls's position, usually interpreted as excessively rationalistic, individualistic, abstract, and Kantian, does rely, she argues, on empathy, benevolence, and equal concern for others as for the self if the parties are to come up with the principles they choose.[45] In arguing that at the centre of Rawls's work is a voice of responsibility, care, and concern for others, Okin attempts to deconstruct the dichotomy between care and justice that has been erected by many feminist philosophers.[46]

While feminist theorists clearly differ in their understandings of the relationship between justice and care, few would suggest that an ethic of care can replace or eclipse the moral problems that justice seeks to address. Certainly, the idea of 'justice' is neither superficial nor morally expendable; moreover, the current global social, economic, and political context is certainly not one in which questions of justice no longer need to be addressed. Nor is 'justice' irrelevant to an interpersonal, relational view of ethics; indeed, the concept of justice, in general, arises out of relational conditions in which most human beings have the opportunity, the capacity, and, for too many, the inclination to treat each other badly.[47]

While most theories of justice do, then, clearly involve some notion of human beings living in relationships, the particular type of 'justice thinking' that is normally contrasted with 'care thinking' starts from the belief that the best way to ensure justice is to respect the autonomy and individual rights of persons through the application of generalizable rules and principles. It also maintains that individuals, as moral legislators, should have a degree of emotional independence, in the sense of being able to distance themselves from their personal affections and interests when making political decisions.[48] Finally, on this account, it is the capacity for rationally autonomous moral agency that makes a being a person and makes persons matter morally. Thus, as the Kantian view has been developed, respect for persons has come to be thought of primarily in terms of respect for each individual's equal, basic human rights—the rights that protect the defining capacity of persons—and especially respect for the fundamental right of each person to live her life as she sees fit.[49]

justice

Thus, it is not the idea of 'justice' as such, but the individualist, atomistic ontology, the liberal-impartial view of persons as 'generalized' rather than 'concrete', and the concomitant reliance on abstract moral principles which are corrected by the care perspective. That said, however, it is not the case that we must jettison all of the moral notions regarding self and other associated with justice ethics. For example, the ideas of 'self-esteem' and 'respect' may be integral to both justice and care. Citing self-esteem as a basic presupposition of liberal theory, Susan James nevertheless notes that self-esteem, which is required to be able 'to speak in one's own voice', depends heavily on the approval of others for one's continued sense of self.[50] Similarly, Claudia Card suggests that self-esteem is contingent upon primary personal relationships and upon the sense we develop of ourselves in such relationships—our sense of ourselves as capable of faithfulness, understanding, warmth, and empathy, as endowed with the qualities we would want in a personal affiliate, not only the qualities that it is rational to want in a 'fellow citizen'.[51] Thus, paradoxically, one of the vital conditions of liberal-impartiality—the emotional autonomy and independence of the moral agent—can be seen as being ensured only through self-esteem, which itself acts as an intermediary between the poles of emotional dependence and independence and thus requires, at least to some degree, an adequate sense of caring, based on attentiveness and understanding.

Moreover, Robin Dillon's notion of respect, when joined with care, ensures that care does not descend into arbitrary preference based on emotion. Although we might like something for no reason, she argues, we cannot respect something for no reason, nor for any old reason. Respecting something requires having a certain kind of reason, namely, that I believe that there is some feature, characteristic, or fact about it that makes it deserving of my attention and some further response.[52] An ethics of care that is enriched with notions such as self-esteem and respect is one in which care and justice are no longer fixed in a dichotomous relationship; indeed, it is a new kind of moral thinking in which a strong sense of self goes hand in hand with the valuing of human attachment and the focus on abstract, impersonal, distanced relations is replaced by a focus on real, concrete, particular relations.

In thinking about the difference between justice and care, perhaps we would do well to remember that theorizing about justice is, in fact, a response to the existence of *injustice* in the world. Perhaps, as Judith Shklar has suggested, it is injustice, rather than justice, with which we should be most concerned. As she has pointed out, felt injustice is a personal experience, and it is evoked by particular incidents. It may well be that our subjective, personal experiences are too various and incommunicable to be fitted into general rules of conduct or, in other words, into any abstract theory of justice; this may be why, moreover, our attempts to impose them tend to backfire. Perhaps we are too ignorant (of others) and too diverse to be fitted into any single normative scheme. If injustice is, then, as complex and intractable as seems likely, a less rule-bound phenomenology, she suggests, may be a better way of exploring the matter.[53]

Shklar has argued that the emphasis in political theory on constructing what she calls the 'normal model' of justice has resulted in a lack of serious attention to the idea of 'injustice'. There is an absence, she claims, of any 'elaborate or serious understanding of injustice as a personal and political experience or as a part of all societies known to history'. Most injustices, she argues, occur continuously within the framework of an established polity with an operative system of law, in normal times. They are 'banal historical realities' which remind us that the 'self-confident intellectual and moral claims of the normal model' are unwarranted.[54]

> [I]n its cognitive complacency the normal model forgets the irrationality, cupidity, fear, indifference, aggression and inequality that give injustice its power. The normal model of justice, to which we cling, is not really given to investigating the character of injustice or its victims. It does not tell us everything we should know about either one. Indeed, its very aims prevent us from doing so. The ethical ends of a theory of justice, as of justice itself . . . respond to the requirements of juridical rationality, impersonality, fairness, impartiality. Probity in this case acts as an inhibition to speculation.
>
> The tasks of political theory are, however, quite different and less circumscribed. They can and should raise every possible question about injustice as a *personal characteristic, as a relation between individuals, and as a political phenomenon.* Above all, political theory cannot turn away from the sense of in-

> justice that is an integral part of our *social and personal experiences, whether private or public,* and that plays an essential part in democratic theory and practice.[55]

In the language of moral and political theory, 'care' is not the same as 'justice'. But that is not to say that, from a critical perspective of care, we can neither deplore injustice nor respond to it. Indeed, given the scope and intensity of injustice and human suffering in the global context today, no serious approach to international ethics can ignore injustice; rather, we simply must question the need, and indeed the possibility, of delivering *theories* of justice and instead consider seriously how all moral agents can learn to care about the needs of real others, and how healthy social relations, both within and between communities, might best be maintained and promoted.

From Private to Public and Beyond

While the debates rage on about the alleged essentialism of care, the plausibility of gendering moral orientations, and care's potential for reinforcing oppressive stereotypes, perhaps the most important critique of care ethics for the purposes of this book involves the claim that care is a moral orientation for the private, or intimate, sphere of life, and thus that it has no bearing on public, or indeed international, social relations.

It is not surprising that advocates of rights-based ethics, and liberal theories of justice more generally, tend to be hostile to the idea of a morality of care for precisely this reason. Caring about particular persons, it is argued, may indeed be a fact of life, but it is an inappropriate way to define morality, especially our moral relations to strangers. Indeed, a common response to the notion of care is to make what Margaret Walker calls the 'separate spheres' move of endorsing particularism for personal or intimate relations and universalism for the large-scale or genuinely administrative context, or for dealings with unknown or little-known persons.[56] Impartialist critics of care argue that while care for others in the context of relationships may constitute a genuinely distinct set of concerns or mode of thought and motivation from that found in impartialist morality, and while these can be deeply important to individuals' lives, nevertheless such concerns are not moral but only personal ones. Caring may be important, but actions which flow directly from it are in that respect without moral significance.[57]

Grace Clement devotes substantial space in her recent book to an effort to broaden the conventional boundaries of care. She focuses on the public/private dichotomy and argues that the public sphere shares features usually understood as private and thus calls for an ethic of care. Her first argument draws on Robert Goodin's *Protecting the Vulnerable;* following Goodin, Clement argues that our obligations to care for family and friends are based on the particular vulnerability of our family and friends to our actions and choices. We have special obligations to our family and friends because we can affect their interests to a great extent. But, she argues, many people beyond our family and friends are also particularly vulnerable to our actions and choices, and thus the ethics of care has implications beyond our sphere of personal relations.[58] Clement summarizes:

> First, our care obligations within the private sphere are based on our friends' and family members' vulnerabilities to us. Second, people beyond our private sphere are also vulnerable to our actions and choices, and thus we also have care obligations to them. This argument challenges one aspect of the public/private dichotomy . . . by showing that the moral concerns that call for an ethic of care are present in public as well as in private.[59]

While I am sympathetic to the project of seeking to demonstrate that care ethics is applicable to public as well as private moral contexts, Clement's argument here could be seen as potentially damaging. First, it is not clear on what grounds she has determined that caring emerges specifically out of others' vulnerability to us (other than the fact that Goodin says so). This does not seem to have been an assumption of any previous theorists of care, nor indeed of Clement herself in the rest of her book. How can we justify this assumption? Do I care about my family and friends because they are vulnerable to me? Do I act morally because I recognize that if I 'withdrew' my care, they would be hurt and abandoned? Or do I care about them simply because those relationships in themselves, and the attention which they demand, are inseparable from my moral responses of care and love? Do I not care because I understand myself in relation to those other persons, and because I recognize the moral value and the shared importance of listening, attending, and responding to those others? The notion of vulnerability is tied, not to the ethics of care, but rather to the other moral concept raised by Clement, via Goodin, in this argument: *obligations.* Indeed, Clement uses a phrase—'obligations to care'—which is surely undermining: to use such a phrase is ultimately to make concessions to Kantian ethics and to admit that morality is always, ultimately, a question of obligations.

Clement also suggests that we could 'interpret care priorities in terms of positive rights'.[60] But just as one might criticize the idea of 'obligations to care', one might also object to concessions to rights which suggest that the language of rights is ultimately necessary to interpret the moral priorities of care. Indeed, it could be argued that the opposite strategy is desirable: care theorists should assert the futility of arguing for substantive moral goods and basic needs in rights language and instead reassert the language of care to address the moral priorities of food, shelter, and proper health care.[61]

In spite of these limitations, many of Clement's other suggestions for moving caring beyond the private sphere are both creative and feasible. For example, she claims that while public policy decisions may not allow for attention to be paid to particular features of individuals, they do allow for attention to distinguishing features of groups. This is an important argument: 'The fact that we do not know the individual particularities of the members of such a group would not prevent us from focusing on the group's special needs in making public policy'. In this form, she argues, the concrete standpoint of care is possible in the public sphere. The contextual emphasis of the ethics of care need not limit it to the sphere of personal relations.[62]

Clement's most valuable insight, however, is surely her point that it is a mistake to limit morality to conflict resolution or, in other words, to the construction of abstract principles of right; the importance of an ethics of care, she argues, is its focus on preventing conflict. Thus, to prevent conflict, crime, and injustice, we need an ethics of care and its recognition of the importance of human connection in helping to *avoid* injustice.[63]

Writers like Clement and Tronto have clearly made inroads towards the acceptance of care as a morality which extends beyond the private sphere and personal relationships and has a public, and indeed a political, relevance. The purpose of a rights- or obligation-based ethics is to define some criterion or procedure which allows us to derive all and only the things we are obliged to do.[64] Many moral problems, however, require more from an ethics than a procedural framework for the application of rules designed to adjudicate, fairly, among competing claims. Much of modern Western moral theory, as well as most of what passes for 'ethics' in international relations, is about the resolution of conflict through the use of moral concepts like rights and obligations, reciprocity and fairness. But, as Clement argues, it is a mistake to limit morality to conflict resolution. Ethics may also be about the creation of a society in which certain types of conflicts no longer occur.

Thus, rather than providing tidily argued, philosophically rigorous justifications for the existence of universal rights or universal obligations (based on the moral standing of individuals as human beings), care ethics asks not only *why* should I care, but also *how* should I care, and how can I best promote caring personal and social relations among others. This kind of ethics focuses less on providing principles to establish right and wrong and more on examining the actual, concrete conditions within moral relations that can and do occur, and seeking to understand the nature of those moral relations. An ethics of care takes seriously both the problem of motivation and the problem of the nature of moral responses, rather than focusing solely on the derivation of principles of right action. Thus, an ethics of care must, in the context of social and political relations, seek to uncover the relationships which exist among and within groups while, at the same time, maintaining a critical stance towards those relations. It should not be taken for granted, moreover, that we know *how* to care for others; care ethics involves learning how to listen and be attentive and responsive to the needs and suffering of others. This, in turn, involves a thorough understanding of how relations are constructed and how difference is perceived and maintained through institutions and structures in societies. In this way, an ethics of care for the global context must be a critical ethics which eschews complacency about our abilities to respond morally, and especially about our rational competence to acknowledge individuals' moral standing on the basis of their humanity alone.

Understood in this way, the ethics of care can be seen to relate not only to personal and intimate relations among particular individuals but to all kinds of institutional and structural relations in and across societies. As Eva F. Kittay argues,

> Each intimate relationship is in turn embedded in ties among members of neighbours, religious and ethnic groups, fellow citizens, all of which are deeply affected but not entirely determined by the political system and economic circumstances. Connecting these relationships to a vibrant sense of responsibility would engage wide circles of people, including even public-policy makers and voters, who would need to consider what social and economic structures are necessary to permit continuous, caring human relationships especially responsive to those most dependent on such care.[65]

Bringing care into the public, and indeed the global, realm is not about 'privatizing' the responsibilities of the state so that it falls to overworked, underpaid 'carers' to maintain decency in the world. The polity cannot take for granted the contribution made by caregivers to maintaining the social and political order; on the contrary, it 'must take upon itself the primary responsibility of maintaining structures that will support the principles of care'.[66] Moreover, to ensure that the full impact of the ethics of care is felt, it is crucial that its relevance not be seen as limited to those with whom we have an existing relationship of either intimacy or propinquity. As Tronto argues, if caring is used as an excuse to narrow the scope of our moral activity so as to be concerned only with those immediately around us, then it has little to recommend it as a moral theory. Rather, she argues, we must question the ways in which we, and others, are responsible for our narrow sphere, and hence for who receives our care. To say that we will care for a stranger at our door but not for starving children in Africa is to ignore the ways in which the modern world is intertwined and the ways in which hundreds of prior public and private decisions affect where we find ourselves and which strangers show up at our doors.[67]

Conceiving of care as both a moral orientation and a practice that informs our daily lives removes the focus from the individual and recognizes that human well-being relies on the giving and receiving of care. Because care forces us to think concretely about people's real needs and to evaluate how those needs will be met, it introduces questions about what we value into the public, and ultimately the international, sphere. Questioning who is and who is not cared for in the world will force us to explore the role of social relations and structural constraints in determining who can and cannot lead a dignified and fulfilled life. This is not an abstract ethics about the application of rules, but a phenomenology of moral life which recognizes that addressing moral problems involves, first, an understanding of identities, relationships, and contexts, and second, a degree of social coordination and co-operation in order to try to answer questions and disputes about who cares for whom, and about how responsibilities will be discharged. The ethics of care focuses not on the moment of rational moral judgement or of pure moral will, but on the permanent background to decision-making, which may often be characterized by apparent inaction—waiting, listening, focusing attention.[68] Bringing care into international relations would remove the focus from an ostensibly separate 'moral dimension' to politics, characterized by the need to make 'moral' decisions in the face of economic and political priorities. The ethics of care would focus instead on the continuous background of interpersonal and social contexts in which all human relations occur, offering us a better starting point for thinking about the claims, entitlements, needs, interests, and dignity of persons.

If we are going to integrate care into our moral and political vocabulary, it cannot simply be to claim that we have a responsibility to care only for those individuals with whom we have a close or personal relationship, such as our own children; to do so would be to leave in place the boundary that separates private from public life, so that, in the international arena, we could be satisfied that our duties extended only to respecting others' individual rights. Moral responses cannot be divided up into those which are appropriate for those to whom we have a 'special' relationship and those which apply, more generally, to 'all human beings'. As Tronto argues, by focusing on care, we focus on the process by which life is sustained; we focus on human actors acting. By starting from the premise that these practices are central, we are able to place them at the center of our moral and political universe.[69]

The ethics of care undermines the individualistic moral logic that leads us to believe that rights and obligations are somehow disconnected from the networks of social relations in which actors—from individuals to states—are situated. Thus, enquiry into the question of our moral responses to situations of human suffering would no longer be seen as solely a problem of justification, or of resolving the conflict between universal moral duty and individual self-interest; rather, it becomes an exercise in understanding how human suffering and exclusion are shaped by a series of collective social, political, and economic decisions and social and economic relations. The enquiry would also look at the nature of those moral responses, and at how we might *learn* to care, rather than just provide a justification for why we *ought* to care. It should, then, help us to come to an understanding that we, as moral agents and potential carers, are not isolated from the moral situations which surround us in society. Finally, an approach to ethics based on caring involves a recognition that accepting our social responsibilities, performing our public services, and cultivating the moral virtues needed to care adequately for others may be, in fact, an altogether better way of attending to our own interests, broadly defined, than focusing narrowly on our individual rights. To illustrate this idea, Charlotte Bunch uses the example of a woman from West Africa who explained that gaining 'the right' to an abortion in her country had to be based on getting the community to understand that a woman's control over her body is in the interest of the community. She felt that she couldn't argue that women have this as an individual right because her culture didn't conceive of individual rights as taking precedence over the community.[70]

Whether it is in the context of the family, the community, or the nation-state, we must struggle to preserve what Margaret Walker has called 'a lively sense of the moral incompleteness or inadequacy' of principled, generalized treatment of individual human beings.[71] Deontological ethics upholds what Walker has called 'the standard discursive forms of moral philosophy', including the stark absence of the second person and the plural in projections of philosophical deliberation; the virtual exclusion of collaborative and communicative modes of formulating and negotiating moral problems; and reliance on schematic examples in which the few 'morally relevant' factors have already been selected and the social-political context has been effaced. An alternative view of ethics, informed by the idea of care, would force us to be more discerning in the construction and consideration of representations of our moral situations. An ethics which breaks down the barriers between ethics and politics would necessarily consider questions like: What actual community of moral responsibility does this representation of moral thinking purport to represent? Who does it actually represent? What communicative strategies does it support? Who will be in a position (concretely, socially) to deploy these strategies? Who is in a position to transmit and enforce the rules which constrain them? In what forms of activity or endeavour will they have (or fail to have) an application? Who is served by these activities?[72]

The ethics of care, then, must not be seen as too partial or too parochial to play a role beyond the personal and the private sphere. The criticism that care ethics is too particularized—too connected to private and particular circumstances—should not lead us to reject care outright; rather, it should motivate the development of a political theory of care which can respond to wider moral concerns. Joan Tronto has suggested that the impoverishment of our vocabulary for discussing caring may be a result of the way caring is 'privatized', and thus placed beneath our social vision for societies. She points out that the need to rethink appropriate forms of caring raises broad questions about the shape of social and political institutions in society.[73] That is not to say, however, that the answer to the question 'Who cares for whom?' is either transparent or unproblematic; indeed, it is not only a moral but *a social and political question*, which requires an analysis of the social construction of roles, relationships, communities, and institutions in their different sociopolitical contexts.

Notes

1. Virginia Held, 'Introduction', in Virginia Held and Alison Jaggar, eds., *Justice and Care: Essential Readings in Feminist Ethics*, Boulder, CO: Westview Press, 1995, p. 1.

2. Susan Hekman, *Moral Voices, Moral Selves: Carol Gilligan and Feminist Moral Theory*, Cambridge: Polity Press, 1995, pp. 62, 67.

3. Here I would include Bernard Williams, Richard Rorty, and Lawrence Blum. It could be argued that communitarians—such as Alisdair McIntyre, Michael Sandel, and Charles Taylor—are also members of this 'alternative' community of moral theorists. I do not include them in this discussion, however, largely because, as I argue in chapter 4, I see many flaws in the communitarian argument and would argue that much communitarian theorizing represents not a rejection but a modification of liberal or cosmopolitan moral reasoning. It should also be clarified that a critical ethics of care for the global context need not be explicitly feminist; in other words, it need not have as its sole or even primary purpose to highlight the particularly feminine characteristics or experiences of women or to advance a moral theory which makes clear the kind of social and political changes necessary to end male domination. This is not to say, of course, that the argument for a critical ethics of care does not serve these important goals, or that it has not been influenced by feminist theorists who were directly motivated by these valid concerns. It is simply to say that a critical ethics of care need not be uniquely and solely 'feminine' ethics, nor need it be limited to serving 'feminist' ends; rather, it may indeed express a hitherto unrecognized

yet important way of understanding morality, which may prove to be emancipatory not only for women but for marginalized and excluded peoples everywhere.

4. Larry May, Marilyn Friedman, and Andy Clark, eds., *Mind and Morals: Essays on Ethics and Cognitive Science,* Cambridge, MA: MIT Press, 1996, p. 1.

5. Ibid.

6. Lawrence Blum, *Moral Perception and Particularity,* Cambridge: Cambridge University Press, 1994, p. 3.

7. Iris Murdoch, *Existentialists and Mystics: Writings on Philosophy and Literature,* London: Chatto & Windus, 1997, p. 337.

8. Nancy Chodorow, *The Reproduction of Mothering: Psychoanalysis and the Sociology of Gender,* Berkeley: University of California Press, 1978, p. 7.

9. Quoted in Gayle Rubin, 'The Traffic in Women: Notes on the "Political Economy" of Sex', in Reyna Reiter, ed., *Toward an Anthropology of Women* (1975), p. 8.

10. Chodorow, *The Reproduction of Mothering,* p. 9.

11. Ibid., p. 38. Object-relations theory describes the self as something which is created through relations with others, rather than existing separately with a fixed, essential core. As Susan Hekman points out, the radical component of object-relations theory is its claim that the separate, autonomous self that is the cornerstone of the modernist self is itself a product of relational forces. See Susan Hekman, *Moral Voices, Moral Selves,* p. 73.

12. Lois McNay, *Foucault and Feminism: Power, Gender, and the Self,* Cambridge: Polity Press, 1992, p. 95.

13. Ibid., p. 96.

14. Carol Gilligan, *In a Different Voice: Psychological Theory and Women's Development,* 2nd ed., Cambridge, MA: Harvard University Press, 1993, pp. 1–2.

15. Ibid., p. 27.

16. Ibid., pp. 28–29.

17. Annette C. Baier, *Moral Prejudices: Essays on Ethics,* Cambridge, MA: Harvard University Press, 1994; Marilyn Friedman, *What Are Friends For?: Feminist Perspectives on Personal Relationships and Moral Theory,* Ithaca, NY: Cornell University Press, 1993; Virginia Held, *Feminist Morality: Transforming Culture, Society, and Politics.* Chicago: University of Chicago Press, 1993; Joan Tronto, *Moral Boundaries: A Political Argument for an Ethic of Care,* London: Routledge, 1993.

18. Susan James, 'The Good-Enough Citizen: Female Citizenship and Independence', in Susan James and Gisela Bock, eds., *Beyond Equality and Difference,* London: Routledge, 1992; Alison Jaggar, 'Caring as a Feminist Practice of Moral Reasoning', in Held and Jaggar, *Justice and Care;* and Susan Moller Okin, 'Reason and Feeling in Thinking About Justice', in Cass R. Sunstein, ed., *Feminism and Political Theory,* Chicago: University of Chicago Press, 1990. This is by no means an exhaustive list of individuals who have written on care or on feminist ethics more broadly conceived. Other important works in the literature on care include Nel Noddings, *Caring: A Feminine Approach to Ethics and Moral Education,* Berkeley: University of California Press, 1984; Claudia Card, ed., *Feminist Ethics,* Lawrence: University of Kansas Press, 1991; Eve Browning Cole and Susan Coultrap-McQuin, eds., *Explorations in Feminist Ethics: Theory and Practice,* Bloomington: Indiana University Press, 1992; Alison M. Jaggar, *Feminist Politics and Human Nature,*

Totowa, NJ: Rowman, 1983; Hekman, *Moral Voices;* and Margaret Urban Walker, *Moral Understandings: A Feminist Study in Ethics,* New York: Routledge, 1998.

19. Blum, *Moral Perception and Particularity,* pp. 215–216.

20. Murdoch, *Existentialists and Mystics,* pp. 159, 357–358.

21. Seyla Benhabib, *Situating the Self: Gender, Community, and Postmodernism in Contemporary Ethics,* Cambridge: Polity Press, 1992, pp. 179–180.

22. Hekman, *Moral Voices,* p. 7.

23. Ibid., p. 1.

24. Ibid., p. 22.

25. Quoted in Tronto, *Moral Boundaries,* pp. 87–88.

26. Brian Barry, *Justice as Impartiality,* Oxford: Oxford University Press, 1995, pp. 252–256.

27. O'Neill, 'Justice, Gender, and International Boundaries', p. 55.

28. Tronto, *Moral Boundaries,* p. 61.

29. Sarah Lucia Hoagland, 'Some Thoughts About "Caring"', in Card, *Feminist Ethics,* p. 247.

30. Sara Ruddick, *Maternal Thinking: Towards a Politics of Peace,* New York: Women's Press, 1989, p. 123.

31. Ibid., p. 12.

32. Ibid., p. 131.

33. Sandra Harding, 'The Instability of the Analytical Categories of Feminist Theory', in Helen Crowley and Susan Himmelweit, eds., *Knowing Women: Feminism and Knowledge,* Cambridge: Polity Press, 1992, pp. 338–354.

34. Linda J. Nicholson, 'Women, Morality, and History', in Mary Jeanne Larrabee, ed., *An Ethic of Care: Feminist and Interdisciplinary Perspectives,* London: Routledge, 1993, p. 99.

35. Blum, *Moral Perception,* p. 142.

36. Okin refers to this argument in 'Reason and Feeling in Thinking About Justice', in Sunstein, *Feminism and Political Theory,* p. 34. See Susan Moller Okin, 'Thinking Like a Woman', in Deborah Rhode, ed., *Theoretical Perspectives on Sexual Difference,* New Haven, CT: Yale University Press, 1990.

37. Carol Gilligan, 'Reply to Critics', in Larrabee, *An Ethic of Care,* p. 209.

38. Tronto, *Moral Boundaries,* pp. 63, 91.

39. Joan Tronto, 'Women and Caring: What Can Feminists Learn About Morality from Caring?', in Held and Jaggar, *Justice and Care,* p. 112.

40. Ibid.

41. Marilyn Friedman, 'Beyond Caring: The De-Moralization of Gender', in Held and Jaggar, *Justice and Care,* p. 63.

42. Gertrude Nunner-Winkler, 'Two Moralities? A Critical Discussion of an Ethic of Care and Responsibility Versus an Ethic of Rights and Justice', in Larrabee, *An Ethic of Care,* p. 143.

43. Friedman, 'Beyond Caring', p. 66.

44. Okin, 'Reason and Feeling', pp. 34–35.

45. Ibid., p. 29.

46. Ibid., p. 17.

47. Friedman, *What Are Friends For?,* p. 133.

48. James, 'The Good Enough Citizen', p. 59.

49. Robin S. Dillon, 'Care and Respect', in Cole and Coultrap-McQuin, *Explorations in Feminist Ethics,* p. 74.

50. James, 'The Good Enough Citizen', p. 60.

51. Claudia Card, 'Gender and Moral Luck', in Held and Jaggar, *Justice and Care,* p. 91.

52. Dillon, 'Care and Respect', p. 71.

53. Judith Shklar, *The Faces of Injustice,* New Haven, CT: Yale University Press, 1990, pp. 27–28.

54. Ibid., pp. 19–20.

55. Ibid., pp. 49–50, italics added.

56. Walker, 'Moral Understandings', p. 147.

57. Blum, 'Gilligan and Kohlberg', p. 53.

58. Grace Clement, *Care, Autonomy, and Justice: Feminism and the Ethic of Care,* Boulder, CO: Westview Press, 1996, p. 73.

59. Ibid., p. 75.

60. Ibid., p. 81.

61. I have argued this point at length elsewhere. See Fiona Robinson, 'The Limits of a Rights-Based Approach to International Ethics', in Tony Evans, ed., *Human Rights Fifty Years On: A Reappraisal,* Manchester: Manchester University Press, 1998.

62. Clement, *Care, Autonomy, and Justice*, p. 80.

63. Ibid., p. 82.

64. Charles Taylor, *Sources of the Self,* Cambridge: Cambridge University Press, 1989, p. 79.

65. Quoted in Martha Minow and Mary Lyndon Shanley, 'Revisioning the Family: Relational Rights and Responsibilities', in Mary Lyndon Shanley and Uma Narayan, eds., *Reconstructing Political Theory: Feminist Perspectives,* Cambridge: Polity Press, 1997, pp. 102–103.

66. Ibid., p. 102.

67. Tronto, 'Women and Caring', pp. 111–112.

68. On this point, see Murdoch, *Existentialists and Mystics,* p. 159.

69. Ibid., pp. 154–155.

70. Charlotte Bunch, 'A Global Perspective on Feminist Ethics and Diversity', in Cole and Coultrap-McQuin, *Explorations in Feminist Ethics,* p. 184.

71. Walker, 'Moral Understandings', p. 147.

72. Ibid., p. 148.

73. Tronto, 'Women and Caring', p. 113.

3

Ethical Reasoning and the Global Context of Care

Beyond Theories, Rules, and Justification

As well as being inspired by and largely based upon the substantive ideas regarding moral relations emerging from feminist ethics, the critical approach to ethics in international relations put forward in this book is informed by a profound scepticism about the usefulness of that elaborate, thoroughgoing, and ambitious kind of structure known as 'ethical theory', which may be defined as 'a theoretical account of what ethical thought and practice are, which . . . implies a general test for the correctness of ethical beliefs and principles'.[1] Thus, the arguments in this book are influenced by the suggestion that there may be a way of doing moral philosophy that starts from the ways in which we experience our ethical life. As Bernard Williams has argued,

> Such a philosophy would reflect on what we believe, feel, take for granted; the ways in which we confront obligations and recognise responsibility; the sentiments of guilt and shame. It would involve a phenomenology of the ethical life. This could be a good philosophy, but it would be unlikely to yield an ethical theory.[2]

These suggestions for an alternative way of thinking about morality stem from Williams's deep scepticism about what he calls 'philosophical ethics'. 'The resources of most modern moral philosophy', he argues, are not well adjusted to the modern world'.[3]

This scepticism may be seen as part of wider misgivings about what Jean Bethke Elshtain has called 'grand, formalizable, universal theory'[4] and what Geoffrey Hawthorn has described as 'fixed pictures of the social world'.[5] Thus, as Williams has expressed doubt about the ethical theory, Hawthorn expresses a similar unease about theory in history and the social sciences, and Elshtain about the possibility of theory in international relations. These writers share a tendency to see the world as composed of concrete, historical particulars—'the inelegant, messy, dense, historically suffused world'[6]—and are critical of the way in which social and political theories, like the moral theories from which many of them derive, have made a habit of abstracting and categorizing agents and generalizing their experience and judgement.[7]

This insistence on context and particularity in thinking about ethics also resonates strongly in American pragmatist philosophy, which, as has been argued recently, bears many similarities to much feminist thought.[8] As Charlene Haddock Seigfried has argued, for pragmatists, philosophical reflection begins and ends with experience, as it does for many feminists. For both, experience is inextricably personal and social. Both pragmatism and feminism reject philosophizing as an intellectual game that takes purely logical analysis as its special task.[9] She points to the pragmatist goal of philosophical discourse—shared understanding and communal problem-solving rather than forced conclusions—arguing that such a goal values inclusiveness and community over exaggerated claims of autonomy and detachment.[10] This is not an argument for a kind of empirical ethics, nor is it a capitulation to moral relativism. Rather, it is an insistence that, when thinking about ethics, we remember that it is real people, living real lives, about whom we are debating. A world full of structural, institutional, and psychological obstacles to the development of moral relations is the context in which the possibilities of international ethics must be discussed.

Not surprisingly, because they derive from the same traditions of thought about the aims and purpose of theory, both 'ethics' and 'international relations' have been notorious for the construction of such abstract, principled, generalizable theories. To counter this tendency, I attempt in this book not to formulate a grand theory of international ethics but rather to make a plea for 'theoretical modesty' based on the recognition that 'whatever we believe we know, we know in virtue of the ways in which our interests connect with the world', and that what matters is our experience: 'our experience of ourselves and others as particular agents of practical reason in what is, for any actual practice, an equally particular and often recalcitrant world'.[11] As has been suggested, the fact that many of them approach ethics in this way is one reason, among many, why the recent works of a number of feminist moral philosophers provide the richest and most compelling starting points for thinking about morality and moral relations in the context of contemporary global relations.

Care is a practice rather than a set of rules or principles. As a result, care's moral qualities take a more ambiguous form than a list of carefully designed moral precepts.[12] However, it should be said that this practicality is, in itself, a defining feature of care. Because it is a practical rather than a theoretical, principled morality, care ethics must refer to particular contexts—specifically, particular relations among concrete individuals. In general, the focus has been on the types of moral responses that emerge from within close, personal relationships, such as those between mothers, or 'mothering persons', and children.

Another defining feature of care is its special 'relational' nature; of course, all moral theories are, in some measure, relational—even individualistic moral concepts like 'rights' require the interaction between moral agents and subjects to make them coherent. Care ethics, however, starts from a relational ontology—that is, from the position of a self delineated through connection, and of life as dependent on this connection and based on a bond of attachment rather than a contract of agreement.[13] Clearly, this differs from the individualistic ontology and rights-based ethics of liberalism; from the liberal-contractarian perspective, relationships and social co-operation exist only to further the ends of the independent, autonomous members of the society. Moreover, although care ethics may seem to have much in common with the communitarian critique of liberalism, communitarian philosophy as a whole is a perilous ally for feminist theory. In their focus on established communities—families, neighbourhoods, nation-states—communitarians foster an uncritical and often conservative approach which differs radically from the aims of care ethics.[14]

While the form of care ethics may be described as 'practical/contextual' and 'relational/interpersonal', the substantive moral content of care ethics is normally said to focus on three elements: attentiveness, responsibility, and responsiveness.[15] These elements are clearly related to the form of care ethics described earlier. A moral practice which is profoundly contextual and focuses on the moral situations arising out of concrete relationships is necessarily one which is attentive and responsive to the needs, claims, fears, and hopes of particular moral subjects. It must be attentive insofar as it can assume no 'ideal', abstract, or universal moral situation but must listen to and learn from the particular standpoint of real individuals. It must be responsive insofar as it is a practical morality—a morality which has a concrete vision of agency and action. Finally, it takes responsibility as its primary moral value because it argues that moral action and social change require a recognition of individual and shared responsibilities.

Moral reasoning and ethical enquiry which take care as its starting point do not seek to construct a moral theory at all. Instead, the ethics of care comprises 'a collection of perceptive, imaginative, appreciative and expressive skills and capacities which put and keep us in unimpeded contact with the realities of ourselves and specific others'.[16] A critical ethics of care does not seek to arrive at an account of moral philosophy which presents a justification for action dependent on the application of principles and rules; rather, it is, as Walker suggests, a phenomenology which starts from the ways in which we experience our ethical lives: as 'human beings connected in various ways . . . responding to each other by engaging together in a search for shareable interpretations of their responsibilities'.[17] Such an approach, I would argue, is particularly useful and relevant in an era when grand, formal theories seem increasingly unable to offer useful guidance about how human beings ought to live their lives.

It is important to note, however, that an ethics which rejects the construction and use of principled moral theories need not necessarily lead to a descent into radical moral relativism or antifoundationalism. Certainly, an ethics of care is neither categorical nor universal-prescriptive; it does not demand that we 'care' wholly, and equally, about all individuals at all times in all places, nor does it regard a moral response as an act of pure will or judgement. Rather, it relies on existing and potential relations among moral agents and the capacity of those agents to learn how to listen and respond to the needs of others. As such, however, the ethics of care may seem to offer no criteria for judging the relative validity of those moral claims—precisely what moral theories which rely on principles do provide. It does not seem to provide an answer to the question that plagues normative theorists of international relations: how to arrive at global or universal norms/values in a world of particular, competing, and often incommensurable value systems.

Because the idea of care does not present itself as a unified ethical theory, it does not provide us with universalizable *rules* or *principles* for handling moral dilemmas and situations of conflict. Thus, we cannot easily isolate and articulate the answers of the 'care perspective' to the moral problems associated with, say, global poverty or intervention. This differs from the cosmopolitan or communitarian responses to such questions: neat, although minimal, answers may be determined according to their respective positions regarding the *scope* of our moral *obligations* and the source of moral value and the related epistemological status of moral claims. For example, where our obligations to our fellow citizens take priority over our obligations to 'humanity' as such, the ethical starting point of communitarians on the question of global poverty is clear. Care ethics also differs from, for example, Kantian or Habermasian solutions to the problem of particular interests and the claims of justice. From these perspectives, universal principles—the prerequisites for justice on a global scale—can be derived through individual rationality or open dialogue and communication.

From the starting point of an ethics of care, however, no such formulaic answers are possible. Depending on one's perspective, this may be seen as a strength or a weakness. The potential weakness, as I mentioned earlier, is that it provides no easy answers about how to judge between right and wrong, or as to where, and to whom, our moral obligations lie; it does not tell us we must care about everyone, nor does it offer us rules for judging whom we should care for in situations where values and interests conflict. But in spite of this, the ethics of care cannot be conflated with the doctrine of moral relativism. Indeed, the two are incommensurable: they cannot be compared because they are concerned with fundamentally different questions.

Moral relativism tells us that there can be no criteria for judging between moral systems or for ascertaining a single objective truth. By contrast, relational approaches—like a critical ethics of care—are simply not concerned with establishing such criteria; rather, they start from the position that knowledge and identities are forged in relationship and that meaning is social rather than natural, mutable rather than fixed.[18] Understanding ethics from the perspective of care helps to explain what motivates individuals to care about others; from this perspective, we can understand formulations of difference and patterns of exclusion as existing in and through social relations, and we can locate moral feelings in the particular relationships which promote an understanding and awareness of others as unique, irreplaceable, concrete individuals.

Such an ethics does not tell us, however, that the existence of a relationship is the primary criterion for judging what, or who, is morally right or wrong. An ethics of care does not valorize 'normal ties'; it does not claim that one must, for example, maintain an existing relationship with, and continue to 'care about', a rapist because he happens to be one's brother. A caring approach to such a situation would, however, require a sensitivity to the relationships involved—between the perpetrator, the victim, and their webs of relations—and an attempt to understand why and how personal and social relations broke down, and how, if at all, they might be restored. It would examine the context of the given moral situation and use relationships—relationships not only of intimacy but of power—as a starting point for thinking about responses. It would ask who has been harmed by the situation, what relationships have been disrupted, who has been abandoned, left alone, or hurt. Moreover, the type of moral response that arises is not one based on the necessity of fulfilling a *duty* or seeking to be *fair;* rather, it is a mode of responsiveness which may vary according to the nature of the particular moral situation. Contrary to the claims of some critics, care ethics does not preclude the possibility—indeed, the frequent necessity—of judging between right and wrong. What it denies is that there are some principles which can allow us to determine what is right and wrong in all, or at least all similar, moral situations.

Indeed, the ethics of care may defend itself against the charge that it cannot tell us what to do by challenging the pretence that abstract norms ever 'tell us' what to do. Rules appear to be clear guides to action only after all that makes a given context unique has been subtracted. An attention to contextual detail, by contrast, neither rejects normative considerations nor alters them on a premise that any value is as good as another. Indeed, a commitment to paying closer attention to the relationship between particular contexts and particular values may contain, in itself, some measure of moral value. As Martha Minow has argued: 'denying the multiplicity of moral perspectives and demands does not make them go away; instead, it marks a rigid either/or thinking that constrains moral understanding'.[19] This is similar to the pragmatist approach, which denies that universalist and relativist approaches to morality are the only two options. In pragmatism, 'values are categorized as relative to context but not relativistic, as applying to more situations than those in which they initially arose without falling into false universalism, and as being objectively identifiable despite their origins in the uniqueness of each subject'.[20]

By shaping an understanding of care which can help us to cope with the moral problems of international relations, relational thinking transcends the limitations which have brought criticisms from both feminist and nonfeminist theorists. Indeed, while most writers on normative theory are fond of reminding us why ethics must be *brought in* or included in the study of international relations, it is worth thinking not just about what ethics can bring to international relations but about what international relations can bring to ethics. As a discipline with its share of abstract theories, but also one which is intensely concerned with the worst situations of human suffering—war and violent conflict, poverty and injustice, environmental degradation—international relations simply cannot avoid addressing (as ethics has often succeeded in doing) the difficult and often messy business of living in this world. Remembering that international relations first emerged as a discipline concerned with ending the violence and destruction caused by war, it becomes clear that what international relations can bring to ethics is the stark reminder that 'styles of moral thinking are not primarily philosophical brain teasers, data begging for the maximally elegant theoretical construction'.[21] As Bernard Williams has argued, 'the only serious enterprise is living, and we have to live after the reflection; moreover (though the distinction of theory and practice encourages us to forget it), we have to live during it as well'.[22]

The Global Context of Care

The previous chapter explored some of the key debates surrounding the ethics of care, including the claim that care might have moral relevance beyond strictly personal, intimate relationships. The remainder of this chapter explores in more detail the responses to, and potential for, the development of the ethics of care for the global context.

In spite of what might be called the intuitive links between the relational/interpersonal morality of care and the interdependent nature of the contemporary globalizing world, the question of the global dimensions of care has been met by feminist theorists with a mixture of compromise and silence. Indeed, the idea of 'globalizing care' is rarely explicitly addressed; more often than not, theorists are concerned with overcoming the 'problem' of parochialism often seen to be inherent in the theory of care, rather than with seeing the global implications of care as a new and challenging avenue to be explored.

The apparent particularism and parochialism of care have often made it difficult for even the advocates of care ethics to imagine how caring could be translated into a world in which many of the most pressing problems are distinctly global problems. Care does not, at first sight, seem to respond well to distance. This, of course, contrasts starkly with justice ethics or rights-based moral reasoning, for which 'distance' ensures impartiality and is therefore fundamental to sound moral judgement. Given that it is a morality of closeness rather than distance, how useful could an ethics of care be when applied to the global context? 'How difficult is it to translate care and moral responsibility from family and intimates, to public and especially to international levels?'[23]

Joan Tronto, for example, argues that parochialism is one of the 'dangers of care'. She claims that

> those who are enmeshed in ongoing, continuing relationships of care are likely to see the caring relationships that they are engaged in, and which they know best, as the most important. . . . Care as a political ideal could quickly become a way to argue that everyone should cultivate one's own garden, and let others take care of themselves, too.

Although Tronto goes on to articulate some radical ideas for 'politicizing' care, as well as to vehemently criticize the claim that the ethics of care should remain in the 'private' sphere, she seems to feel compelled to capitulate to justice ethics where the global context is concerned. Her solution to this dilemma—indeed, the only solution she claims she can see—is to 'insist that care needs to be connected to a theory of justice and to be relentlessly democratic in its disposition'.[24] Thus, it would seem that while an ethic of care may be useful in the domestic context of the democratic polity (the modern liberal democratic nation-state), only an ethic of justice can adequately address and respond to the unique problems of moral relations across borders.

Similarly, Marilyn Friedman argues that global moral concerns raise a unique problem for the conception of a self whose identity is defined in terms of relationships to certain others; specifically, it leads us to ask whether concern for distant and unknown people is an immediate moral motivation of the social self. Ultimately, she suggests, this vision of the self is unable to ground the widest sort of concern for others; this, in turn, forces us to 'confront the apparent fragility of the human motivation of global concern'.[25] Thus, her unique formulation of care—her feminist partialist view—is disabled when it confronts the international dimensions of these moral questions.

Alison Jaggar argues that when we try to make care applicable to large-scale social or global issues by 'enlarging our moral imagination', we reduce care to 'a moral motive, not a distinctive mode of moral response', which is 'incompatible with the characteristically interactive and personal relation that defines care thinking'.[26] Caring about distant others, she argues, can amount to a 'form of colonization', since the distance that separates us from these others removes the interpersonal element of care. Nel Noddings, who has addressed this question specifically, argues that when others are too distant or too numerous for personal caring relations to be established with them, we must either press their neighbours to care for them or seek to empower them to help themselves: 'I have to trust others to do the direct work of caring when I cannot be present'.[27]

Virginia Held's thoughts on what care might mean for 'distant others' are slightly more encouraging. Held argues that, to be adequate, moral theories must pay attention to the neglected realm of particular others in the actual relationships and actual contexts of women's experiences. A result of such a focus might be that the salient moral problems would then be seen as 'how we ought best to guide or to maintain or to reshape the relationships, both close and more distant, that we have, or might have, with actual other human beings. Particular others can be actual children in need in distant continents or the anticipated children of generations not yet even close to being born'.[28] In discussing the possibilities of moral relations across distances of space and time, Held hints at the possibility that an ethic of care might have dimensions beyond the family and domestic society.

The alleged parochialism of care, like its alleged essentialism and alleged antifeminism, are all just that: allegations, even fears, which emerge from the widespread perception that care is primarily, if not exclusively, a morality of the private sphere. Thus, it is hardly surprising that theorists have been reluctant or unable to think about the global implications of care. Indeed, it has proven difficult enough to wrench care from the private sphere of home and family relationships and into the public sphere of domestic politics. Given that it is a morality of closeness rather than distance, how useful could an ethics of care possibly be, then, when applied to the global context? Surely it is precisely that distance—

the physical/spatial, cultural, and psychological distance between moral agents—that we must address and accommodate in thinking about international or *global* ethics?

According to many theorists of globalization and global social change, however, the contemporary world order is marked by a profound change in what distance means. The notion of the 'shrinking world' suggests that, in some important way, distances are effectively being reduced, and that this shrinking, in turn, has a disembedding effect on *places*—the physical settings of social activity as situated geographically. The result, then, is the 'fostering of relations between "absent" others, locationally distant from any given situation of face-to-face interaction'.[29] While this process is often described as a feature of modernity (where modernity is seen as the modes of social life and organization which emerged in Europe from about the seventeenth century onwards), it is a process which has profoundly accelerated in the contemporary period of late or high modernity.[30]

It is precisely these sorts of transformations that Joan Tronto has in mind when, eschewing the strict deontological separation between 'is' and 'ought', she asks, '[W]hat changes in life that have occurred by the end of the twentieth century might change our perceptions of adequate moral argument?'[31] It is clear that these processes of change are significant for ethics; ironically, however, the most common reaction to globalization has been to return to the universalism of Kant. Notwithstanding the controversy over globalization, it cannot be denied that the contemporary world is increasingly interdependent; today we defy both time and space through advances in communications, transportation, and information technology. More than ever before, the world is 'a single place', comprising human beings equally vulnerable to, for example, ecological threats; clearly, this is a world in which the idea of 'humanity' has, for many people, increasing relevance. It is perhaps not surprising that a cosmopolitan ethics has many attractions in a world which is in some ways more threatening, and in others, more united.

It could also be argued, however, that this vision of a united humanity is largely illusory, and that what is important about the contemporary global situation is that it forces us to confront the unique paradox of increasing interrelatedness in the context of profound differences. Globalization has not replaced the exclusionary mechanisms of the modern international system; it is still characterized by sovereign statehood, nationalisms, and a highly unequal global economy. Indeed, in spite of the rhetoric of globalization, a globalizing world may even be a world in which existing asymmetries in power and well-being are exacerbated. A global ethics, if it is to be at all useful, must address difference and exclusion; I would argue, specifically, that it must address difference by seeing it as constituted in and through relationships. It must adopt a critical perspective on knowledge and power, rejecting the notion of impartiality and recognizing that the 'norm' is actually an unstated but specific point of reference, and that the status quo cannot be unquestioningly accepted as natural, uncoerced, or good.[32] An era of globalization is indeed one that is characterized by new relationships and profound interdependence; it is also, however, characterized by radical differences, perceptions of differences that are affected by power relations, and patterns of exclusion. An ethics for such an era cannot remain at a distance, adopt a 'view from nowhere', or remain behind a 'veil of ignorance', viewing global actors as autonomous, equal participants in contractual political, economic, and moral relations. An era of global interdependence demands a *relational* ethics which places the highest value on the promotion, restoration, or creation of good social and personal relations and gives priority to the needs and concerns of 'concrete' rather than 'generalizable' others.

It is a critical ethics of care which can provide the most fruitful starting point for thinking about morality and moral responsiveness in the world today. What this means is not simply that the powerful must learn to 'care about' the suffering and the destitute in what could possibly—although not necessarily—become a paternalistic act which preserves existing power relations. It means that those who are powerful have a responsibility to approach moral problems by looking carefully at where, why, and how the structures of existing social and personal relations have led to exclusion and marginalization, as well as at how attachments may have degenerated or broken down so as to cause suffering. This kind of moral thinking encourages us to see such problems not only as moral but also as social and political. To care for others and to foster caring relations within and among families, social groups, and political communities involves the ability to recognize persons as concrete and unique (rather than as idealized, independent agents) and to learn how to focus attention on others. In the context of North-South relations, for example, strategies based on caring would eschew both paternalism and 'charity', on the one hand, and the false rhetoric of 'partnership' and formal equality on the other.[33] Instead, strategies for the eradication of poverty and the promotion of human well-being would start from the premise that responding morally to others is a capacity which is learned. This involves a recognition that moral response is not a rational act of will, but an ability to focus attention on another and to recognize the other as real. Such recognition is neither natural nor presocial, but rather something that emerges out of connections and attachments. In the context of North-South relations, then, strategies would require sustained and continued attention to the lives, relations, and communities of people in developing countries, rather than to their individual rights, or to the scope and nature of our obligations to them. Specific projects not only would seek to understand and learn about the nature of social relations within a given community but would attempt to build relations among members of those communities and members of agencies and institutions in the North. Building these relations would be done with the conviction that human beings can learn to focus and refocus their attention, to revise what they regard as 'important', and to rethink what 'counts' both as morally valuable and, simply, as moral.

Only a *critical,* politicized ethics of care will be useful in the realm of international relations. Alison Jaggar has correctly observed that, in much writing on care, the emphasis on the quality of individual relations seems to preclude the capacity of caring to address the structural oppositions between the interests of social groups that make caring difficult or unlikely between members of those groups. She also suggests that care thinking seems unable to focus on the social causes of many individual problems, such as widespread homelessness and hunger, both of which, she notes, have disproportionately severe effects on women.[34] Onora O'Neill articulates the problem in terms of the advantages of justice ethics over the ethics of care: 'Justice matters for impoverished providers because their predicament is one of institutionally structured poverty, which cannot be banished by idealizing an ethic of care and insisting on its place in face-to-face relationships'.[35]

These criticisms must be taken seriously. Any approach to ethics which claims to address the moral problems of international relations cannot overlook the structural causes of patterns of moral inclusion and exclusion on a global scale. An ethics of care must not only be about reflecting upon and promoting relations which motivate and encourage the moral qualities of attentiveness and communication among moral agents. It must also reflect critically on why certain global structures inhibit the creation and development of such relations, and on whether patterns of 'community-making', and hence exclusion, serve to undermine the ability of moral agents to identify and understand others as 'real' individuals—with real, special, unique lives.

Thus, what is required for the global context is not a narrow or 'orthodox' understanding of care as a moral orientation or disposition, but a relational ethics supported by a critical awareness of the structures of exclusion and oppression which restrict our ability to recognize or relate to others as particular individuals, thwart the development of caring relations, and inhibit the ability of individual persons to speak freely in their own voices. A useful ethics in the context of international relations must be one, as Joan Tronto has argued, which breaks down the boundaries between morality and politics.[36] An ethics of care is not about the application of a universal principle ('We all must care about all others') nor is it about a sentimental ideal ('A more caring world will be a better world'). Rather, it is a starting point for transforming the values and practices of international society; thus, it requires an examination of the contexts in which caring does or does not take place, and a commitment to the creation of more humanly responsive institutions which can be shaped to embody expressive and communicative possibilities between actors on a global scale.[37] When an ethics of care is combined with a critical examination of how structural features of institutionalized relations enable or deform the abilities of all concerned to hear and to be heard, an ethics of care can combat exclusion and oppression in the international system. Seen in this way, the 'relational turn'—in thinking about ethics—represents not a denial or lack of interest in conflict, power, domination, and oppression, but rather a focus on the 'interpersonal and social contexts in which these and all other human relations occur'.[38]

Joan Tronto has argued that, in the context of American society, care can provide us with a 'critical standpoint', in that it 'becomes a tool for critical political analysis when we use this concept to reveal relationships of power'.[39] This is equally true in the context of international relations and the global political economy. A useful global ethics must be profoundly aware of the context in which caring relations are created and sustained. It must be a critical morality which reflects on and seeks to expose the structures of exclusion and oppression which inhibit the creation of caring relations or render individuals unable to speak in their own voice. Indeed, it is because weak individuals and groups are often unable to speak in their own voice that contractarian ethics—which relies on consent—and liberal theories—which assume autonomy and formal equality—are often inadequate. A relational morality should encourage, not emotional or economic dependence, but interdependence, through the creation of a sense of self-esteem and mutual respect and an atmosphere of trust and responsibility among moral agents who recognize and respond to each other as concrete others.

Thus, while international ethics must not ignore care, so care ethics must not ignore or subvert, but must embrace the dilemmas of *global* moral relations. We cannot afford to dismiss the wider implications of care ethics simply because it is an idea which takes as its ethical starting point the contextualized relationships between particular, concrete others—such as those between a mother and child, or between friends. The suggestion that care ethics is inappropriate in large-scale or genuinely administrative contexts, or for dealing with unknown or little-known persons (precisely the contexts with which the theory of international relations must be concerned) demonstrates a narrow reading of 'care' and a limited moral imagination. We must not be led by such a reading to dismiss the role of caring in international relations; instead, we must acknowledge the necessity of rethinking and reconstructing care ethics in the face of the inadequacy of strictly rights-based or justice ethics. Indeed, we must recognize that the suggestion that only an impersonal, impartial, universal-prescriptive ethics is useful in large-scale contexts is what maintains and upholds our disposition to 'keep strangers strange and outsiders outside'; it is this disposition towards distant others which must be overcome.[40]

It is sometimes argued that relations across large distances—especially global or transnational relations—require mediating institutions, which necessarily depersonalize relations, therefore rendering care inappropriate or impossible as a type of moral response. However, as Margaret Walker argues, distancing, depersonalizing, or paternalistic attitudes may not really be the only resorts if *roles and institutions can be shaped to embody expressive and communicative possibilities.* She points out that more humanly responsive institutions are often said to be impractical. But, she argues, if moral-practical intelligence is understood consistently in terms of caring, it may instead be correct to say that certain incorrigibly impersonal or depersonalizing institutions are too morally impractical to be tolerated. Thus, *it is crucial to examine how structural features of institutionalized relations combine with typical situations to enable or deform the abilities of all concerned to hear and to be heard.*[41]

Some advocates of rights-based contractarian or obligation-centred Kantian styles of ethical reasoning argue that individual rights, guaranteed through the social contract and enshrined in law, or universal duties, guaranteed through the categorical imperative, provide a 'safety net' for individuals who are alone and disempowered—those for whom no one cares. Certainly, this is a strength of such traditions; one should not dismiss outright the rhetorical appeal, and indeed the progressive force, of the human rights discourse. However, as Onora O'Neill has argued, the discourse about rights often makes do with a remarkably indeterminate view of agency.[42] Proclaiming that the poor, the needy, and the powerless have rights tells us very little about why they are unable to exercise those rights, and about who is responsible for what sort of action to alter their state of poverty or powerlessness. Moreover, even a view of global morality as universal obligations must rely on a highly implausible picture of moral motivation, and it does not, in fact, tell us very much about the actual content or nature of those obligations. While a wholesale rejection of notions of individual rights and obligations is surely undesirable, one may still accept the profound moral incompleteness of an ethics dominated by these concepts. In a world which appears to have been little moved by the repeated verbal bludgeoning of human rights declarations, universalistic references to 'human dignity', and the shared nature of all 'humanity', an ethics of care offers us the opportunity to move beyond the rhetoric of cosmopolitanism and the exclusionary and often conservative ethics of communitarianism. Care transcends the moral idea of communities—whether they are particular nation-states or the 'global community of humankind'—giving priority instead to 'voicing and hearing, to being answerable in and for specific encounters and relationships'.[43] Learning how to care adequately is about not striving to be an autonomous, moral agent who responds impartially to the moral claims of all individuals. Instead, it is about 'sensitivity and responsiveness to another person's emotional states, individuating differences, specific uniqueness and whole particularity'.[44]

Because it is an *interpersonal* view of ethics, care allows problems of individual self-interest versus universal rules to recede into a region more like background, out-of-focus insolubility, or relative unimportance.[45] Indeed, a critical ethics of care could eclipse the quintessential problem of international relations theory: resolving the conflict between our 'egoistic' roles and duties as citizens and our 'altruistic' roles and duties as human beings. This problem, framed in terms of the cosmopolitan-communitarian debate in normative international relations theory, dominates the literature on international ethics. This debate, and the liberal-contractualist ethics on which both perspectives are based, are the subject of the next chapter.

Notes

1. Bernard Williams, *Ethics and the Limits of Philosophy,* 2nd ed., London: Fontana, 1993, p. 72.
2. Ibid., p. 93.
3. Ibid., p. 197.
4. Jean Bethke Elshtain, 'International Politics and Political Theory', in Ken Booth and Steve Smith, eds., *International Relations Theory Today,* Cambridge: Polity Press, 1995, p. 271.
5. Geoffrey Hawthorn, *Plausible Worlds: Possibility and Understanding in History and the Social Sciences,* Cambridge: Cambridge University Press, 1992, p. 182.
6. Elshtain, 'International Politics', p. 272.
7. Hawthorn, *Plausible Worlds,* p. 35.
8. See Charlene Haddock Seigfried, *Pragmatism and Feminism: Reweaving the Social Fabric,* Chicago: University of Chicago Press, 1996.
9. Ibid., p. 37.
10. Ibid., p. 32.
11. Hawthorn, *Plausible Worlds,* pp. 183–184.
12. Joan Tronto, *Moral Boundaries: A Political Argument for an Ethic of Care,* London: Routledge, 1993, pp. 126–127.
13. Carol Gilligan, *In a Different Voice: Psychological Theory and Women's Development,* 2nd ed., Cambridge, MA: Harvard University Press, 1993, pp. 35, 57.
14. Marilyn Friedman, *What Are Friends For: Feminist Perspectives on Personal Relationships and Moral Theory,* Ithaca, NY: Cornell University Press, 1993, p. 233.

15. Joan Tronto (*Moral Boundaries*) identifies four elements: attentiveness, responsiveness, competence, and responsibility. Margaret Urban Walker ('Moral Understandings: Alternative "Epistemology" for a Feminist Ethics', in Virginia Held and Alison Jaggar, eds., *Justice and Care: Essential Readings in Feminist Ethics,* Boulder, CO: Westview, 1995) isolates three elements of attention, contextual and narrative appreciation, and communication.

16. Walker, 'Moral Understandings', p. 145.

17. Ibid., p. 144.

18. Martha Minow, *Making All the Difference: Inclusion, Exclusion, and American Law,* Ithaca, NY: Cornell University Press, 1990, p. 222.

19. Ibid.

20. Siegfried, *Pragmatism and Feminism,* p. 217.

21. Walker, 'Moral Understandings', p. 147.

22. Williams, *Ethics and the Limits of Philosophy,* p. 117.

23. Jan Jindy Pettman, *Worlding Women: A Feminist International Politics,* London: Routledge, 1996, p. 119.

24. Tronto, *Moral Boundaries,* pp. 170–171.

25. Friedman, *What Are Friends For?,* pp. 87–88.

26. Jaggar, 'Caring as a Feminist Practice', p. 197.

27. Nel Noddings, 'The Alleged Parochialism of Caring', *American Philosophical Association Newsletter on Feminism and Philosophy* 90, no. 2, Winter 1991: 97–98.

28. Held, *Feminist Morality: Transforming Culture, Society and Politics.* Chicago: University of Chicago Press, 1993.

29. Anthony Giddens, *The Consequences of Modernity,* Cambridge: Polity Press, 1990, p. 18.

30. Ibid., p. 1.

31. Tronto, *Moral Boundaries,* p. 57.

32. Minow, *Making All the Difference,* pp. 50–70.

33. Laura Macdonald, 'Unequal Partnerships: The Politics of Canada's Relations with the Third World', *Studies in Political Economy,* no. 47, Summer 1995: 124–135. I am grateful to Laura Macdonald for bringing to my attention the changing moral strategies of NGOs (non-governmental organizations) in their relations with peoples in the South.

34. Jaggar, 'Caring as a Feminist Practice', pp. 196–197.

35. O'Neill, 'Justice, Gender, and International Boundaries', p. 60.

36. Tronto, *Moral Boundaries,* pp. 6–9.

37. Walker, 'Moral Understandings' , p. 147.

38. Minow, *Making All the Difference,* p. 198.

39. Tronto, *Moral Boundaries,* pp. 172–173.

40. Walker, 'Moral Understandings', p. 147.

41. Ibid.

42. O'Neill, *Faces of Hunger,* pp. 118–119.

43. Minow, *Making All the Difference,* p. 145.

44. Marilyn Friedman, 'Beyond Caring: The De-Moralisation of Gender', in Held and Jaggar, *Justice and Care,* p. 71.

45. Virginia Held, *Feminist Morality,* p. 59.

4

Traditions of International Ethics: A Critical Reappraisal

The languages of rights and liberalism are probably the most frequently used in contemporary international politics. The language of rights, in particular, has become predominant. . . . The contractarian vocabulary—of agreement, reciprocity, contractual obligation, and especially 'fairness'—is widely used in popular debate on international issues, particularly when the issues are economic ones.

David R. Mapel and Terry Nardin, 'Convergence and Divergence in International Ethics', 1992 (pp. 318–319)

Chapters 2 and 3 traced the development of the literature on the ethics of care and explored the questions and controversies surrounding feminist ethics and the idea of globalizing care. The notion of care as a feminine or even feminist morality was rejected, based on the argument that the gendering of moral outlooks can reinforce gender stereotypes by essentializing and naturalizing, rather than problematizing, socially constructed norms surrounding gender roles. On the question of the compatibility of justice ethics and the ethics of care, it was argued that notions of care cannot simply be added to liberal-contractarian or rights-based theories of justice in an effort to remedy the shortcomings of these approaches. What is required, instead, is a reshaping of the idea and goals of ethics in order that they may address not only the real needs and concerns of particular persons but the normative and structural constraints which erect exclusive moral boundaries and inhibit the creation of caring relations both within and between social groups.

Finally, on the alleged parochialism of care, it was suggested that this assumption—that the ethics of care focuses on the 'micro' moral dilemmas of particular and, specifically, intimate relations among concrete individuals, thus obfuscating the wider, often structural causes and implications of moral situations which generate the need for caring responses—is indeed a *potential* but not *necessarily an unavoidable* limitation of care ethics. However, it was argued that any useful approach to ethics in the context of global social and political relations *must* take seriously the wider structural and institutional obstacles to caring, as well as the extent to which all relations are infused with power and contain at least the potential for exploitation and domination.

Before developing that argument, this chapter looks more closely at the dominant traditions in international ethics and at how an adherence to these traditions of ethical reasoning has produced a narrow and limited debate. First, it explores the defining principles and historical development of liberal contractarianism and rights-based ethics; the aim of this section is to demonstrate the extent to which the central norms of the international system of states—including autonomy, reciprocity, non-intervention, and more broadly, the idea of freedom—may be traced to this tradition in moral and political theory. As will be shown, liberal contractarian notions of rights, justice, fairness, reciprocity, and non-interference are crucial elements of most contemporary accounts, both cosmopolitan and communitarian, of international ethics.

The second section explores in more detail the opposition between cosmopolitan and communitarian approaches to normative international relations theory. First, it discusses the deontological, liberal, universalist ethics which defines the cosmopolitan position; second, it examines the distinctive visions of the self and the nature of moral relations which characterize communitarianism. It is suggested that, in many respects, the social view of the self espoused by many communitarian philosophers is a welcome antidote to the metaphysical grandness of Kantian ethics and the rational individualism of liberal-contractarianism. However, it will be shown that, as a normative theory of international relations, communitarianism has many limitations; because 'political community' has regularly been understood as synonymous with 'nation-state', this focus on preexisting, established communities has obscured the possibility of alternative communities, and hence, of a vision of global ethics which could emerge from a communitarian understanding of ethics and politics.[1] Cosmopolitan perspectives, moreover, ignore both the *particularity* and the *connectedness* of persons and focus instead on their moral status as *human beings*. By regarding persons as abstract and autonomous, rather than concrete and attached, these approaches overlook a crucial facet of moral motivation and an important feature of what adequate moral responsiveness actually means. It is a feature of the dominant Western ethical perspectives that morality is regarded as wholly distinct from politics; within Kantian and rights-based moral theory, social and political dimensions of moral problems are systematically obfuscated and little or no reference is made to the relationships—personal, social, and political—and the structures—economic, social, and political—in which the moral problems of international relations are embedded.

The contribution of both cosmopolitan and communitarian perspectives to moral enquiry in the context of international relations will always be limited. For although we may apply these perspectives to particular ethical issues in international relations, they cannot go very far towards actually helping us to understand the suffering or the needs of real persons in moral crises. Because they are preoccupied with the question of the source of moral value and the question of the scope of our rights and obligations, they reduce what is a complex world composed of overlapping networks of personal and social relations to a world made up only of 'men' and 'citizens'. In assuming that the recognition of a shared identity is a necessary prerequisite for the recognition of rights and obligations, and in asserting that morality, in the context of international relations, can be subsumed within the moral concepts of rights and obligations, these approaches ignore the fact that moral relations and responses are a continuous part of all our connections with others, and that we use a vast range of moral qualities—including care, trust, and patience—in our everyday relations with others.

Liberalism and Contractarianism

> *It would be no exaggeration to say that this assumption—that the only coherent idea of liberty is the negative one of being unconstrained—has underpinned the entire development of modern contractarian thought.*
>
> **Quentin Skinner, 'The Idea of Negative Liberty', 1984 (p. 194)**

Political philosophers would, no doubt, find it odd that Machiavelli and Hobbes are often introduced to students of international relations as representatives of a shared view on the nature of international politics; they are, students are told, the 'founding fathers of realism'. Machiavelli, it is said, brought us the idea that princes must act to protect themselves and their territories and never be swayed by the demands of morality. Hobbes, moreover, introduced the model of anarchy, as described in his 'state of nature', and confirmed the naturally competitive and warring nature of all participants living under this anarchical structure. Many political theorists, however, would make more of the differences between these two philosophers than the similarities. For example, Hobbes's individualistic, contractarian style of political reasoning, and the view of 'negative liberty' to which it gave rise, is often contrasted with the revived classical republicanism of Machiavelli and the corresponding view of freedom as inextricably linked with civic duties. As R. B. J. Walker has noted, however, it is characteristic of international relations theory that the writings of political philosophers have been narrowed and even caricatured in order to demonstrate the desired historical antecedent.[2] Thus, the civic republican notion of freedom articulated by Machiavelli has been lost in realism's conceptual development and contemporary self-portrayal as an amoral theory of power politics. There may indeed be, in contemporary realist theory, claims about the primacy of the state which echo these arguments regarding civic participation, liberty, and virtue; when presented in realism, however, they have been purged of their normative content, and the values associated with freedom and responsibility become subordinated to the demands of power and politics.

Hobbes, too, is presented as a realist in international relations theory; his 'state of nature' provides the definitive model of the anarchical international system. Again, however, it is rarely seen as contradictory that while orthodox international relations theory strongly associates Hobbes with realism, political theorists recognize him as an early liberal (or, at least, the first to articulate what have become central liberal values). Perhaps there are fewer differences between realist and liberal approaches than orthodox international relations theory has traditionally suggested; the strong, negative view of liberty as the right to non-interference which is reminiscent of Hobbes is a defining feature of certain strands of both liberal and realist accounts.

The following section argues that it is a Hobbesian liberalism—accompanied by the Hobbesian assumption that 'any theory of negative liberty must in effect be a theory of individual rights'—which has determined both the type of moral reasoning and the specific moral categories which define the nature of relationships in the international system.[3] These contractual concepts and categories may also be said to characterize the dominant mode of moral reasoning in Western ethics. As Annette Baier notes, modern moral philosophy has concentrated on the morality of fairly cool relationships between those who are deemed to be roughly equal in power to determine the rules and to instigate sanctions against rule breakers.[4] Because it leaves the power relations and organizing principles of the international system fundamentally unchallenged, liberal contractarianism—the ethics of rights and obligations—is the acceptable voice of morality in international relations. To understand international ethics solely in these terms is to overestimate seriously the ability of this type of moral reasoning to address the moral issues raised in contemporary international relations.

For liberal theorists in the classical contractarian tradition, the widest possible area of individual freedom is required to protect the individual from arbitrary power. In this view, freedom is ensured by minimizing the interference of the state. The wider the area of non-interference, the wider the individual's freedom. This, Isaiah Berlin argues, is what the classical English political philosophers meant when they used this word: simply, that there ought to exist a certain minimal area of personal freedom which must on no account be violated; 'for if it is overstepped, the individual will find himself in an area too narrow for even that minimum development possible to pursue, and even to conceive, the various ends which men hold good or right or sacred'.[5] Liberty is guaranteed through a system of individual rights, which exist in order to ensure that individuals are subject to no other vision of the good life than their own.

The individualism inherent in the theory of negative liberty—the claim that the ideal human condition is one in which each individual is surrounded by a kind of 'invisible fence' which separates and protects him from the interference of the state and other groups in society—leads to an emphasis on individual rights over any other moral values. Indeed, it is characteristic of the liberal position to advocate a society in which citizens should be able to exercise their human and civil rights without the threat of intrusion—physical or psychological—by others. This is based on a strong belief that the individual is the best and only judge of his or her own good, on the grounds that 'he has privileged access to the contents of his own mind', and that society should be governed by a set of minimal rules, the purpose of which is not to dictate but to facilitate the seeking of these individual ends.[6] Thus, Brian Barry has described liberalism as 'the vision of society as made up of independent, autonomous units who co-operate only when the terms of co-operation are such as to make it further the ends of each of the parties'.[7]

The very fact that some measure of co-operation is necessary, moreover, is what introduces the need for a contract. Contractarian arguments use a procedure of collective rational choice to show how legitimate political institutions might arise.[8] Early contractarian arguments were employed to explain the move from arbitrary to rational rule. Civil society was conceived to be the outcome of individual negotiation; individuals surrender their inherent, absolute rights of liberty in order to obtain a condition of civility conducive to their utility. Because of their natural equality and liberty, individuals can construct society only through free, individual exchanges of equivalent benefits; reciprocity makes social life possible, and consent gives force to obligations.[9] Thus, while in the state of nature individuals are free to exercise their natural rights, it is only through the social contract and the creation of civil society that the reciprocal relationship between rights and duties is formed. By freely entering into the contract, we consent to sovereign rule as a form of self-rule; at the same time, we enter into a moral relationship with society as a whole in which we see rights and duties as two sides of the contractarian coin.

The early contractarian political theorists, including Hobbes and Locke, argued that the law preserves our liberty essentially by coercing other people. It prevents them from interfering with our acknowledged rights, helps us to draw around ourselves a circle within which they may not trespass, and prevents us at the same time from interfering with their freedom in just the same way. Our freedom—or, in other words, our rights—are our natural possession, a property of ourselves.[10] Thus, in Hobbes's words,

> Liberty, or Freedome, signifieth (properly) the absence of Opposition; . . . And according to this proper, and generally received meaning of the word, A FREE-MAN, is he, that in those things, which by his strength and wit he is able to do, is not hindred to doe what he has a will to.[11]

Initially, most contractarian arguments conceived of social contracts as having force only within particular political communities; thus, classical contractarianism generally held, first, that circumstances of distributive or social justice principally arise between members of a co-operative scheme, and second, that the state is the largest such scheme.[12] Thus, it might be said that the classical contractarians were not contractarians of international ethics, precisely because they thought that sufficient reciprocity did not exist in international affairs.[13] However, as Linklater points out, international obligations are not necessarily incompatible with statist contractarianism. The importance of a relatively stable international condition may give rise to a variety of international practices. Diplomacy, international law, and the balance of power (crucial elements of the modern states system) reflect the capacity of particularistic political entities to articulate their separate interests. Through the operation of mutual consent, states can extend the web of social relations; reciprocity facilitates the development of a society of states.[14]

Moreover, it could be argued that it is the philosophy of Kant which has provided the strongest and most enduring statement of the union of contractarianism and deontological universalism. That said, it is certainly the case that important differences exist between Kantian and contractarian views of morality. In the latter view, our obligations are dependent on what others have done—if you have benefited me, I should benefit you in turn—whereas for Kant, our duties are categorical. Thus, it could be argued that reciprocity and fairness invoke a more social understanding of morality, whereas for Kant, obligations are grounded in a metaphysical notion of the self and in the idea of autonomy.[15] In spite of this, however, Kant's *international political theory* demonstrates a conscious attempt to eliminate the gap between contractarianism and universalism. As Linklater argues, the fiction of a social contract, which Kant employs in his analyses of just domestic and international arrangements, overcomes the distinction between actual consent which empirical men might give and the rational consent which they would give if they fully observed the moral law. Here the contract will be used to determine what would emerge from the rational consent of autonomous individuals.[16] Thus, Kant posits a contract which elicits the rational consent of moral agents.[17]

Certainly, Kant's ethics has provided the groundwork for a number of leading contemporary accounts of justice, including that of John Rawls. As Shapiro has convincingly argued, the primary concern of such contemporary liberals has been to find a way to hold on to the ontological conception of the individual of the seventeenth-century writers but simultaneously to find an alternative moral basis that both acknowledges the centrality of that individual's freedom and limits his power to act in any way he pleases. This has been attempted, he argues, principally by embracing a version of Kant's ethics that appears both to acknowledge the centrality of the autonomous individual and to generate universal moral injunctions.[18]

Not surprisingly, because of their universalist aspirations, Kantian versions of contractarianism have been attractive to theorists of international ethics. Charles Beitz, for example, constructs an argument for a Kantian, cosmopolitan conception of international morality which is concerned with the moral relations of members of a universal community in which state boundaries have a merely derivative significance. He reasons that if global economic and political interdependence is shown to be supported by a global scheme of social co-operation, we should not view national boundaries as having fundamental moral significance. Since boundaries are not coextensive with the scope of social co-operation, they do not mark the limits of social obligations.[19] Thus, Beitz takes what may be called a Kantian contractual position: the moral terms of contractarianism are united with a universal code of obligations to all human beings.

Michael Walzer takes a very different contractarian position in *Spheres of Justice*. Arguing from a communitarian position, Walzer presents what he describes as a 'radically particularist' account of justice. At the outset, he flatly denies that the global market can be described as a 'complete distributive system', and hence he rejects the assumption that there is only one distributive system that philosophy can rightly encompass.[20] For Walzer, the political community is probably the closest we can come to a world of common meanings; in taking the globe as the setting for a theory of justice, we would have to imagine what does not yet exist: a community that includes all men and women everywhere.[21] Walzer rejects the notion of 'natural' or 'human' rights. He asserts that men and women do indeed have *some* rights, but that they do not follow from our common humanity. They follow, he argues, from shared conceptions of social goods; they are local and particular in character.[22] Moreover, although he claims that the purpose of a community goes beyond socially contracted rights and obligations (that is, what the members of the political community 'owe to one another and to no one else'), he suggests that 'contract' and 'community'—'mutual aid' and *'amour social'*—are reciprocal and mutually reinforcing concepts. 'Mutual provision', he claims, 'breeds mutuality'.[23] Thus, in spite of his communitarian approach, his pluralism, and his insistence on limiting the scope, or 'sphere', of justice, Walzer's language is unmistakably contractarian:

> Here, then, is a more precise account of the social contract: it is an agreement to redistribute the resources of the members in accordance with some shared understanding of their needs, subject to ongoing political determination in detail. The contract is a moral bond. It connects the strong and the weak, the lucky and the unlucky, the rich and the poor, creating a union that transcends all differences of interest, drawing its strength from history, culture, religion, language and so on.[24]

The relevance of the contractarian tradition to international relations may be found not only in the accounts of justice described earlier but in the conventional understanding of the international system of sovereign states. As Beitz notes, the conception of international relations as a state of nature could be viewed as an application of the analogy of states and persons. Another application, moreover, is the idea that states, like persons, have a right to be respected as sovereign entities.[25] The liberal idea of the 'sovereign' man—rational and therefore prepared to enter into contractual relations with other self-interested, rational parties—mirrors the conventional understanding of the sovereign state. Indeed, the non-intervention principle has often been explained with reference to an analogy with personal liberty. Wolff claims: 'Nations are regarded as individual free persons living in a state of nature'. He argues that nations, like persons, are moral equals: 'Since by nature all nations are equal, since moreover all men are equal in a moral sense whose rights and obligations are the same; the rights and obligations of all nations are also by nature the same'.[26] Indeed, this characterization of international relations—as a state of nature analogous to the one which social contract theorists presumed to have existed formerly among individuals—is deeply embedded within the Western political tradition and continues to be reflected within contemporary accounts of the structure of international society.[27]

Although, in international society, the contract is incomplete and the system is said to be anarchic, the structure of the international system is still presumed to be one in which a contractarian model of relations, based on a kind of prudential reciprocity, applies. In the reciprocal relationship between mutually disinterested sovereign states, I observe your territorial integrity (negative liberty) because in doing so I reinforce a system in which you are expected to observe mine. In this way, the claims of states are the international equivalent of those basic rights of individuals that are familiar in the domestic arena, including the right to security (of the territory) and the right to liberty (of the independent polity).[28]

Despite the fact that contemporary realist and liberal theories seek to distance their arguments from normative considerations, the influence of liberal and contractarian political philosophy is evident not only in what is addressed in these theories but also in what is taken for granted. Whether they are explicit attempts to theorize about justice and moral relations or assertions of universal norms that guide the international system of states, orthodox theories of international relations, despite their positivist methodology and epistemology, have been heavily influenced by the liberal-contractarian tradition of thought. It is not a coincidence, furthermore, that this tradition has maintained a central place in Anglo-American ethics and political theory. The idea of the contract is pervasive in Western society, not only as a moral concept but as a practical solution to virtually all moral and legal dilemmas. As Virginia Held points out, 'contemporary Western society is in the grip of contractual thinking. Realities are interpreted in contractual terms, and goals are formulated in terms of rational contracts. Leading current conceptions of rationality begin with assumptions that human beings are independent, self-interested, or mutually disinterested individuals'.[29]

Certainly, there is much that is attractive about the idea of a contract. As Annette Baier notes, a contract enables us to make explicit just what we count on another person to do, in return for what, and should they not do just that, what damages can be extracted from them. The beauty of promise and contract is explicitness.[30] Similarly, in international relations, contract sets out the rules of the game—the rights to non-interference enjoyed by states and the duties owed by other states to respect those rights. In spite of the simplicity of this moral framework, however, many feminist theorists, including Baier, have questioned the idea of contract, arguing, in Virginia Held's words, that, 'when examined, the assumption and conceptions of contractual thinking seem highly questionable. As descriptions of reality they can be seriously misleading. . . . As expressions of normative concern, moreover, contractual theories hold out an impoverished view of human aspiration'.[31]

For example, it has been argued that a conception of moral relations as contractual presupposes both an equality of power and a natural separateness from others. Indeed, it is a typical feature of dominant moral theories that relationships between equals, or those who are deemed equal in some important sense, have been the relations that morality is primarily concerned to regulate. Relationships between those who are clearly unequal in power, including large and small states, parents and children, earlier and later generations, have had to be shunted to the bottom of the agenda and then dealt with by some sort of promotion of the weaker, so that an appearance of virtual equality is achieved.[32] When relations between agents are clearly unequal, however, a moral code designed for those equal in power will be at best nonfunctional, at worst an offensive pretence of equality which actually breeds further inequality. Such criticisms are not meant to minimize the importance of relationships of mutual respect among anonymous, autonomous agents, but rather to question the completeness of a moral philosophy which confines itself to such relations. As Annette Baier suggests, a complete moral philosophy would tell us how and why we should act and feel toward others in relationships of shifting and varying power asymmetry and shifting and varying intimacy.[33]

Liberal contractarian accounts of ethics and politics are dependent on the notion of individual rights; rights, moreover, are intimately connected to the view of freedom as negative liberty and, in the international context, to claims regarding non-interference and non-intervention. Indeed, as the epigraph to this chapter suggests, the languages of rights and liberalism are probably the most frequently used in contemporary international politics. Mapel and Nardin describe the language of rights, in particular, as 'predominant'.[34] But this idea of 'rights', so central to the liberal contractarian tradition, is only one moral concept among many. Indeed, as Baier argues, to focus on rights at the expense of other, more fundamental moral concepts is to overlook the fact that these other moral categories are necessary for the creation of a morally decent society. For example, rather than capturing the social nature of public life, the language of rights pushes us, she argues, to see the participants in a moral community as 'single, clamorous living human beings, not as families, clans, tribes, groups, classes, churches, congregations, nations or peoples'.[35]

Seen from this perspective, the idea of rights as negative liberties—those rights created in a contractual relationship to ensure mutual respect for a principle of non-interference—offers an impoverished account of moral relations. If the right to life simply means that no one kills me and I kill no one, it overlooks those individuals whose ability to exercise a right to life depends on more than simply being allowed a certain amount of personal freedom. Again, Baier's example is instructive:

> In a sense it is correct that, in order for [my right to life] to be respected, all that must be done by others is that they not kill me. But although what that means may seem clear enough when I am a reasonably tough adult, it was less clear when I was a helpless newborn, and will be less clear when I am a helpless incapacitated old person.[36]

Feminist theorists also reject the abstract, individualist conception of the self and society so prominent in modern liberal thought; feminists tend to pose a conception of a self whose identity and nature are defined by her contingent and particular attachments. They argue that the negative picture of freedom and morality put forward by rights-based ethics and the morality of justice is at once profoundly inadequate and morally impoverished, not only because it neglects the social self and the importance of attachment, but also because it is highly gendered, thus excluding the experiences and insights of many women.

Certainly, one could construct a strong case against these feminist critics by claiming that human rights—the key moral category in the liberal contractarian tradition—are no longer limited to the rights to personal negative liberty advocated by the natural rights theorists. Indeed, it could be argued that a conceptualization of international ethics as characterized only by negative liberty, rights, and non-interference is a caricature—a straw man. Today the idea of international human rights embodies not only civil and political but also economic and social rights, which seek to uphold our claims to vital goods such as economic security, welfare, and cultural autonomy.

The counterargument, however, would suggest that the classification of these goods as rights is dubious. Not all moral contexts can be adequately addressed using the language of rights; rights are not ends in themselves, but guarantees of freedom which allow individuals to pursue chosen ends without obstruction. Because they are ultimately about social responsibility and care, goods such as economic and social security, the fulfilment of basic human needs, and the cultural survival of groups cannot be expressed adequately in the language of rights. As Roger Rigterink has argued, the notion that rights can be defeated only by other rights led to the profusion of alleged rights. He claims that positive rights have been 'invented' by philosophers who recognized that a multitude of moral concerns—what he calls concerns of care—could not be addressed as long as rights were conceived of in the traditional Lockean fashion as freedoms.[37]

Clearly, our moral vocabulary must extend beyond rights if we are to create a full and rich language which is capable of addressing the variety of moral problems confronting the international community. Baier emphasizes this when she highlights rights as a moral concept which is parasitic on other less individualist moral concepts. Indeed, as she observes, '[i]t is only as participants in a co-operative practice that we can have any rights. The concept of responsibility, of being properly responsive to our fellow co-operators, is the more fundamental one'.[38] Responsibilities, in this sense, are qualitatively different from the minimal duty to respect others' rights. While rights intrinsically belong to individual units—persons or states—responsibilities, including very important ones such as those to future generations or to poor and distant strangers, must be addressed collectively through co-operation. Rights, then, must be supported by the responsibilities that we co-operatively discharge and by the individual responsibilities that we recognize, including responsibilities to co-operate in order to maintain common goods, such as civilized speech and civilized ways of settling disputes.[39] Taking her own analogy further, Baier argues that, 'Rights do define a sort of individualist tip of the iceberg of morality, one that takes no extra organization to stay afloat, but that is because it is supported by the submerged floating mass of co-operatively discharged responsibilities and socially divided labour'.[40]

This is not to suggest that the idea of rights can be completely discarded in favour of relational strategies. Indeed, as Martha Minow argues, in the search for commonalities and connections between people, the real divisions, conflicts, and disagreements must not be overlooked. What is important about the language of rights is that it enables individuals and groups to demand attention from others for points of view that have been neglected. But locating rights *within relationships* protects against the faulty pretence that people are already equal and free.[41]

Rights-based liberal contractualism assumes the existence of rational moral agents, of roughly equal standing, who know their interests and can meaningfully consent to terms of agreement. Certainly, rights may be criticized for their individualism, in that they assume the existence of a society made up of abstract, atomistic individuals who co-operate for mutual gain; this conception overlooks the social nature of identity and the moral significance of personal and social relations with particular others. But rights-based ethics is also prone to a kind of methodological individualism that ignores the wider obstacles—oppressive and exploitative social and economic structures and cultural norms—that can prevent individuals from claiming their rights. Rights-based ethics assumes that all human beings can claim rights, and that those claims will be undistorted by the environment in which they are made. The discourse of human rights does not build in an analysis of the structures of power and dependency which infuse relations in the global context. As O'Neill argues, idealized pictures of justice have tended to overlook the import of economic power: by idealizing the capacities and the mutual independence of those involved in market transactions, they obscure why the weak may be able to dissent from arrangements proposed by the strong.[42]

In liberal-contractarian accounts of international relations, as in the moral and political philosophy of deontological liberalism, the notion of freedom is not problematized; it is unquestioningly assumed that a person's negative liberty to pursue his own ends without interference is an important good, and that it is better to have more of it rather than less.[43] Owing to the dominance of liberal-contractarian accounts in international ethics, the intrinsic moral and political value of this autonomy is taken for granted. This emphasis on liberty and non-interference, however, could also be interpreted as facilitating a culture of indifference and neglect—as maintaining what Walzer calls the 'member/stranger' distinction and upholding the myth that all moral questions can be answered within the moral categories of negative liberty and rights. In the contemporary world order, states' rights to autonomy and self-determination are regarded as necessary to ensure liberty and self-determination for individuals; especially since 1945 and the period of decolonization that followed, it has been prescribed as a universal value for all states and persons. Thus, sovereign man and sovereign states 'are defined not by connection or relationships but by autonomy in decision-making and freedom from the power of others'.[44]

Certainly, there would appear to be sound, practical reasons why a negative account of liberty and a contractual account of relationships are the only acceptable, or indeed conceivable, options in the international system. In an anarchical—rather than hierarchical—system, it would seem that the only way to maintain order is to formulate and rigorously apply a principle of non-intervention, couched in the profoundly normative, universalized notion of self-determination. States can thus enjoy the right to pursue their own political, economic, and social policies and must act in accordance with the corresponding obligation to respect the autonomy of other states. To act according to any other principles would be to open the floodgates to accusations of moral and cultural imperialism, inconsistency, and economic and political manipulation of weak states by strong states. The problem with this normative framework, however, is its grounding in a misconceived ontological account of the nature of actors in the international system. Although liberal and neo-liberal theories in international relations, which posit the existence of a world of 'complex interdependence', argue that co-operation is both possible and desirable in the international system, the meaning of co-operation still entails the fulfilment of individual, separate interests. Far from being closely related to the relational thinking of much feminist theory, as Keohane has suggested, neo-liberal approaches still rely on an individualist ontology and the rational determination of individual preferences and interests.[45] Thus, as David Long has argued, the so-called debate between neo-realism and neo-liberalism all too quickly becomes an attempt to reconcile a modified liberal international theory with realism in international relations.[46] Ultimately, both approaches remain within the parameters of orthodoxy, offering a highly limited scope for understanding the nature of relations between actors on the global stage.

Cosmopolitanism and Communitarianism

The previous section argued that international relations theory is dominated by the moral and political thought of liberalism—specifically, rights-based contractual liberalism—and that the central principles and guiding assumptions of this approach to ethics can be found in both cosmopolitan and communitarian arguments about justice. This is not to say, however, that cosmopolitan and communitarian approaches to international ethics may be reduced to theories which define social, political, and moral relations in terms of contracts. Indeed, both of these approaches represent very broad categories within which a number of different perspectives may be subsumed. Their importance for the argument of this section, however, lies in the fact that, together, they have defined, and indeed limited, the analytical structure within which the normative debate in international relations now seems to take place. This section examines the adequacy of the cosmopolitan and communitarian positions in international relations theory in an attempt to illustrate that the construction of this debate in terms of these allegedly antithetical perspectives is theoretically intractable, and that ultimately the overwhelming focus on the sources of moral value and the scope of moral obligations has very little to contribute to the practical questions of moral relations in the global order.

It is important to note that communitarianism first emerged as a critique of liberal-individualism and, in particular, liberal theories of justice. This dispute has operated primarily in two philosophic domains—political philosophy and the 'metaphysical' theory of the self.[47] The most influential of these critiques has been Michael Sandel's *Liberalism and the Limits of Justice* (1982), which argues against John Rawls's hugely important book, *A Theory of Justice* (1971). In his critique, Sandel concentrates on Rawls's construction of the subject and, specifically, Rawls's claim that his concept of the self avoids the pitfalls of both Kant's radically disembodied subject, on the one hand, and the notion of the self as radically situated on the other. Sandel argues that Rawls seeks to maintain an individualistic vision of individuals as 'distinct persons' while at the same time arguing for a concept of justice which requires a constituent concept of community that his concept of the subject precludes; this, Sandel claims, is what ultimately makes his entire argument incoherent. Sandel proposes what he calls a 'wider subject'—one marked by constitutive community, a common vocabulary of discourse, and a background of implicit practices and understandings. He argues that the relationships we form, such as family, community, and nation, are both definitive and constitutive subjects. Thus, the self is constituted in part by aspirations and attachments and is open to growth and transformation in the light of revised self-understandings.[48]

Sandel's critique has been extremely influential in the rise of communitarianism as a critique not only in political philosophy but also in international relations.[49] But it has been pointed out that the portrayal of liberalism and communitarianism is based, in part, on a confusion. Charles Taylor has argued that it is quite possible to be an ontological 'holist' while advocating the 'individualist' values of rights and freedoms.[50] Clearly, Sandel's conception of the community does not preclude some of the virtues of liberalism, most notably freedom and equality. As Susan Hekman argues, this communitarian vision sees advantages in the communality denied by liberal society, yet each wants to retain the 'good' elements of individualism in the self and the community they advocate. Hekman argues convincingly that what is missing is any attempt to forge a discourse which avoids the polarities of the two dichotomies.[51]

This problem is equally visible in the international relations discourse. Moreover, cosmopolitanism and communitarianism share a common, paralyzing limitation which arises from what Hekman calls their 'sexism'—their shared conviction that morality, like politics and international relations, belongs only in the public sphere; thus, moral relations are between either abstract individuals in the context of the universal 'community' of humankind, or between encumbered, socially constructed individuals in the political community—usually, the nation-state. Other types of relations—specifically, relations and attachments among particular, concrete persons within, for example, families or social movements—are overlooked. The preoccupation with the dichotomy between universal and particular values and obligations thus thwarts the ability of moral enquiry in international relations to address the important questions about how we should act in order to mitigate human suffering.

Kantian Ethics and Cosmopolitanism

In the context of international relations, it is Kant's deontological ethics which provides us with the most authoritative statement of the cosmopolitan position. Cosmopolitanism is characterized by a refusal to regard existing political structures as the source of ultimate value.[52] Moreover, it is founded on a belief in the *universalizability* of moral principles, and it takes the *scope* of morality to be universal and thus unrestricted by spatial or temporal boundaries.

Kant's ethics relies heavily on the primacy of reason and duty. Kant believed absolutely in man's capacity for moral self-direction (autonomy) and his intrinsic quality as a supremely free agent who, when rid of dependence and oppression, is clearly able to see, by virtue of his reason, where his moral duty lies. As Geoffrey Hawthorn explains:

> [Man's moral duty] lies . . . in unconditional or categorical imperatives, in directives to action which may be held to apply unconditionally to all men. If they may be held to be universally applicable they may be held to be

> rational, without inconsistency, and thus to conform to a law, a law, he says at one point, of nature, but a law of course of our own nature. Our morality is our duty, and our duty lies in obeying the rational law that we ourselves create.[53]

Thus, it is the autonomous, rational agent who accepts the categorical demands of the moral law, which takes the form of the categorical imperative: 'Act only in such a way that I can also will that my maxim should become a universal law'.[54] Moreover, the idea of autonomy—that the rational will is subject to laws it makes itself—links to the idea of a kingdom of ends, within which all rational agents are treated as ends in themselves, rather than as means.

Contemporary ethics in the Kantian tradition has focused on the importance of the principle of impartiality. Brian Barry, for example, has developed a theory of justice as impartiality which is derived from Kantian principles. Thomas Nagel, moreover, has presented human moral psychology in terms of a constant conflict between two standpoints—the 'impersonal' and the 'personal' perspectives. Nagel argues that the impersonal standpoint in each of us produces a powerful demand for universal impartiality and equality, while the personal standpoint gives rise to individualistic motives and requirements which present obstacles to the pursuit and realization of such ideals.[55] Because we are all individual human beings with our own subjective standpoints, we see things, as Nagel puts it, *'from here'*; but because we are also rational, we are able to think about the world in abstraction from our particular position in it to obtain, as Nagel has put it elsewhere, 'the view from nowhere'.[56] What is needed, says Nagel, is some general method of resolving the inner conflict that can be applied universally and is acceptable to everyone in light of the universality of that conflict.[57] It is important to note that Nagel departs from Kant in the admission that the domain in which impartiality and impersonality reign supreme has some limits; in his view, impartiality is not (legitimately) ubiquitous. However, it must also be noted that he is centrally concerned with calling for a stronger role for the objective, impersonal perspective in our lives; thus, despite the fact that we are often motivated by personal, subjective concerns, these are regarded as lying outside morality and thus as standing in opposition to our objective, impersonal, and hence truly moral concerns.[58]

The most common line of attack on morality as impartiality is made by asking a question of practical, as opposed to meta-ethical importance: How is it possible to be impartial? Can we devote literally equal amounts of time, energy, and resources to all persons, that is, to all persons in the world? Clearly, critics argue, such an effort would be impossibly demanding.[59] Although this practical problem is an obvious one, it could legitimately be argued that it forms the least damaging criticism of impartiality, insofar as most contemporary impartialists make it clear that impartiality need not require each of us to devote the entirety of our resources to helping the world's needy; rather, it is simply upheld as a criterion of adequate moral justification.[60] This is what Brian Barry is arguing in his distinction between 'first-order' and 'second-order' impartiality. Indeed, Barry denies that 'impartiality is a "view from nowhere", an arbitrary imposition that might appeal to "men from Mars" but has little to offer to human beings'.[61] Thus, first-order impartiality means 'not being motivated by private concerns', such that 'to be impartial you must not do for one person what you would not do for anyone else'; this has the implication that, for example, 'children should not be regarded as having special claims against their parents, or that a fully conscientious man would toss a coin to determine whether he should rescue from a burning building his wife or a total stranger'.[62] This is contrasted with second-order impartiality, which applies only to the (political and legal) rules of a society and calls for 'principles and rules that are capable of forming the basis of free agreement for people seeking agreement on reasonable terms'. Barry argues that most critiques of impartiality are mistakenly directed towards first-order impartiality, since it is only second-order impartiality that most advocates of impartiality seek to defend. Indeed, he describes first-order impartiality as a 'pathological overextension' of an idea which is valid only within certain limits.

But it is precisely those 'limits', and the boundaries that Barry draws between public and private life—and more specifically, between public and private morality—which must be challenged. He claims that the principles of justice designed for the basic structure of a society cannot be deployed directly to address other moral questions. He cites Thomas Hill, who argues that we must distinguish 'the liberal aim of establishing a constitution and economic order that mutually respecting citizens can publicly affirm without judging one another's individual ways of life' from the appropriate 'moral guidelines for friendship, family, charity, personal integrity, and so forth'.[63] This takes us back to the familiar argument that 'justice ethics' is required in the public sphere, while any concessions to the importance of relationships and the value of particular persons insist on their relegation to the so-called private sphere. It is a central argument of this book that this separation is untenable; the establishment and maintenance of trusting and attentive personal and social relations is a crucial element of morality in all spheres of life.

In spite of such efforts to mitigate the supposed demands of impartiality, it has been argued that all versions of impartial reason foster 'a rather outlandish moral illusion'—the illusion of homogeneity among moral subjects. Impartiality relies on the fact that, insofar as we are moral subjects, we are all the same, for we have the same rational faculty. But, as Diana Meyers argues, moral subjects are unique, and this uniqueness cannot be addressed by asking the question 'Would I want to be treated like that?' Because people are not all like oneself, posing this question—however useful it may be—is not a sufficient basis for moral reflection. Indeed, Meyers claims, only by also asking 'What is it like to be you?' can we sufficiently respond to the difference and uniqueness of moral subjects.[64]

Cosmopolitan ethics relies on a Kantian-based morality of duty, guided by the principles of impartiality and universality. Indeed, the only acceptable ethical principles are ones which can be accepted by all, either because they are apparent to all rational moral agents through reason or because they are based on principles that cannot reasonably be rejected. All of this is possible, moreover, in spite of the pronounced diversity of individuals, cultures, societies, and indeed moralities in the world today. Thus, to satisfy the requirements of impartiality and universality, ethical principles must be sufficiently abstract and unspecified in order to be acceptable to all. As Hawthorn has argued, this high level of abstraction results in the most serious deficiencies of Kant's ethics:

> One [deficiency] is that in stipulating conditions that have to be met for a moral injunction, the imperative only stipulates what is unacceptable. It does not point to the ends that we should pursue. A second, related to this, is that Kantian ethics are parasitic. They prescribe a test for injunctions, but no way of generating them.[65]

Moreover, Kantian ethics must insist on the radical separation of moral from nonmoral, impersonal from personal, and must reduce complex persons with multifaceted identities, ties, and commitments to rational, presocial individuals—members of the community of humankind. Virginia Held has noted that, because of these requirements, absolutist ethics has had no place for 'the domain of particular others'. In this domain, says Held,

> the self is already constituted to an important degree by relations with others, and these relations may be much more salient and significant than the interests of the 'all others' or 'everyone' of traditional moral theory. They are not what a universal point of view or a view from nowhere could provide. They are characteristically actual flesh-and-blood other human beings for whom we have actual feelings and with whom we have real ties.[66]

While Held is directing this criticism at universalist-prescriptive ethics from her own position as a feminist moral theorist, this criticism could also have been articulated by the most prominent critics of deontological and cosmopolitan ethics—the communitarians.

Moral Particularism and Communitarianism

From the perspective of moral universalism, the notion that morality could possibly be directed towards particular others—groups and individuals—is not just morally wrong, it is inconceivable. To the moral universalist, ethical judgement occurs through reason. While the universalist may admit that all individuals have personal or egoistic desires and concerns, the moral—the impersonal, public realm—must be governed by impartiality, so that justice and fairness may prevail. Thus, from this perspective, to locate intrinsic moral value in one's citizenship is to subvert the universalist aims of cosmopolitanism; to the universalist, ethical particularism is simply an irrational outlook which elevates our existing prejudices to the status of objective truths.[67]

For the moral particularist, however, particularity is justified by conceptualizing the individual as 'encumbered' by her 'central aspirations and attachments',[68] or as one who has 'personal commitments that are not necessarily egoistic but are narrower than those imposed by a universal concern or respect for rights',[69] or as one whose 'identity is always partly defined in conversation with others or through the common understanding which underlies the practices in our society'.[70] For the moral particularist, there is an overt recognition of the role of social contexts, group commitments, and even personal relationships in defining moral boundaries; in this view, the individual cannot be understood as ontologically prior to her culture, history, or social position.

Although most ethical universalists are advocates of the principle of impartiality, it does not follow from this that most ethical particularists are advocates of partiality. Indeed, the ethical particularist—for example, the communitarian who believes that the limits of justice are the limits of the nation-state—will argue that impartiality must be extended only to members of that particular political community. Agents are still required to be impartial, but this particularist impartiality does not require a perspective of universality. This drawing of moral boundaries around families, communities, and nationalities acknowledges the futility of basing morality on a set of principles which will guide our ethical behaviour regardless of our communities and loyalties.

Contemporary communitarians have been influenced by a number of different philosophers and movements. Most often cited are the German Romantics—Herder, Fichte, Schiller, and ultimately, Hegel. German Romanticism has been described as a 'revolt against reason', specifically, the notion that 'the richness of cultural experience could be replaced by the cold reason'.[71] It has been described as a belief in two propositions: that we live in a world that we ourselves create, and that the principle of creativity is plenitude, infinite variety.[72] Hegel, too, reacted against Kant and his rationalist, formal philosophy but also sought to preserve the autonomy of the individual—the great achievement of Enlightenment thought—while situating this individual in a communitarian context.[73]

Linklater argues that it is precisely the incorporation of individualism and universalism within a theory of the history of social and political life which makes the Hegelian system philosophically superior to its Kantian predecessor.

> Kantianism breaks down because its categories do not supply an adequate account of the conditions of their own existence, and because its philosophical categories are stated in abstraction from the social conditions which make them possible. Hegelianism, on the other hand, sought to incorporate the history of categories within a theory of the development of their cultural contexts and within a statement of the history of human subjects.[74]

Not surprisingly, the Kantian/Hegelian controversy sounds suspiciously like the Rawls/Sandel dispute described earlier. Indeed, as Linklater demonstrates in his historical account of this debate, the contemporary 'cosmopolitan/communitarian' debate in international relations theory—what he calls the conflict between 'men and citizens'—may be traced from the Greek idea of the *polis* and the Stoic/Christian idea of a universal humanity, through the ethical and political theories of the Enlightenment and the Romantic/Hegelian reaction, up to the contemporary disputes between the critical theory of Jürgen Habermas and the postmodernism of Michel Foucault. In international relations theory, contemporary communitarianism starts from the position that value stems from the community, and that the individual finds meaning in life by virtue of his or her membership in a political community.[75]

While communitarians recognize the value of a number of traditional or established communities, their work tends to focus on one type of community—that which is created by the modern nation-state. Because communitarianism typically takes the form of a critique of liberal theories of justice, and because these original liberal theories focused on justice in its domestic context, that is, within the political community, communitarian critics naturally concentrate on the value of membership within that community.[76] Indeed, Walzer uses 'countries' and 'political communities' interchangeably, and analogizes 'neighbourhoods', 'clubs', and 'families' to illustrate his arguments about members, strangers, and admissions.[77]

In some recent work, communitarian theorists in international relations have attempted to transcend this association of community with nation-state.[78] Given the analytical and normative priority assumed by the nation-state in international relations, however, this conflation of 'community' with 'nation-state' has been difficult to overcome. As R. B. J. Walker notes, 'the principle of state sovereignty already expresses a theory of ethics, one in which ontological and political puzzles are resolved simultaneously. It affirms that the good life, guided by universal principles, can only occur within particularistic political communities'.[79] Thus, whether we use the term 'communitarian' or not, the central normative debate in international relations has been, and continues to be, over our obligations, identities, and responsibilities as citizens of nation-states, and our obligations, identities, and responsibilities as human beings.[80]

The communitarian vision of the self as encumbered or socially embedded in relationships would certainly appear to be a more adequate basis from which to begin thinking about moral communities and moral responsibilities among individuals. In spite of its merits, however, the particular brand of statist communitarianism which has dominated normative debates in international relations has had a deleterious effect on our ability to understand political communities as anything other than territorially enclosed, preexisting, formal-legal entities: in short, modern nation-states. Statist communitarianism has systematically obscured the possibility of alternative communities, and hence of a vision of global responsibilities or justice which could emerge from a communitarian understanding of ethics and politics. As Janna Thompson notes, in their criticism of the transcendent, impartial self, communitarians have seemed to erect an 'insurmountable barrier in the way of any attempt to formulate an international theory of justice'.[81]

Yet communitarianism, it could be argued, is inadequate not only as a normative international political theory but also as an ethical theory. Communitarianism has traditionally focused on preexisting, established relations or communities as the sites of moral values. By sanctioning traditional relationships, however, communitarians are promoting a moral conservatism. For communitarians, special relationships are accorded ethical significance in order to fulfil socially assigned responsibilities in the context of traditional relationship practices that define the starting points of individual moral identity. In this sense, they endorse a complacency about the social traditions which define our relationships. These traditions, however, may be morally problematic, as Marilyn Friedman has suggested. First, she argues, such relationship traditions are sometimes exclusionary, and they often stigmatize any kind of relationship that falls outside of conventional bounds. Second, relationship traditions, accepted uncritically, may harbour the potential for abuse and exploitation. Third, many people lack the resources to care for their own effectively; thus, 'the social practices by which we each favor only our respective own, if untempered by any methods for redistributing caretaking resources, would result in gravely inadequate care for many of the world's people'. These problems, argues Friedman, are often disregarded by communitarians in their haste to endorse the partiality featured in those relationships.[82] Thus, while feminists are, like communitarians, sympathetic to a conception of the self as social and an emphasis on the importance of social relationships, the feminist critique of liberal justice differs significantly from the communitarian critique. A view that all human selves are constituted by their social and communal relationships does not itself entail a critique of these highly individualistic selves, nor does it promote the moral value of caring personal and social relations, as many feminist moral and political philosophers have done.

As an alternative to the cosmopolitan conception of identity and the nature of community, communitarianism may be convincing; as an ethical or political theory, however, it is problematic. Within the primary constitutive political community—the nation-state—the uncritical particularism of communitarianism admits that there may be bonds—attachments which allow us to gain an insight into others' identities, needs, and interests and which give the members of that community moral standing. However, for communitarians, the *scope* of morality is limited; beyond the community, others are identified as distinctly *other,* and the possibility of shared understandings, justice, and moral co-operation is undermined.

The construction of the debate as a standoff between two apparently incompatible positions obscures the many similarities between cosmopolitanism and communitarianism. Just as Brown and Linklater argued that Hegel sought to retain the 'great achievement' of Enlightenment thought—the autonomy of the individual—so too can we argue that contemporary communitarians seek to retain that which they see as 'good' in the individualism of liberalism, namely, that which ensures the freedom of the moral and political agent. Indeed, Thomas A. Spragens, Jr., argues that nothing in communitarianism is at odds with the fundamental elements of the liberal tradition. Communitarians, he points out, simply flesh out the liberal framework with a conception of the good society, and for this reason, they have as much right as their competitors to lay claim to the liberal tradition.[83]

Finally, there is yet another reason why it would be misguided to assume that communitarianism is fundamentally antithetical to deontological liberalism or cosmopolitanism. Despite the fact that the internationalist, cosmopolitan commitments that were implicit in the ideals of deontological liberalism have repeatedly been targets of communitarian criticism, it is evident that the practice of liberalism has fallen rather short of its universalist aspirations. Indeed, it has not been universalistic, but clearly subordinated to the boundaries and demands of nation-states. Thus, while it may be the case that liberals have not, generally, been willing to take differences seriously, it is also the case that they have taken differences between sovereign states remarkably seriously.[84]

It would seem that we are left with two rather unappealing alternatives in our quest to develop a global ethics for the contemporary world order. The dichotomous relationship between cosmopolitanism and communitarianism—the apparent either-or choice between men and citizens—constructs a debate that is insoluble; it could be argued that the construction of such a debate obscures any way of moving forward. In the desperate and ill-founded attempt to build rigorous and enduring moral theories, both cosmopolitans and communitarians have obfuscated the original question which motivated the need for theorizing. Defining the limits and nature of our moral relations with others is, or should be, motivated by a desire to understand how those limits were constructed, to address and reduce marginalization and exclusion, and to understand the nature of moral motivation. Thus, to think about moral communities is to think about the recognition of difference, and about the moral significance of that difference. Moral universalism asks us to eradicate difference and to understand both identity and community in terms of our shared humanity. Communitarianism asks us to valorize difference and to understand identity and community as given—dictated by history, culture, and formal-legal boundaries. As such, both positions offer us neither an adequate method of critique nor a practical way forward. While Kantian ethics, ever wary of committing the naturalistic fallacy, tells us what ought to be rather than what is, its pronouncements on how to get to that place are suitable only for ideally rational, individuated, similar agents. While communitarian ethics appears to tell us what is and, often, that this is indeed how things ought to be, it is imbued with a disturbing moral complacency about the configuration of moral boundaries; all of this, moreover, is couched within a language that is often unmistakably liberal.

The dominant approaches in Western ethics—Kantian, neo-Kantian, liberal-contractarian, and rights-based theories—all rely on a high level of abstraction in their moral reasoning. These traditions are primarily concerned with arriving at principles or rules of right action—of justifying, for example, aid to distant people by constructing principles which answer the questions 'Do we have a duty to help?' and 'What rights do individuals have?' or by calculating an answer to the question 'How can we bring about the greatest good?' In international theory, such approaches exhibit a deep concern and interest in the search for rational principles and moral rules concerning obligation, human rights, reciprocity, and justice.[85] Thus, Kantian approaches focus on the obligations of moral agents, arguing that the demands of moral duty are not conditional on particular social structures or practices; rather, they emerge out of a conception of practical reasons which insists only that moral agents must act only on principles that can be adopted by any plurality of potentially interacting beings.[86] But as Roger Spegele argues, such approaches are flawed because their understanding of moral reasoning either falsifies our moral experience or fails to account for a range of moral phenomena which are of decisive importance for understanding the relation of ethics to international relations.[87]

In an effort to propel international ethics beyond this stasis, the next chapter explores the nature of the contemporary global system, including the changes associated with globalization. If international ethics is to move away from justifications towards what Shklar has called 'a less rule-bound phenomenology', or what Williams has described as a 'phenomenology of the ethical life', it must examine the actual circumstances in which existing and potential moral relations occur at the global level.

Notes

1. See Fiona Robinson, 'Rethinking Ethics in an Era of Globalisation', Sussex Papers in International Relations, no. 2, Brighton, 1996, p. 13.

2. See R. B. J. Walker, *Inside/Outside: International Relations as Political Theory,* Cambridge: Cambridge University Press, 1993, pp. 31–32.

3. On the relationship between the Hobbesian conception of liberty and individual rights, see Richard Tuck, *Natural Rights Theories: Their Origin and Development,* Cambridge: Cambridge University Press, 1979.

4. Annette Baier, 'Trust and Antitrust', in *Moral Prejudices: Essays on Ethics,* Cambridge, MA: Harvard University Press, 1994, p. 116.

5. Isaiah Berlin, 'Two Concepts of Liberty', in *Four Essays on Liberty,* Oxford: Oxford University Press, 1969, pp. 123–124.

6. Ian Shapiro, *The Evolution of Rights in Liberal Theory,* Cambridge: Cambridge University Press, 1986, p. 275.

7. Brian Barry, *The Liberal Theory of Justice,* Oxford: Clarendon Press, 1974, p. 166.

8. David R. Mapel, 'The Contractarian Tradition and International Ethics', in Terry Nardin and David R. Mapel, eds., *Traditions of International Ethics,* Cambridge: Cambridge University Press, 1992, p. 181.

9. Andrew Linklater, *Men and Citizens in the Theory of International Relations,* London: Macmillan, 1990, p. 42.

10. Quentin Skinner, 'The Paradoxes of Political Liberty', in David Miller, ed., *Liberty,* Oxford: Oxford University Press, 1991, pp. 199–200.

11. Thomas Hobbes, *Leviathan,* ed. Richard Tuck, Cambridge: Cambridge University Press, 1991 , pp. 14–16.
12. Mapel, 'The Contractarian Tradition', p. 193.
13. Ibid., p. 197.
14. Linklater, *Men and Citizens,* p. 46.
15. I am indebted to David Miller for this insight.
16. Linklater, *Men and Citizens,* p. 103.
17. Ibid., p. 119.
18. Shapiro, *The Evolution of Rights,* p. 276.
19. Charles Beitz, *Political Theory and International Relations,* Princeton, NJ: Princeton University Press, 1979, p. 151.
20. Michael Walzer, *Spheres of Justice: A Defence of Pluralism and Equality,* Oxford: Oxford University Press, 1983, pp. 4–5.
21. Ibid., p. 29.
22. Ibid., p. xv.
23. Ibid., pp. 64–65.
24. Ibid., pp. 82–83.
25. Beitz, *Political Theory,* p. 69.
26. C. Wolff, quoted in ibid., p. 75.
27. Linklater, *Men and Citizens,* p. 47.
28. R. J. Vincent, 'The Idea of Rights in International Ethics', in Nardin and Mapel, *Traditions of International Ethics,* pp. 256–257.
29. Virginia Held, *Feminist Morality: Transforming Culture, Society, and Politics.* Chicago: University of Chicago Press, 1993, pp. 193–194.
30. Baier, *Moral Prejudices,* p. 117.
31. Held, *Feminist Morality,* p. 194.
32. Baier, *Moral Prejudices,* p. 28.
33. Ibid., pp. 116–120.
34. Mapel and Nardin, 'Convergence and Divergence', pp. 318–319.
35. Baier, *Moral Prejudices,* p. 237.
36. Ibid., p. 242.
37. Roger J. Rigterink, 'Warning: The Surgeon Moralist Has Determined that Claims of Rights Can Be Detrimental to Everyone's Health', in Eve Browning Cole and Susan Coultrap-McQuin, eds., *Explorations in Feminist Ethics: Theory and Practice,* Bloomington: Indiana University Press, 1992, p. 42.
38. Baier, *Moral Prejudices,* p. 243.
39. Ibid., p. 246.
40. Ibid., p. 241.
41. Minow, *Making All the Difference,* p. 389, my italics.
42. Onora O'Neill, 'Justice, Gender, and International Boundaries', in Robin Attfield and Barry Wilkins, eds., *International Justice and the Third World,* London: Routledge, 1992.
43. Beitz, *Political Theory,* pp. 75–76.
44. V. Spike Peterson and Anne Sisson Runyan, *Global Gender Issues,* Boulder, CO: Westview Press, 1993, p. 34.
45. See Robert Keohane, 'International Relations Theory: Contributions from a Feminist Standpoint', in Rebecca Grant and Kathleen Newland, eds., *Gender in In-*

ternational Relations, London: Macmillan, 1991; for a critique of this article, see Cynthia Weber, 'Good Girls, Little Girls, and Bad Girls: Male Paranoia in Robert Keohane's Critique of Feminist International Relations', *Millennium: Journal of International Studies* 23, no. 2, 1993: 337–348.

46. David Long, 'The Harvard School of Liberal International Theory: A Case for Closure', *Millennium: Journal of International Studies* 24, no. 3, 1995: 500.

47. Lawrence A. Blum, *Moral Perception and Particularity,* Cambridge: Cambridge University Press, 1994, p. 98.

48. Susan Hekman, *Moral Voices, Moral Selves: Carol Gilligan and Feminist Moral Theory,* Cambridge: Polity Press, 1995, p. 52. See Michael Sandel, *Liberalism and the Limits of Justice,* Cambridge: Cambridge University Press, 1982.

49. Two other influential philosophers, presenting slightly different versions of communitarianism, are Alistair MacIntyre and Charles Taylor.

50. Charles Taylor, 'Cross-Purposes: The Liberal-Communitarian Debate', in *Philosophical Arguments,* Cambridge, MA: Harvard University Press, 1995, pp. 181–186.

51. Hekman, *Moral Voices,* p. 56.

52. Chris Brown, *International Relations Theory: New Normative Approaches,* Hemel Hempstead: Harvester Wheatsheaf, 1992, p. 24.

53. Geoffrey Hawthorn, *Enlightenment and Despair: A History of Social Theory,* 2nd ed., Cambridge: Cambridge University Press, 1987, p. 34.

54. Immanuel Kant, *The Groundwork of the Metaphysic of Morals,* translated and analyzed by H. J. Paton, London: Routledge, 1991, p. 67.

55. Thomas Nagel, *Equality and Partiality,* Cambridge: Cambridge University Press, 1991, p. 4.

56. This is a reference to the title of Nagel's 1986 book *The View from Nowhere* (Oxford: Oxford University Press), in which the above subjective/objective distinction is discussed in greater detail.

57. Nagel, *Equality and Partiality,* p. 17.

58. Blum, *Moral Perception,* pp. 15–16.

59. Friedman, *What Are Friends For?,* p. 81.

60. Ibid., p. 82.

61. Brian Barry, *Justice as Impartiality,* Oxford: Oxford University Press, 1995, p. 255.

62. Ibid., p. 194.

63. Ibid., p. 216.

64. Diana T. Meyers, *Subjection and Subjectivity: Psychoanalytic Feminism and Moral Philosophy,* London: Routledge, 1994, pp. 169, 39.

65. Hawthorn, *Enlightenment and Despair,* p. 35.

66. Held, *Feminist Morality,* pp. 57–58.

67. David Miller, 'The Ethical Significance of Nationality', *Ethics* 98, no. 4, 1988: 705–722, 650.

68. Michael Sandel, 'Justice and the Good', in Michael Sandel, ed., *Liberalism and Its Critics,* Oxford: Blackwell, 1984, p. 18.

69. Bernard Williams, *Moral Luck,* Cambridge: Cambridge University Press, 1981, p. 18.

70. Charles Taylor, 'Atomism', in Will Kymlicka, ed., *Justice in Political Philosophy,* Aldershot: Edward Elgar, 1992, p. 205.
71. Brown, *International Relations Theory,* p. 60.
72. Hawthorn, *Enlightenment and Despair,* p. 37.
73. Brown, *International Relations Theory,* p. 60.
74. Linklater, *Men and Citizens,* pp. 149–150.
75. Brown, *International Relations Theory,* p. 55.
76. Sandel's *Liberalism and the Limits of Justice* may be seen as a response to Rawls's *Theory of Justice;* Walzer's *Spheres of Justice* may be seen as a response to Nozick's *Anarchy, State, and Utopia.*
77. Walzer, *Spheres of Justice,* pp. 35–42.
78. Brown (*International Relations Theory,* p. 186) argues convincingly that 'those communitarian theories that assume the communities are a given are . . . unhelpful when it comes to the attempt to enlarge the sense of community. It may be that individuals are constituted by their communities . . . but this constitutive function need not be exclusive and exclusionary'. Similarly, in her analysis of the nation as community (*Justice and World Order: A Philosophical Inquiry,* London: Routledge, 1992, pp. 186–187), Janna Thompson argues that a satisfactory conception of the nation must be useful in accounting for the national loyalties that people actually have, though it need not endorse everything that people believe about nations. She envisages the nation, not as a homogeneous, 'thick', constitutive community, but rather as a 'society of overlapping communities'.
79. Walker, *Inside/Outside,* p. 64.
80. This debate is explored extensively by Linklater in *Men and Citizens.* He refers to our 'double existence as men and citizens' (p. 36), and to the 'dichotomy between citizenship and humanity' as a 'fragmented moral experience' (p. 37). See also 'Symposium on Duties Beyond Borders', a special issue of *Ethics* (98, no. 4, 1988), especially the articles by O'Neill, Miller, and Goodin; and Thompson, *Justice and World Order.*
81. Thompson, *Justice and World Order,* p. 19.
82. Friedman, *What Are Friends For?,* p. 75.
83. Thomas A. Spragens, Jr., 'Communitarian Liberalism', in Amitai Etzioni, ed., *New Communitarian Thinking: Persons, Virtues, Institutions, and Communities,* Charlottesville: University of Virginia Press, 1995, p. 51.
84. O'Neill, 'Justice, Gender, and International Boundaries', p. 56.
85. Roger Spegele, *Political Realism in International Relations,* Cambridge: Cambridge University Press, 1996, p. 193.
86. As Onora O'Neill explains, according to the Kantian view, any principle of action that is adopted by all members of such pluralities alters the world that they share and becomes a background condition of their action. This is why certain principles of action which can coherently be held by one agent cannot be coherently proposed as principles for all. For example, principles of deception and coercion are non-universalizable, for if they were to be adopted by everyone, they would undermine themselves, making all projects of deception or coercion incoherent. See O'Neill, 'Justice, Gender, and International Boundaries', p. 64.
87. Spegele, *Political Realism,* p. 193.

5

Globalization, Moral Relations, and the Ethics of Care

This chapter explores the wider structural and institutional context of moral relations on a global scale, focusing on arguments from international relations theorists about globalization and the international system. The purpose of the chapter, then, is to explore the actual conditions for moral relations in the global context and, specifically, for the development of a global ethics of care; it seeks to determine the ethical implications, if any, of a world which is characterized by increasing interdependence and relations across borders yet, paradoxically, at the same time presents obstacles to the creation of inclusive relations due to structures of exclusion and increasing asymmetries in access to power and levels of well-being.

The first section examines the responses to arguments about globalization from normative theorists of international relations and moral and political philosophers; these responses are concerned not only with the social, political, and economic aspects of globalization but with how, if at all, globalization affects our understanding of ethics and moral relations in the contemporary world. Most of these arguments focus on the unifying aspects of globalization—the claims that, in an era of globalization, difference and distance are giving way to homogenization and integration. From there, these normative arguments assert that the potential for universal consensus, and thus the recognition of universal rights and obligations, has increased significantly, and that the possibility of achieving a truly global moral community is now realizable.

It is suggested that these claims are flawed for several reasons. First, they overemphasize the extent to which globalization can be regarded as a progressive phenomenon characterized by homogenization and greater inclusivity; second, they seek to procure a normative argument from an essentially empirical one; and finally, they rest on the implicit belief that the eradication of difference is a necessary precondition for moral relations. The central argument of this chapter is that, although in an era of globalization social relations are characterized by systematic patterns of exclusion, this does not preclude the possibility of moral relations and, indeed, of moral relations based on care. In spite of—or in some cases, due to—the processes of globalization, the contemporary world order is characterized by the legacy of 'old' nationalisms and the rise of 'new', ethnic nationalisms, a robust and enduring commitment to state sovereignty, and asymmetries in levels of power and well-being in the global capitalist economy. Rather than gloss over difference at a global level, or seek to theorize it out of existence, we should use it as the starting point for our exploration of moral relations at the global level. As Margaret Urban Walker has argued, '[d]ivisions, instabilities, conflicts of authority, and diverse experiences of social reality provide occasions and materials for critical, and possibly transformative, moral thinking'.[1]

An ethics of care does not require the existence of moral agents whose similarities outweigh their differences, or who are prepared to see in one another only their shared humanity. On the contrary, an ethics of care is based on attentiveness and responsiveness to others and their differences. Moreover, a critical ethics of care (discussed at length in chapter 6) rests on a relational ontology which allows us to see difference as existing only in relational terms. Thus, at the end of this chapter, it is suggested that although a globalizing world does indeed demand an ethics which is relational and interpersonal—in order to address the moral implications of interdependence—it cannot be an 'orthodox' ethics of care. The recognition of difference and particularity must not signal a descent into moral relativism or a kind of 'micro' ethics, but rather it must encourage a commitment to tackle the ways in which difference is assigned and oppression and exclusion are justified. A useful ethics for the contemporary global context must be able to address the structures and processes which lead to the institutionalization of exclusion.

Globalization, Values, and Duties: Universalist Arguments

In the last couple of decades, allusions to 'globalization', 'global change', and an emerging 'global society' have become more and more prevalent in both academic literature and political rhetoric. Most theories of globalization begin from the observation that relations and connections—social, cultural, economic, and political—between actors across the globe are far 'closer', more 'intense', and more frequent today than they were only half a century ago. In international relations, Keohane and Nye argued more than twenty years ago that as the role of the international society steadily increased in importance, there would be a simultaneous devaluing of the role of the nation-state; they described the territorial state, which has been dominant in world politics for the four centuries since feudal times ended, as being eclipsed by nonterritorial actors, such as multinational corporations, transnational social movements, and international organizations.[2] Most recent writing on globalization, in contrast, regards contemporary global relations, processes, and transactions as both qualitatively and quantitatively different from mere 'interdependence', which, like 'internationalization', remains wedded to the idea of discrete entities—usually nation-states—which have simply increased their level of interaction.

Thus, theorists of globalization seek to emphasize the idea of the world becoming a *single place.* Jan Aarte Scholte has defined globalization as processes whereby social relations acquire relatively distanceless and borderless qualities, so that human lives are increasingly played out in the world as a single place. Scholte is careful to distinguish globalization from internationalization, the latter referring to a process of intensifying connections between national domains. The central difference, then, is in the nature of time, space, and distance:

> Whereas international links (for example, trade in cocoa) require people to cross considerable distances in comparatively long time intervals, global connections (for example, satellite newscasts) are effectively distanceless and instantaneous. Global phenomena can extend across the world at the same time and can move between places in no time; they are in this sense supraterritorial. While the patterns of 'international' interdependence are strongly influenced by national-state divisions, the lines of 'global' interconnections often have little correspondence to territorial boundaries.[3]

Other theorists of globalization have also focused on the changing nature of time and space. Anthony Giddens has defined globalization as 'the intensification of world-wide social relations which link distant localities in such a way that local happenings are shaped by events occurring many miles away and vice versa'.[4] Globalization, then, refers to that process whereby the relations between local and distant forms and events become stretched, insofar as the modes of connection between different social contexts or regions become networked across the earth's surface as a whole. These ideas are built around the notion of what Giddens calls 'time-space distanciation': the condition under which time and space are organized to connect presence and absence. What were once clearly defined societies now possess a greater ability to span time and space; they are 'interwoven with ties and connections which cross cut the socio-political system of the state and the cultural order of the nation'.[5]

In response to this focus on the changing nature of time and space, the intensity of global social relations, and the potential changes in political organization, theorists have been motivated to explore the effects of these changes on the scope and nature of values, norms, and moral obligations. The dominant, indeed popular, trend has been to link the idea of the world as a 'single place' with the convergence of values and a new human unity—a universal 'community of humankind'. It is argued that, if territoriality and, specifically, borders between nation-states are deemed to be less significant—in terms of economics, governance, and civil society—then the simple fact that one is Egyptian or English or Guyanese can also be seen as less significant in terms of identity, community, and the development of values and obligations. The proliferation of transnational social movements and transnational ideologies, along with the rise of a global 'risk culture', are all said to lead to changes in identity and new solidarities, including a global solidarity of humankind.

This new solidarity and inclusiveness is supported by the spread, and increasing dominance, of Western liberal values. It is often argued that the end of the cold war has brought with it an explicit and renewed commitment to liberalism in Western thought. Famously, Francis Fukuyama has recently proclaimed the 'end of history', based on the argument that the collapse of the Soviet Union demonstrates the demise of any serious ideological challenge to liberalism.[6] Moreover, it has been argued that liberalism, within the international realm, although limited by the states system, is of growing importance because of its dominance as a value system against which state forms are legitimized.[7] When these ideas are coupled with calls for the Western states to take an increasingly active responsibility in world affairs—especially with regard to issues such as human rights and democracy—globalization quickly becomes perceived as a set of processes which are founded on the universalization of liberal norms and values.[8]

Arguments connecting globalization to the convergence of values and moral universalism, described in terms of either universal obligations (that is, universal in scope) or universalizable principles of justice (those which could be accepted, rationally, by all), generally take two forms. First, there are those Kantian arguments which are fundamentally deontological; in these arguments, globalization or no globalization, morality is based on the rational discernment of universal obligations. The existence or the lack of a global consensus on norms and values does not preclude the need to distinguish between right and wrong, between good and bad, and to set out some objective universal standards of human treatment or universal principles of justice upon which all peoples *could,* theoretically, agree. Kantians offer tests based on principles of practical reason to determine what principles could or could not be universalized. Increased interdependence may lead us to now have real, rather than notional, confrontations with distant others. The demands of practical reason, moreover, may compel us to recognize the moral standing of these others, others whom, in an era of globalization, we cannot ignore. But in spite of this, it is the demands of reason, then, rather than of globalization or interdependence, which ensure that moral obligations are not only universalizable but also universal in scope—in other words, all human beings have moral standing. Globalization, even when characterized as increased co-operation or as a global convergence of norms and values, plays no part in this moral reasoning. The purpose of ethics, then, is critique; ethics must prescribe, not describe.

The serious limitations inherent in these cosmopolitan theories confine their moral arguments to the question of whether we have obligations to distant strangers and, if so, whether globalization can be said to have some bearing on the scope of our obligations—beyond, say, national boundaries. Certainly, the premise, made strongly by Kantians, that essentially empirical propositions about the nature of the global system cannot lead directly to normative claims about ethics—and, specifically, about moral obligations—is both valid and important; one neither entails nor is entailed by the other. That said, however, the Kantian distinction between 'is' and 'ought', between the empirical and the normative, or between 'facts' and 'values', remains questionable. Where the social world is concerned, and particularly in the study of globalization, the best investigations recognize the interdependence and indivisibility of 'theory' and 'practice' and demonstrate the extent to which globalization is both influenced and constituted by our perceptions of it. Moreover, while one might accept, on its own terms, the argument that empirical conditions—co-operation, interdependence, globalization—can neither cause nor vindicate moral claims—that is, make them right or wrong—one may still object to this preoccupation with epistemological certainty. Certainly, this kind of ethics can always stand apart from, and provide a point of critique against, ordinary behaviour or 'commonsense morality'. But what we must ask is whether it can actually be useful in the real world of concrete persons, persons who do require motivation to act, and whose moral situations are not abstract puzzles to be solved but real dilemmas involving real people and relationships.

More commonly, however, Kantian arguments do not take this strictly deontological position; rather, they seek to create a moral argument out of an empirical one. In these arguments, the existence of an increasingly interdependent world, or a thoroughly globalized capitalist economy, is said to create not only social, political, and economic bonds but moral ones; a truly global community both creates shared norms and the potential for consensus regarding principles of justice and creates the demand for such principles as we become reciprocally obligated to the members of a global network of social interaction. Thus, empirical arguments surrounding 'interdependence', or now more commonly, 'globalization', are often used as a starting point for the construction of universalist or cosmopolitan ethical positions or of arguments for the development of global obligations or responsibility. Usually, these arguments refer to the enhanced international mobility of capital and the de facto requirements of co-operation among states in areas such as environmental protection and conservation. It follows from this that political interaction—and even, in some cases, democratic participation and citizenship—must now be exercised at levels higher than the nation-state, at the regional or even the global level. The corresponding moral argument claims that there is no reason to think of people's moral obligations as confined within national or state boundaries. The creation of a cosmopolitan moral framework is necessary in order to ensure that human rights are protected and that our duties to people outside the borders of our own state are effectively discharged.[9]

Even though, as David Miller notes, the moral argument and the allegedly empirical argument are frequently run together in practice, it must be recognized that these two arguments are independent from one another.[10] In the context of the contemporary world, we must be wary of linking normative arguments about obligations or justice to so-called empirical arguments about globalization. This is not to suggest that it is easy, or indeed possible, to distinguish between empirical and normative knowledge; on the contrary, those theorists who seek to link ethical arguments to 'facts' about globalization in fact assume the separateness of empirical and normative arguments and often 'read' the 'reality' of globalization in such a way as to emerge with the desired ethical argument. If objective judgements about the nature of the world are impossible, then it will be impossible to emerge with a universal-prescriptive ethical theory about the moral implications of globalizing trends in the world today.

The following section explores two arguments which aim to link arguments about globalization—about economic interdependence and the emergence of a global civil society—with moral arguments about global justice and global responsibility. It will be shown that these arguments are untenable, and that thinking about our moral responses to and in the contemporary world must recognize the contingent and partial nature of any one interpretation of that world and put that recognition at the forefront of its ethical framework.

Economic Interdependence and Global Justice

In 1979 Charles Beitz argued that the world is not made up of self-sufficient states; rather, he claimed, states participate in complex international economic, political, and cultural relationships that suggest the existence of a global scheme for social co-operation.[11] Thus, to arrive at his own principles of international justice, Beitz relied on the methods adopted by John Rawls but took them further, such that the 'difference principle' would apply equally within international society:

> The appropriation of scarce resources by some requires a justification against the competing claims of others and the needs of future generations. Not knowing the resource endowments of their own societies, the parties would agree on a resource redistribution principle which would give each national society a fair chance to develop just political institutions and an economy capable of satisfying its members' basic needs.[12]

Thus, the parties involved would be acknowledging that 'persons of diverse citizenship have distributive obligations to one another analogous to those of citizens of the same state'.[13] These claims are based on Beitz's conviction that the world may plausibly be described as a single society, characterized by a global scheme of social co-operation.

Beitz's original argument has been widely criticized, based on the unconvincing nature of his central premise: that obligations—moral and especially distributive—emerge out of the realities of global economic interdependence. The empirical proposition that the world is becoming more interdependent does not entail the moral argument of cosmopolitan ethics; there is no simple formula whereby interdependence can be said to lead directly to universal moral obligations, moral impartiality on a global scale, or the creation of truly universal values. Indeed, there is no reason why the integration of sovereign nation-states in, for example, the global economy should make them recognize that they have equal moral obligations to one another. While it may be the case that, given the influence exerted on other countries through economic interdependence and the lack of democratic control of peoples to influence the decisions which will affect them, a system of wider democratic participation and greater accountability ought to be set up, it is not necessarily the case that interdependence will make nation-states less competitive. Liberal arguments linking economic interdependence to peace and, ultimately, justice are inherently flawed in that they overlook the nature of power relations within the global capitalist economy; indeed, participation in an integrated political economy is likely to make states and economic actors more competitive, rather than lead them to recognize their obligations to greater global distribution of resources.

Interestingly, however, in his later work Beitz concedes the problems in his argument and adopts a much more strictly Kantian view. In a 1983 paper, Beitz acknowledges that this argument—that the system of global trade and investment, organized within a structure of international institutions and conventions, constitutes a scheme of social co-operation, and that, moreover, this suggests that the principles of international justice should apply to the world at large—is flawed. And yet, although he accepts that this argument 'misses the point', he still accepts its conclusions, arguing that the possibility of global justice ultimately resides in the essential 'capacity to form, revise and pursue a conception of the good'.[14] He recognizes that if his is to be a truly Kantian account, then it will recognize that human beings possess the powers of practical reasoning necessary for moral judgement regardless of whether they belong, now or in the future, to a common co-operative scheme, thus, he concedes, 'the argument for construing the original position globally need not depend on my claim about the existence of international social cooperation'.[15]

In another paper on the universalist/particularist debate surrounding the question of sovereignty and morality, Beitz continues along these lines, suggesting that the claims of particularism, at the level of moral agency, are so obviously true that 'one suspects one has missed the point'.[16] What he finds so puzzling and perplexing, however, is the claim that this conception of ethical agency is necessarily connected to a particularist understanding of the moral point of view. Questions of moral learning and motivation, he argues, are distinct from questions of the nature of morality or, as he puts it, the 'moral point of view': '[T]he fact that our communal relationships play a major role, even a constitutive role, in defining us as moral agents does not imply that we are or should regard ourselves as incapable of achieving the degree of detachment or objectivity that the notion of impartial judgement requires'.[17]

Here, Beitz is adopting Kantian practical reasoning and the demands of impartiality to support his cosmopolitan arguments; thus, the significance of interdependence, or any empirical changes in global political, economic, or social relations, is minimized. While this shift may avoid the obvious dangers of conflating an empirical argument with a moral one, Beitz's argument remains a limited account of global ethics, insofar as it is preoccupied with the justification of universal obligations over particular—or in this case, national—duties, which is seen to be a precondition for moral engagement and the achievement of international justice. As argued later in this chapter, this preoccupation is flawed, insofar as it ignores the extent to which moral relations continually occur in the absence of any unified moral community. Ultimately, moreover, it tells us very little about how interdependence and globalization might usefully help us to rethink the nature of moral relations and the appropriateness of our moral responses across borders.

The Global Dialogical Moral Community

A similar yet more sophisticated moral argument linking moral obligations to globalization is Seyla Benhabib's arguments for a 'global dialogical moral community'. Benhabib starts from an interpretation of the 'facts' of globalization: she claims that in the last two decades the world has 'grown together', and that the globe has 'become unified to a hitherto unprecedented degree'.[18] From this starting point, she invokes Bernard Williams's interesting distinction between what he called *real* and *notional* confrontations: 'A real confrontation between two divergent outlooks occurs at a given time if there is a group of people for whom each of the outlooks is a real option. A notional confrontation, by contrast, occurs when some people know about two divergent outlooks, but at least one of these outlooks does not present a real option'.[19] The moral difference between the two, according to Williams, is that only in the context of real confrontations can the language of appraisal be used. Thus, we can make moral judgements only on ways of being which are, at least potentially, real to us. Notional confrontations, however, elude judgement and are governed by the relativism of distance, whether temporal or spatial.

Using this idea, Benhabib argues that the condition of global interdependence in which we find ourselves today has practically transformed all cross-cultural communication and exchange in the present to *real* confrontation.

> As a consequence of the world-wide development of means of transportation and communication, in the wake of the emergence of international markets of labour, capital and finance, with the multiplying and increasing effects of local activities on a global scale . . . today the real confrontation of different cultures has produced not only a community of conversation but a community of interdependence. . . . Twentieth-century development has diminished the cultural distances of the present. It is at the level of real confrontations that the most pressing moral issues on a global scale today arise.[20]

In this context, she argues, the articulation of a pluralistically enlightened ethical universalism on a global scale emerges both as a possibility and a necessity. She claims that 'in the global situation that we are in, our interactions with others are largely real and no longer notional. We have become moral contemporaries, caught in a net of interdependence, and our contemporaneous actions will also have tremendous uncontemporaneous consequences. This global situation creates a new community, a "community of interdependence"'. One of the moral imperatives of the present, she argues, is to translate the community of interdependence into a community of conversation across cultures.[21]

Benhabib uses arguments derived from Habermasian discourse ethics to articulate the moral imperative which emerges from this situation. A community of interdependence becomes a moral community, she claims, if it resolves to settle those issues of common concern to all via dialogical procedures in which all are participants. This 'all' refers to all of humanity, not because one has to invoke some philosophically essentialist theory of human nature, but because the condition of planetary interdependence has created a situation of 'world-wide reciprocal exchange, influence and interaction'. And yet, in spite of the emphasis she places on the empirical conditions of globalization, Benhabib admits that her argument is derived from Kant; '[T]he principle of a dialogical global community based on norms of universal respect and egalitarian reciprocity is not new; its honourable ancestor', she explains, 'is Kant's idea of the "republican constitution", which, when conceptualized as a principle of interaction among nations, yields the cosmopolitan point of view'. According to Kant's ethics, then, the moral law cannot exist in nature; for it is only through their reasoning capacity that human beings can at all articulate and act according to the principle of treating other human beings as ends and never only as means.[22]

This argument put forward by Benhabib is very close to the practical approach to moral standing put forward by Onora O'Neill. O'Neill argues that we make complicated assumptions about others with whom we interact, and that on that basis it would be incoherent to deny them moral standing. In an era of globalization, she argues, we make regular, complex assumptions about others across borders: we trade and negotiate, translate and settle payments, pollute the environment and contribute to its renewal, and so on.[23] Thus, she relies on the existence of these interactions, these assumptions, and the practical reasoning that follows to demonstrate that distant others have moral standing; the scope of our moral obligations is a problem, O'Neill argues, which simply *cannot be solved* at the level of theoretical reason.

Clearly, the approaches put forward by Benhabib and O'Neill do not fall into the trap of Beitz's early argument, insofar as they do not actually claim that moral obligations emerge *because of* the existence of an interdependent world. Where globalization and interdependence are concerned, their claims are more modest. While it is our interactions with others—our real confrontations, to use Benhabib's favoured term—which demonstrate, practically, that we must regard others are real moral agents with moral standing, it is the Kantian moral law, which exists independently of nature but is knowable only through the autonomous insight of the rational human subject, from which the universal obligations to all human beings are derived.

As with Beitz's approach, however, these arguments end up focusing their energies on proving that the argument for moral relativism across distance is unsustainable. This, as I have already argued, is a highly limited exercise, for it overlooks essential questions of motivation and of the nature of moral response and action. Moreover, especially in Benhabib's argument, it is predicated on over-inflated claims regarding 'planetary interdependence' and 'world-wide reciprocal exchange, influence and interaction'.[24] Using empirical arguments about globalization, these moral arguments seek to theorize away our differences by claiming that interdependence creates a kind of moral community characterized by a basic level of consensus, that is, that we all recognize one another as human because we engage in real confrontations. Thus, the preconditions for moral relations exist. The following sections argue, however, that while globalization has had an important effect on the nature of global social relations, it is important to regard with caution any claim to mutual *interdependence* and *reciprocity* in influence and interaction.

Identity and Community in an Era of Globalization

Like some of the accounts described earlier, most cosmopolitan normative arguments about global ethics or justice begin with, or at least rely implicitly upon, the idea of a world community, characterized by the development not just of global common interests and interactions but also of a worldwide consciousness of common identity. The basic premise is that the world is moving in the direction of such a community, albeit, as Brown has argued, with a 'faltering step because of the context between forces representing common interests and common identity and those representing the old, particularistic, order'.[25]

It is increasingly accepted that the exploration of identity is crucial to the analysis of both ethics and international relations. Experiences of identity—of recognizing and accepting the self, of observing and seeking *sameness,* and of acknowledging *difference* and classifying it as other—are generally accepted as fundamental processes of human social and psychological development. Indeed, it has been observed that, even in very young children, a striking feature of their interpersonal relations is the delight which they exhibit on discovering similarities between themselves and another. In doing so, a child situates herself alongside another: that is to say, a child finds, rather than is found, a place within a social group. In slightly older children, the emphasis on sameness and conformity gives way somewhat to a motif of individuality, which separates the child, as an individual person, from the other. As James argues, questions of identity are fundamentally social as well as psychological; for any particular child, she argues, it is her participation in a tangled web of social relationships which helps shape the identity and sense of self she assumes as she moves towards adulthood to become a person in society.[26]

Clearly, in giving ourselves personhood—recognizing that we are unique individuals—we are making the basic distinction between self and other. When we form group identities, we recognize that certain individuals are different from ourselves; however, perhaps more significantly, we simultaneously identify them as being, in some important way, 'like us'. Such group-forming activities are clearly as fundamental to human beings as is the initial differentiation between self and other. Furthermore, the formation and development of personal and collective identities are not entirely separate or distinct processes. As William Connolly points out, every stable way of life invokes claims to collective identity that enter in various ways into the interior identifications and resistances of those who share it.[27] Simply put, your membership in a particular group is, in fact, part of who you are.

In the modern era, political identity has been defined preeminently in terms of nationality and citizenship. Although often conflated, it should be made clear that the idea of the nation is distinct from the idea of the state. The term 'nation' describes a collection of people who regard themselves as united by the bonds of history, language, and culture; it is, as Anderson has famously claimed, an 'imagined community' which is ideally, though by no means necessarily, coterminous with the boundaries of the state.[28] The state, then, by contrast, is the formal-legal entity which is defined by political sovereignty. Thus, while our citizenship refers, technically, to our belonging to a particular state, our nationality may not correspond to our citizenship. Quebecois in Canada, Scots or Welsh in the United Kingdom, and Basques in Spain are just a few of the most well-known examples of this.

However, while the ideas of nation and state are certainly distinct, any definition of nations and nationalism will be, as Ernest Gellner points out, 'parasitic on a prior and assumed definition of the state'.[29] In international relations, the modern nation-state is normally thought to be a product of the Peace of Westphalia in 1648; it could be argued, however, that the modern nation-state, roughly as we know it, emerged around the time of the French Revolution. Indeed, the rise of nationalism in Europe was closely linked to the consolidation of state borders. Today the modern nation-state suggests a definite social space, a fairly well demarcated and bounded territory, with which the members are thought to identify and to which they feel they belong.[30] Thus, the notion of citizenship is often conflated with nationality, where citizenship is seen as that which completes an otherwise incomplete personal identity.

Frost describes Hegel's account of the relationship between the individual and the state: it is through their participation in the state, as citizens, that people come to know themselves to be constituted parts of a whole rather than alienated individuals. To become a whole, free, and fully ethical self a person has to be a citizen of a good state.[31] In her account of Rousseau and the idea of sovereignty, Anne Norton suggests that the citizen was seen as great insofar as his individual will recapitulates that of the sovereign. He is made whole by the accordance of his will to the will of the whole. The citizen's regard for himself follows from his participation in sovereignty.[32] In her discussion of sovereignty, war, and sacrifice, Jean Elshtain argues that the state has been widely understood as the arena that calls upon and sustains the individual's commitment to universal ethical life, satisfying expansive yearnings through the opportunity to sacrifice 'on behalf of the individuality of the state'.[33]

While nationalism has been recognized as a progressive force which is based on rationalism and secularization, it has been argued that a world of sovereign nation-states depends on the naming of difference and on processes of exclusion. As we recognize differences, we often experience an internal compulsion to define some of them as forms of otherness to be conquered, assimilated, or defiled.[34] While this competitive nature remains evident—despite the end of the cold war and hopes for a 'New World Order'—in security policies which continue to reinforce adversarial military relations among national sovereignties, it is also implicitly present, although perhaps no less threateningly, in the moral and psychological dispositions of individuals.[35] Nationalism is not only a political and cultural doctrine but a moral one, in which the love of home and the sense of belonging that leads to safety are stronger than reason.[36] But as Dunn asks, why should this be so when many of us are all too aware of its moral shabbiness, insofar as it directly violates the official conceptual categories of modern ethics—the universalist heritage of a natural law conceived in terms of either Christianity or secular rationalism?[37]

Spatially, the principle of sovereignty fixes a clear demarcation between life inside and outside a centred community. Within states, universalist aspirations to the good, the true, and the beautiful may be realizable, but only within a spatially delimited territory.[38] Thus, in spite of obvious internal differences in ethnicity, religion, gender, and class within nation-states, the national bond continues to provide the most inclusive community, the most widely accepted boundary within which social intercourse normally takes place, and the limit for distinguishing the 'outsider'.[39] Yet this partiality comes into conflict with the dominant ethical traditions of universalism, as Andrew Linklater points out: 'Throughout the development of the modern system of states the case for the primacy of citizenship has come into conflict with various forms of ethical universalism and their attendant visions of a global community which supersedes the sovereign state'.[40]

The principle of state sovereignty is said to provide its own resolution to the philosophical struggle between universality and particularity. The normative resilience of the nation-state has been convincingly explained in terms of the struggle to reconcile the claims of 'men and citizens'—the claims of a universalist account of humanity and a particularist account of political community. As R. B. J. Walker argues, the tension between the universalist claims of Christianity and empire and the competing claims arising from participation in a particular statist community provides the unavoidable core of early modern political thought. In the struggle to reconcile these claims—of a universalist account of humanity and a particularist account of political community—early modern political thought both affirmed the primacy of the particular—the statist community, but also the individual—and attempted to legitimize accounts of political authority within particular communities through a reinterpretation and secularization of claims to universal reason and natural law.[41] Thus, the principle of state sovereignty affirms that our primary and often overriding political identity emerges through our participation in a particular community, but it also asserts that we retain a connection with 'humanity' through our participation in a broader global—international—system.[42]

In spite of the existence of this international system, the lack of a strong, centred 'global' community has suggested either the 'difficulty or the radical impossibility of established ethical principles that are applicable to international relations'.[43] But in terms of the relations among states, state sovereignty also expresses a normative demand for national self-determination and non-intervention. The principles which emerged out of the Peace of Westphalia in 1648 established a normative system which granted a level of legal equality to nations of manifestly unequal proportions in terms of population, levels of economic and political development, and military capabilities. This 'equality' was ensured through the imperatives of reciprocity and neutrality, which encouraged autonomous national political and cultural development.

Thus, the idea of the nation-state as a causally self-sufficient entity was reinforced, ironically, by the principles governing relations between states. As Murray Forsyth points out, at its conception, at the root of the new system of international law, was the external correlate of the idea of the sovereign territorial state: 'The concept of sovereignty expressed a determination to restrain the imperatives of individual moral conscience, anchored in religious belief, and to accord priority instead to the requirements of peaceful coexistence within a given political space'. It was intended to assert a legal and secular standpoint in the face of a moral and religious one, which had the effect of 'privatizing' and 'neutralizing' the latter.[44]

In the contemporary era, nationality is linked to the international norm of national self-determination, which is, in practice, inextricably linked to the idea of state sovereignty. All three concepts, taken together, remain both important and heavily protected in spite of the rhetoric and reality of globalization and the alleged emergence of global society. Indeed, Paul Hirst and Grahame Thompson argue that in an era when ideas and capital are more mobile, the continued rootedness of populations and the continuing importance of national community will be a potentially explosive mixture. The myth of the culturally homogeneous nation-state is no longer sustainable in the contemporary world, and such homogeneity can no longer be relied upon as an excuse for exclusion. But as the advanced countries 'seek to police the movement of the world's poor and exclude them', they argue, 'the capriciousness of the notions of citizenship and of political community will become ever more evident'. 'Exclusion', they conclude, 'will be a mere fact, with no other logic or legitimacy than that states are fearful of the consequences of large-scale migration'.[45]

Thus, while globalization theorists may argue that the importance of territoriality has receded into the background over the last several decades, citizenship remains an important aspect of both identity and community for most people. As Hirst and Thompson have argued, people are less mobile than money, goods, or ideas; in spite of globalization, then, most people remain 'nationalized', dependent on passports, visas, and residence and labour qualifications.[46]

The principle of state sovereignty has restricted our political identity and created an international system based on exclusion; it has also, however, been understood as a source of moral value, standing in an uneasy, yet cleverly reconciled, relationship to cosmopolitan notions of the universal community of humankind. This is not to suggest, of course, that the distinctly modern notion of the nation-state has ever been the only force which has created group identities which categorize, mystify, and exclude. Religion has done this in the past and continues to do so today. Language and ethnicity and, perhaps to a lesser extent, class and gender have all led to the categorization of persons and the formation of exclusive and excluding groups. Moreover, strong identities such as these which are associated with 'ethnic nations', in states as diverse as the former Yugoslavia and Canada, currently struggle against the hegemony of nation-statism. The artificial 'carve-up' which took place during the colonial 'Scramble for Africa' has led to disunity and ethnic and tribal conflict within many of the present-day nation-states in sub-Saharan Africa.

And yet, in spite of the existence of strong group loyalties and identities corresponding to ethnicity and religion, it remains indisputable that the idea of the modern nation-state has been supported by the belief that it provides the rational, modern answer to questions concerning identity and moral and political community. Moreover, it is evident that, especially in international relations, analyses of culture, class, gender, race, and even individual subjectivity as expressions of modern political identity have been systematically marginalized, primarily because the character and location of modern political identity is already taken for granted in the claims of state sovereignty.[47] The resilience of communities defined in terms of nations and nation-states suggests that there is little evidence to support claims to an emerging world community—based on shared norms, common identity, and the recognition of the moral standing of all members—that is, all human beings. This is not to say, however, that there cannot or should not be moral responses to situations of need and suffering across borders; it is simply to argue that we cannot assume that the processes of globalization will create a seamless, inclusive, universal moral community.

Exclusion in the Global Political Economy

It could be argued that the modes of exclusion which exist in the workings of the global political economy are at once less explicit and more insidious than those which emerge out of the sovereign nation-state. As noted earlier, for the nation-state, territoriality—borders which keep out those whose loyalty cannot be guaranteed—is a precondition of existence, and to a considerable degree the practice of international politics is designed explicitly to maintain exclusivity. By contrast, for economic actors, such as firms, exclusivity is arbitrary and inefficient. National boundaries have no economic rationale and decrease profits. Moreover, international trade and investment clearly create interdependencies and mutual vulnerabilities.[48] It would seem, then, that a thriving global political economy would advocate interdependence rather than autonomy, integration rather than separation.[49] As John Williams has argued, economic liberalism's notion of the harmony of interests does not square easily with an international system in which conflict appears to be a central feature and in which the state retains the right to resort to violence.[50]

There can be no doubt that globalization has had a significant influence on, and indeed has been driven by, changes in the global political economy. The increasing importance of transnational corporations, the mobility of capital, and the spread of production processes all signal a shift from an international to a global political economy. For liberal and neo-liberal theorists, these changes are linked to the spread of liberal values and the increased proclivity for states and international institutions to co-operate for mutual benefit. Moreover, it is the marketing strategies of multinational firms, in conjunction with the media, which contribute to the dissemination and promotion of the idea of a 'global society'. From Microsoft to Coca-Cola, multinational corporations push the idea of a 'small planet'[51] as the basis for their products' appeal. The message seems to be not only that computers and soft drinks are 'global' products in terms of their availability and appeal, but that their consumption may, in some way, contribute to global peace and harmony.[52] These messages, of course, are both misleading and harmful.

As Janna Thompson has noted, it is not difficult to understand why theorists have supposed that economic interdependence between states, or between actors within different states, will encourage peaceful and, eventually, just relations in the world. It is reasonable to believe, as liberal international theory has told us, that states are less likely to act aggressively or unjustly to other states if the well-being and prosperity of a significant part of their populations depend upon the maintenance of mutually beneficial commercial relations. However, she argues, there are serious problems with this idea. Not all agents receive benefits from the world economy, and some agents are economically powerful enough to exploit others. The existence of a global market, then, cannot be conflated with the emergence of a 'global society'. As Thompson wonders, 'Can the fabric of a just world order really be spun out of the cloth of economic self-interest?'[53]

Terms like 'multilateralism' perpetuate the illusion of a 'harmony of interests' in the global economy. As Robert Cox has argued, economic multilateralism arose out of a specific historical context—the negotiation essentially between the United States and Britain for the constitution of the post–World War II economic order.[54] In 1945 the United States was the dominant hegemonic power, accounting for 40 percent of world industrial production and holding 70 percent of world gold reserves. American leaders, recognizing their responsibilities to a liberal international economy, rejected traditional isolationism, arguing that economic nationalism had been a major cause of the Second World War. They argued that free trade would increase global welfare, thereby providing a positive stimulus to peace and security. Liberal values and procedures were embodied in new institutions: the International Monetary Fund (IMF), the General Agreement on Tariffs and Trade (GATT), and the International Bank for Reconstruction and Development (IBRD).[55]

In this context, multilateralism meant, specifically, the structure of the world economy most conducive to capital expansion on a world scale. This appeared, from certain perspectives, to be implicitly compatible with the political idea of multilateralism, which 'had as a primary goal the security and maintenance of economic multilateralism'.[56] It is important to note, however, that when the postwar Anglo-American negotiations took place, Europe and the Soviet Union were devastated by war and what later became known as the Third World was inarticulate in international economic affairs. Thus, these countries were not effective participants in the definition of the concept of multilateralism or in giving substance to it.[57]

Fifty years later, in a truly globalized political economy, the exclusion of the poor continues, and the gap between the richest and the poorest continues to widen. Sub-Saharan African states 'consent' to austerity programmes and 'structural adjustment' within a world in which specific, historically situated liberal norms are widely perceived to embody universally accepted principles of order. Dominant approaches to international political economy—liberal institutional approaches—seek to ensure stability and predictability in the world economy and are thus generally unconcerned with the uneven power relations, or with the relations of structural dependency, that characterize the economic links between North and South. As Cox points out:

> Thus regime theory has much to say about economic cooperation among . . . groupings of advanced capitalist countries with regard to problems common to them. It has correspondingly less to say about attempts to change the structure of world economy, for example, in the Third World demand for a New International Economic Order.[58]

While changes in the global economy represent the increasing spatial reach of companies and the stretching out of social relationships over space, they must also be understood specifically as the stretching out over space of relations of power. As Doreen Massey argues, the spanning of the globe by economic relations has led to new forms and patterns of inequality, not simply to increasing homogeneity or similarity. A global hierarchy is clearly emerging as social and economic power seem inexorably to be increasingly geographically centralized in the few global cities which dominate the world economy.[59]

Exclusion in the global political economy is not limited to the North-South divide; feminist theorists of global political economy have argued that women have been excluded from the global political economy because of the way that both economic and political activity have been defined. Participation in the labour force and the inclusion of production in both national accounts and the measurements of international economic activity have been defined in relation to connection to the market, or to the performance of work for pay or profit. Unremunerated work is not, and the person performing it (usually a woman) is not included because the work is not part of the market of paid exchanges for goods or services and so is not viewed as economically significant.[60] Boundaries between the 'public' and the 'private' serve to exclude women from the former, and thus to exclude them from what counts as 'real' economic activity.

Gender intersects with race and class to multiply women's exclusion in the global political economy. Spike Peterson and Anne Sisson Runyan argue that through colonization this Western public-private division of labour was imposed on many cultures in the Americas, Asia, and Africa from the fifteenth to the twentieth centuries.[61] Moreover, it is evident that the processes of globalization—most notably, the increasing importance of flexibility in labour forces and the relocation of production—have had deleterious consequences for women. Currently, approximately 85 percent of the workers in the world's seventy-nine light-assembly and manufacturing export-processing zones (EPZs—enclaves favoring the activities of multinational corporations), operating in thirty-five countries in the mid-1980s, were women. Thus, it is argued, the gendered division of labour ensures that crises in the world economy are, in great measure, absorbed by mostly poor and working-class women and that male-dominated transnational corporations and Western banks reap large profits at the expense of these women, their families, and their societies.

Even a cursory examination of the contemporary global system and the specific changes associated with globalization—in both the international system of states and the global political economy—reveals the extent to which patterns of exclusion must be seen as structural and systematic, rather than operating simply at the level of individual agents and their arbitrary prejudices or normative preferences. Any account of global ethics or global justice which ignores these patterns of exclusion, and their economic causes, will be, by definition, inadequate. However, it is important to recognize that this is a concern not only for liberal or contractarian ethics or for theories of justice as impartiality or reciprocity. Relational ideas, too, carry risks for vulnerable people if the underlying patterns of power remain unchanged.[62]

Care and Moral Relations in a Globalizing World

The purpose of this chapter has been to illustrate that while globalization is indeed altering the nature of social relations on a global scale, there are dangers associated with the overstatement of shared purposes, universal reciprocal rights and obligations, and the emergence of a unified global society or community. In the contemporary world, the globalization of the world economy brings not only interdependence but also increased competition, deepening hierarchies and patterns of exclusion. Moreover, the importance of nationalistic sentiments and an increased protection of sovereignty—especially in 'new' nations and those states that see themselves as 'excluded' from the community of liberal states—must be recognized as both a part of and a reaction to globalization. In such a world, we must be wary of linking normative arguments about obligations or justice to so-called empirical arguments about globalization. It is a mistake to assume that we need to establish the existence of a homogeneous moral community before we can begin to think about the existence of moral relations. Even those arguments which accord a lesser role to 'real confrontations'—relying on them only to demonstrate the moral standing of all human beings—are unwisely tempted to make the over-inflated claims that the current 'global situation creates a new community', a 'community of interdependence', and that 'the condition of planetary interdependence has created a situation of world-wide reciprocal exchange, influence and interaction'. Such arguments must ultimately rely on Kantian principles in order to provide a foundation for their universalist ethics. These principles—rational self-legislation, practical reason, and autonomous insight—exist 'outside' of nature, and thus independently of globalization. Ultimately, all of the arguments discussed here are reduced to providing a moral justification of universal obligations based on the demands of reason. Certainly, there is little harm in claiming that reason tells us that we should not leave any other human being to starve or suffer, especially, but not only if, we have some real confrontation with her. But it is surely not *all* that ethics can do; nor, indeed, is it all that ethics must do when confronted with the moral demands of a globalizing world.

The changing nature of social relations in an era of globalization must have some bearing on what sorts of moral responses will be appropriate and helpful in situations where real people are suffering. We must eschew the will to establish universal principles of right and wrong which can guide moral decision-making and moral action across time and space, and engage instead in a phenomenological approach which explores the actual nature and conditions of, and possibilities for, moral relations in the global context. This chapter has demonstrated that globalization cannot be regarded as bringing only increased solidarity and homogeneity; rather, globalization is unevenly experienced and may indeed entail the deepening of exclusionary structures and practices and the widening of gaps in levels of well-being between races, genders, and territorial locations. However, while it may be that globalization brings with it a heightened awareness of difference and diversity in the world, we may also argue that it brings an unprecedented opportunity to understand those differences in relational terms. Rather than trying to overcome differences through universalizing solutions, we must recognize that differences that yield social distance and exclusion must be condemned as the self-serving expressions of the more powerful. What we must address now is not how to assimilate difference, but rather the framework itself which makes some differences salient and others unimportant; to do so, moreover, we must adopt a critical epistemology which insists that 'knowledge itself depends on the conceptual scheme or point of view employed'.[63]

The contemporary world remains, and is perhaps increasingly, a world of divisions, exclusions, and boundaries. But this need not suggest that there exist no possibilities for the creation of moral relations across those divisions; although boundaries and categories of some form are inevitable insofar as they are necessary to our efforts to organize perceptions and to form judgements, boundaries may also be seen as points of connection.[64] This is especially true, it could be argued, in a world characterized by increasing globalization. As was suggested in the first section of this chapter, the geography of social relations is indeed changing. In many cases, such relations are increasingly extended across time and space: economic, political, and cultural social relations, each full of power and with internal structures of domination and subordination, are stretched out over the planet at every different level, from the household to the local area to the international.

Doreen Massey has argued that it is from this perspective of changing social relations that it is possible to envisage an alternative interpretation of place and, by implication, of identity, difference, and moral relations. In this interpretation, what gives a place its specificity is not some long internalized history but the fact that it is constructed out of a particular constellation of social relations, meeting and weaving together at a particular locus—a true meeting place. Instead, then, of thinking of places as areas with boundaries around them, they can be imagined as articulated moments in networks of social relations and understandings, but where a large proportion of those relations, experiences, and understandings are constructed on a far larger scale than what we happen to define for that moment as the place itself.[65]

Object-relations theory—discussed in chapter 2—argues that in societies where early child-rearing is almost entirely in the hands of women, the project of identity construction is different for little girls and little boys. In particular, it is different in relation to the issue of boundaries. It is the boy's need—growing up in a society in which genders are constructed as highly differentiated and as unequal—to differentiate himself from his mother, which encourages in him an emphasis, in the construction of a sense of identity, on counterposition and on boundary-drawing. Only by this means, it seems, can his identity be securely established. Given the dominant place of masculine views in this society, it is this defensive and potentially so vulnerable way of establishing a sense of self which becomes generalized in social relations.

This view also reverberates, Massey argues, through our currently dominant notions of place and of home, and very specifically through notions of place as a source of belonging, identity, and security.[66]

> [F]or the new complexities of the geography of social relations to produce fear and anxiety, both personal identity and 'a place called home' have had to be conceptualised in a particular way—as singular and bounded. Of course places can be home, but they do not have to be thought of in that

> way, nor do they have to be places of nostalgia. You may, indeed, have many of them. . . . And what is more, each of these home-places is itself an equally complex product of the ever-shifting geography of social relations present and past.[67]

This approach to places and categories emphasizes not the boundedness of them but the possibility of understanding them as networks of social relations. From this perspective, the possibility of moral progress and political transformation can be seen as lying not in the universalization of values or the creation of a seamless global community of universal obligations, but in the fostering of a relational understanding of identity, difference, and the self. A globalizing world is one in which places and homes may more readily be conceived of as less fixed, and where the increasing intensity of social relations on a global scale may highlight not only differences but also relationships across boundaries.

Margaret Urban Walker's critical, expressive-collaborative model of ethics echoes these ideas. She argues that any notion of a moral community as wholly homogenous is an idealization; even where social meanings are shared or overlapping, social and political communities are likely to be diverse and stratified by social differences. Our social or moral world, she argues, is characterized by 'conditions of imperfect understanding, conflict among and within ourselves, and diverse perceptions from different social positions that include dramatic inequities in material and discursive resources'. While these conflicts can cause 'personal breaches, social fractures, and individual or group violence', they are also opportunities 'to rethink understandings or search for mediating ideas or reconciling procedures within or between communities. They can disturb the superficiality, complacency, or parochialism of moral views'.[68]

Recognizing others as existing in relationship—both to oneself and to others—is a crucial starting point for an ethic of care. Responding with care towards others emerges out of an ability to see the other as a concrete, particular person who exists not as 'other' in an absolute, objective sense, but as another whose uniqueness and particularity emerges through her relations with others. From this perspective, in contrast to the universalist, rule-based ethics described earlier, what is morally significant about globalization is that it highlights the need to think of new ways of responding to difference—ways that resist the compulsion to homogenize and assimilate, but also, importantly, ways that do not approach difference as absolute but as existing only in relational terms.

Without necessarily endorsing in its entirety the theory of gender-based differences in identity and difference-perception put forward by object-relations theorists, it is still possible to acknowledge the persuasiveness of the argument that there exists a mutually reinforcing relationship between individual, psychological dispositions regarding difference and relationships, on the one hand, and the social structures and conditions which endorse and legitimate those understandings on the other. It also suggests that an understanding of gender differences as relational rather than as existing objectively—'out there' to be discovered—could help to undermine the exclusionary and hierarchical aspects of gender difference. This is true, it could be argued, of any type of social difference, whether it is created by nationality, religion, class, or gender. As will be discussed at greater length in the next chapter, a relational approach to social exclusion involves the recognition that power is involved in the naming of difference, and that that power is located in the institutions and structures of the society in question.

From this starting point, paying attention to particular examples of human suffering need not necessarily divert attention from the social structures and privilege that legitimate such behaviour. As has already been pointed out, this is one of the most penetrating criticisms of care ethics—the claim that when an agent is focusing on the concrete specificities of a situation, she is not attending directly to the social institutions that structure it and vice versa.[69] Alison Jaggar argues convincingly that this has been a limitation of many existing interpretations of an ethics of care; must we necessarily accept her claim, however, that, like the ambiguous duck/rabbit figure, it is impossible to focus on both the 'particular' and 'social structures' at once? To be attentive to the concrete specificities of a moral situation—indeed, to care effectively—*is* to acknowledge the wider structural causes of suffering or exclusion. A human being only becomes a particular person when she is understood as a person with an identity—a person who may be both different and similar to the moral agent and to others. This in itself means that that particular person exists, and can be known, only in the context of her relationships both to the moral agent and to other individuals and groups. One cannot even begin to respond morally, indeed, to care for another person, without making sense of this. Close attention to the specificities of moral situations need not obscure perception of the larger social context in which they are embedded if the process of understanding, knowing, and caring for a person who is different from you involves an understanding that difference is actually constructed through relationships which are not personal but social, and which are often characterized by both power and privilege.

Conclusion

It has been the aim of this chapter to explore a number of complex social, political, and economic circumstances which characterize the current era of globalization. Through an analysis of globalization and ethics, the chapter has sought to dispel any notion that universal reciprocal moral obligations, or indeed, a seamless 'global moral community', can be explained by, or will necessarily be the direct consequence of, globalization as characterized by, for example, economic interdependence. The poverty of such an approach is due in large measure to its simplification and reduction of the relationships which exist in the world today. Globalization is neither a simple nor a unitary process; moreover, not all of the relations which characterize its relations will promote care, trust, and responsibility among those involved. There is no simple formula which allows us to bridge the normative gap and prove that interdependence as such will lead to a more caring world, or even to the recognition of obligations, across the chasms of distance and difference.

Yet the untenability of a truly inclusive, cosmopolitan ethics need not imply the inevitability of a world of moral exclusion. The possibility of achieving a new plurality in our own identities and in the nature of our social, political, and moral communities depends not only on circumstances but also on a willingness to adopt a critical attitude to both the structures and the social conventions which have defined the patterns of our social intercourse and demarcated the boundaries of our moral concern. The next chapter demonstrates the importance of these conclusions for a critical ethics of care which integrates the relational ethics of care with a critical account of power relations, difference, and exclusion in the globalizing world order.

Notes

1. Margaret Urban Walker, *Moral Understandings: A Feminist Study in Ethics*, New York: Routledge, 1998, p. 72.

2. Robert Keohane and Joseph Nye, *Power and Interdependence: World Politics in Transition*, Boston: Little, Brown, 1977, p. 3.

3. Jan Aarte Scholte, 'The Globalization of World Politics', in John Baylis and Steve Smith, eds., *The Globalization of World Politics: An Introduction to International Relations*, Oxford: Oxford University Press, 1997, pp. 14–15.

4. Anthony Giddens, *The Consequences of Modernity*, Cambridge: Polity Press, 1990, p. 64.

5. Ibid., p. 14.

6. Francis Fukuyama, *The End of History and the Last Man*, New York: Basic Books, 1992.

7. John Williams, 'Nothing Succeeds Like Success? Legitimacy and International Relations', in Barry Holden, *The Ethical Dimensions of Global Change*, London: Macmillan, 1996, p. 52.

8. Robert Jackson, *Quasi-States: Sovereignty, International Relations, and the Third World*, Cambridge: Cambridge University Press, 1990; see also Martin Shaw, *Global Society and International Relations*, Cambridge: Polity Press, 1994.

9. David Miller, 'Bounded Citizenship', paper presented at the University of Sussex Seminars in Social and Political Thought, 10 October 1996, p. 13.
10. Ibid.
11. Charles Beitz, *Political Theory and International Relations,* Princeton, NJ: Princeton University Press, 1979, p. 144.
12. Ibid., p. 141.
13. Ibid., p. 128.
14. Charles Beitz, 'Cosmopolitan Ideals and National Sentiment', *Journal of Philosophy* 80, no. 10, 1983: 591–600, 595.
15. Ibid., p. 595.
16. Charles Beitz, 'Sovereignty and Morality in International Affairs', in David Held, ed., *Political Theory Today,* Cambridge: Polity Press, 1991, p. 253.
17. Ibid.
18. Seyla Benhabib, 'Cultural Complexity, Moral Interdependence, and the Global Dialogical Community', in Martha Nussbaum and Jonathan Glover, eds., *Women, Culture, and Development: A Study of Human Capabilities,* Oxford: Oxford University Press, 1995, p. 235.
19. Bernard Williams, *Ethics and the Limits of Philosophy,* 2nd ed., London: Fontana, 1993, p. 160.
20. Benhabib, 'Cultural Complexity', p. 249.
21. Ibid., pp. 250–251.
22. Ibid., pp. 251–253.
23. Onora O'Neill, 'Moral Standing and State Boundaries', Christopher Thorne Memorial Lecture, University of Sussex, 5 December 1995.
24. Benhabib, 'Cultural Complexity', p. 251.
25. Chris Brown, 'International Political Theory and the Idea of World Community', in Ken Booth and Steve Smith, eds. *International Relations Theory Today,* Cambridge: Polity Press, 1995, p. 92.
26. Allison James, *Childhood Identities: Self and Social Relationships in the Experience of the Child,* Edinburgh: Edinburgh University Press, 1993, p. 201.
27. William Connolly, *Identity/Difference: Democratic Negotiations of Political Paradox,* Ithaca, NY: Cornell University Press, 1991, p. 158.
28. Benedict Anderson, *Imagined Communities: Reflections on the Origin and Spread of Nationalism,* rev. ed., London: Verso, 1991.
29. Ernest Gellner, *Nations and Nationalism,* Oxford: Blackwell, 1983, p. 4.
30. Anthony Smith, *National Identity,* London: Penguin, 1991, p. 9.
31. Mervyn Frost, *Ethics in International Relations,* Cambridge: Cambridge University Press, 1996, p. 148.
32. Anne Norton, *Reflections on Political Identity,* Baltimore: Johns Hopkins University Press, 1988, p. 32.
33. Jean Bethke Elshtain, 'Sovereignty, Identity, and Sacrifice', in V. Spike Peterson, ed., *Gendered States: Feminist (Re)visions of International Relations Theory,* London: Lynne Rienner, 1992, p. 143.
34. Connolly, *Identity/Difference,* p. 48.
35. Robert C. Johansen, 'Military Policies and the State System as Impediments to Democracy', in David Held, ed., *Prospects for Democracy: North, South, East, West,* Cambridge: Polity Press, 1993, p. 228.

36. Michael Ignatieff, *Blood and Belonging: Journeys into the New Nationalism,* London: Chatto & Windus, 1993, p. 6.

37. John Dunn, *Western Political Theory in the Face of the Future,* Cambridge: Cambridge University Press, 1979, p. 57.

38. R. B. J. Walker, *Inside/Outside: International Relations as Political Theory,* Cambridge: Cambridge University Press, 1993, pp. 61–62.

39. Smith, *National Identity,* p. 144.

40. Andrew Linklater, *Men and Citizens in the Theory of International Relations,* London: Macmillan, p. 207.

41. Walker, *Inside/Outside,* p. 61.

42. Ibid., p. 189.

43. Ibid., p. 63.

44. Murray Forsyth, 'The Tradition of International Law', in Terry Nardin and David Mapel, eds., *Traditions of International Ethics,* Cambridge: Cambridge University Press, 1992, p. 25.

45. Paul Hirst and Grahame Thompson, *Globalization in Question,* Cambridge: Polity Press, 1996, p. 182.

46. Ibid., p. 171.

47. Ibid., p. 11.

48. Rowland Maddock, 'The Global Political Economy', in John Baylis and N. J. Rengger, eds., *Dilemmas of World Politics: International Issues in a Changing World,* Oxford: Oxford University Press, 1992, pp. 107–109.

49. The separate discussion of the states system and the global political economy is an analytical distinction only; in no way am I seeking to uphold the claim that these two systems are wholly distinct or separate. Indeed, I would wish to suggest that the opposition of states and markets is largely illusory—that the opening up of national territories to global market forces does not necessarily lead to inclusion, but often to new forms of exclusion. I am grateful to John Maclean for pointing out the potential for confusion on this point in my analysis.

50. Williams, 'Nothing Succeeds Like Success', p. 58.

51. The IBM marketing slogan 'Solutions for a Small Planet' exemplifies this trend in advertising.

52. I owe this insight to Virginia Held.

53. Janna Thompson, *Justice and World Order: A Philosophical Inquiry,* London: Routledge, 1992, pp. 42–43.

54. Robert Cox, 'Multilateralism and World Order', in Robert Cox with Timothy J. Sinclair, *Approaches to World Order,* Cambridge: Cambridge University Press, 1996, p. 495.

55. Maddock, 'The Global Political Economy', pp. 110–111.

56. Cox, 'Multilateralism', p. 496.

57. Ibid., p. 495.

58. Ibid., p. 509.

59. Doreen Massey, 'A Place Called Home', in *Space, Place, and Gender,* Cambridge: Polity Press, 1992, pp. 158–160.

60. Jill Krause, 'The International Dimension of Gender Inequality and Feminist Politics: A New "Direction" for International Political Economy?' in Andrew

Linklater and John MacMillan, eds., *Boundaries in Question: New Directions in International Relations,* London: Pinter, 1995, p. 130.

61. V. Spike Peterson and Anne Sisson Runyan, *Global Gender Issues,* Boulder, CO: Westview Press, 1993, p. 92.

62. Martha Minow, *Making All the Difference: Inclusion, Exclusion, and American Law,* Ithaca, NY: Cornell University Press, 1990, p. 229.

63. Ibid., p. 224.

64. Ibid., p. 390.

65. Doreen Massey, 'A Global Sense of Place', in *Space, Place, and Gender,* p. 154.

66. Massey, 'A Place Called Home', p. 170.

67. Ibid., p. 172.

68. Walker, *Moral Understandings,* pp. 70–71.

69. Alison M. Jaggar, 'Caring as a Feminist Practice of Moral Reason', in Virginia Held and Alison Jaggar, ed., *Justice and Care: Essential Readings in Feminist Ethics,* Boulder, CO: Westview Press, 1995, p. 195.

6

Global Social Relations and Exclusion: Towards a Critical Ethics of Care

Significantly improving the lives of the world's women certainly requires the empathy, imagination and responsiveness that distinguish care thinking; but it also requires a kind of moral thinking that focuses not only on meeting immediate needs but on problematizing the structures that create those needs or keep them unfulfilled.

Alison Jaggar, 'Caring as a Feminist Practice of Moral Reason', 1995 (p. 197)

Developing a method of attending to relationships without losing sight of larger patterns of power will be critical to those who want to redress the legal treatment of difference.

Martha Minow, *Making All the Difference*, 1990 (p. 229)

The previous chapter explored the nature of the contemporary global system in order to demonstrate that neither liberal-universalist ethics nor conventional versions of the ethics of care can usefully respond to the moral challenges of globalization. It argued that we cannot use arguments about globalization to support a universalist account of global ethics. This claim was made on methodological grounds—citing the confusion over 'empirical' and 'normative' arguments about globalization—and on substantive grounds—in the claim that the current world order, in spite of many globalizing tendencies, is ultimately characterized by renewed nationalisms, a robust legacy of state sovereignty, and an increasingly uneven global capitalist economy. It was suggested that, rather than heralding the arrival of global solidarity and a fully inclusive global society, the contemporary world is, in many ways, characterized by patterns of exclusion. What this means, in the context of international relations, is that the structures, norms, and practices which govern the global system served to exclude, and to marginalize, certain groups. Thus, in addition to the system of nation-states, which is based on the notion of boundaries, groups are marginalized and oppressed through the exclusionary structures of the global political economy, through the gendered nature of international norms and practices, and through the cultural hegemony of Western values. The purpose of this chapter, then, is to construct a critical ethics of care which can address the demands of the contemporary, globalizing world.

Previous chapters have suggested that, in order to provide adequate moral responses in a global context, an ethics of care must build on and make more explicit its relational ontology; moreover, it has also been argued that an ethics of care for international relations must be a critical ethics which refuses to valorize 'normal ties' and is aware of both the potentially exploitative nature of all relationships and the way in which the naming of 'difference', and the processes of social exclusion, are themselves the product of relationships. Thus, a critical ethics of care begins from a relational ontology; it highlights the extent to which people 'live and perceive the world within social relationships' while, at the same time, recognizing that people use relationships to construct and express both power and knowledge.[1] This approach, like orthodox versions of feminist care ethics, values and promotes an understanding of morality characterized by sustained and focused moral attention arising out of the attachments and connections between concrete persons; where it differs from some accounts of the ethics of care, however, is in its explicit recognition 'the potential for violent domination and inequalities in all social relationships'.[2] Thus, while feminist thought has, in the ethics of care, articulated a radical alternative to Kantian and rights-based ethics, it can also offer a useful alternative way of understanding both the nature of and the solutions to moral and social exclusion in the global system. In this way, the ethics of care transcends its perceived limitations as an ethics which is relevant only in the context of physically and emotionally close personal relationships and becomes an ethics which is relevant to the wider moral context of international relations. An account of ethics which is based on the feminist ideas of care, but which also takes account of the social relations and institutional arrangements, norms, and structures through which perceptions of difference and moral boundaries are created can serve to advance the ethics of care beyond the 'personal' and the 'private' and to highlight its relevance in large-scale, institutionalized, or cross-cultural contexts.

This chapter elucidates the relevance of a social relations approach to dismantling exclusionary practices on a global scale to the construction of a global ethics of care. Thus, it emphasizes the importance of locating care within the context of the wider institutions and structures which shape the global order; understood in this way, relational thinking can assist us in exposing the often hidden values and norms which reinforce and reproduce established exclusionary social practices and attitudes. It attempts to show that, when taken as part of a larger, critical-relational approach to moral exclusion, care transcends its perceived limitations as an ethics which is relevant only in the context of physically and emotionally close personal relationships.

The first section explores the problems of exclusionary attitudes and practices and what Minow describes as the 'dilemma of difference'.[3] It focuses on her argument that exclusion and marginalization exist because norms and institutions are structured with 'the included participants in mind, so that the excluded seem not to fit because of something in their own nature'.[4] Although Minow's analysis concentrates on legal norms and practices in the United States, both her diagnosis and prescriptions are relevant to the context of the contemporary global system and to the exclusionary mechanisms of state sovereignty and global capitalism.

The second section addresses approaches to inclusion and exclusion in contemporary international relations theory. Specifically, it explores the Habermasian and Foucauldian accounts of, and responses to, inclusion and exclusion on a global scale. These critical theoretical and postmodern approaches are worthy of discussion here because they have played an important role in challenging the traditional Kantian, rights-based, and communitarian liberal approaches to international ethics discussed in chapter 4. By focusing on the problem of exclusion in international relations, these perspectives have moved beyond the perception of ethics as an 'achieved body of principles, norms and rules' which can be applied to the practical issues of international relations and towards an approach which sees ethics and 'accounts of ethical possibility' as already embedded in the values, norms, organizing principles, and structures of the contemporary international system.[5]

Influenced by the ethics, epistemology, and methodology of Habermas, Andrew Linklater advocates the development of a critical theory of international relations which examines the origins, reproduction, and transformation of the moral boundaries which separate the societies which comprise specific intersocietal systems. Specifically, he suggests that we must employ the method of *ideologiekritique,* developed by the Frankfurt School, in order to challenge spurious grounds for disallowing the other equal moral consideration.[6] Ultimately, this approach seeks to eradicate the exclusionary aspects of the identification of difference in the world through the progressive universalization of values and a reliance on the 'force of the better argument' to propel international society beyond illegitimate forms of moral exclusion and towards the ultimate goal of a thoroughly inclusive moral community—a universal kingdom of ends.

Demonstrating a similar reliance on Habermas, but also the influence of contemporary feminist thought, Seyla Benhabib starts from an explicitly Kantian position, arguing that Habermas's communicative ethics provides us with a method of arriving at universal criteria of normative validity which can be applied to moral situations.[7] However, she recognizes the dangers of over-abstraction and formalism inherent in Habermas's critical theory and advocates as a corrective the application of care ethics. Particularly, she argues that the concrete other of the ethics of care complements the 'generalized other' of the conditions of discursive validation. Thus, Benhabib attempts to create a theoretical bridge between Kantian-inspired, Habermasian discourse ethics and the feminist ethics of care.

In contrast to this Habermasian critical theory is the Foucauldian theory of postmodernists, including Susan Hekman's work in ethics and feminist theory, as well as the political theory of William Connolly.[8] Although, like Benhabib, Hekman is influenced by feminist ethics and seeks to draw a connection between, in her case, feminist ethics and Foucault, both Connolly and Hekman approach the moral problem of inclusion and exclusion through an examination of the self and subjectivity; in this view, overcoming exclusion based on difference requires an understanding of self-identity which is characterized by an ironic recognition of its own contingency, and which rejects both the notion of a true or authentic self and that of a prescribed, exclusive 'we'.

This chapter argues that all of these approaches have much to commend them and that both critical theory and postmodernism have much to contribute to work on ethics and moral reasoning in the context of international relations. It is argued, however, that Habermasian approaches, in spite of their Marxist epistemology, remain wedded to a distinctly Kantian universalism, which ultimately relies on an untenable vision of morality and moral motivation as well as on indefensible arguments regarding the universalization of values and obligations. The Foucauldian ethics of Hekman and Connolly, moreover, with their focus on self-actualization and ethics as aesthetics, advocate a retreat into individual acts of self-creation and re-creation and thus ignore the intrinsically social and interpersonal nature of exclusionary structures and processes.

The final sections of this chapter elaborate on the relational approach to exclusion which is the basis for a critical ethics of care. This approach addresses exclusion by shifting the paradigm we use to conceive of difference from a focus on the distinctions between people to a focus on the *relationships* within which we notice and draw distinctions.[9] Through the application of such a critical, relational approach to the labelling of difference—characterized by a commitment to an ontology based on social relations and a critical epistemology—we can create a bridge between the notion of care and the wider institutional and structural features of the global order. Finally, there is a brief exploration of the work of feminist theorists of global political economy; this work is important and potentially useful to the development of a global ethics in that it offers a critique of the institutions and structures of the global political economy which complements the relational approach to morality offered by the ethics of care.

It should be noted that this approach owes a debt to, but is by no means equivalent to, Marxist epistemology. Because of its critique of capitalism, individualism, and rights-based ethics, care is often regarded as 'a new cast for old models of socialism', and because of its emphasis on the socially constructed, relational self, there is a tendency to draw parallels between these ideas in care ethics and Marxist notions of the self and social relations.[10] Certainly, a critical ethics of care shares with Marxist epistemology a refusal to see social norms and institutions—and indeed, all 'knowledge'—as natural or given, but rather to reject the apparent 'objectivity' of knowledge and to regard all knowledge as socially constructed and historically contingent. Moreover, it is certainly the case that, as Susan Hekman notes, the 'first step that led to the construction of the "anti-Cartesian" subject was taken, ironically, by one of the masters of modernist thought: Karl Marx. By positing a subject that is determined by historical contingencies', she argues, 'Marx laid the groundwork for what would become the twentieth century's constructed subject'.[11]

That said, however, it is also important to recognize that Marxian theories of morality differ markedly from the relational approaches found in feminist ethics. As Seyla Benhabib has argued, the reductionist Marxian tradition views morality as merely an expression of the interests of the ruling classes. On this view, social conflict—between classes or genders—will come to an end with the elimination of the current regime—of capitalism or, in Catherine MacKinnon's words, 'compulsory heterosexuality'.[12] A critical ethics of care, however, eschews such a reductionist view, embracing instead the particularity and diversity of all kinds of social and personal relations. Moreover, it accepts that, as Benhabib claims, there will always be a need to 'protect the commitments of a shared human existence', since the permanent background to all ethical and political enquiry is always one of conflict, compromise, and change.

Difference and Social Relations

In her complex and challenging study of legal reasoning and ethics in the United States, Martha Minow describes the 'dilemma of difference' as 'a choice between integration and separation, as a choice between similar treatment and special treatment, or as a choice between neutrality and accommodation'. This dilemma, she argues, is not an 'accidental problem'; rather, it grows from the ways in which society assigns individuals to categories and, on that basis, determines whom to include in, and whom to exclude from, political, social, and economic activities.[13] In her exploration of the sources of perceptions of difference as justification for exclusionary social practices, Minow cites five 'unstated assumptions' which she says underlie difference dilemmas: (1) that difference is intrinsic, not a comparison; (2) that the 'norm' need not be stated, that is, that we typically adopt an unstated point of reference when assessing others; (3) that an observer can see without a perspective—in other words, can be impartial; (4) that other perspectives are irrelevant; and (5) that the status quo is natural, uncoerced, and good.[14]

Minow argues that both the social and legal constructions of difference at work today in the United States hide from view the relationships among people, relationships marked by power and hierarchy. She claims that it is within these relationships that we each become who we are and make order out of our own lives. Yet, by sorting people and problems into categories, she argues, we each cede power to social definitions that we individually no longer control.[15] One of the most interesting points made by Minow about the difference dilemma is her claim that this dilemma is a symptom of a particular way of looking at the world. 'The problem arises', she says, *'only in a culture that officially condemns the assigned status of inequalities and yet, in practice perpetuates them.'* While Minow is referring, as noted earlier, to the United States, it could be argued that this claim is equally true of the contemporary international system.

The modern system of sovereign nation-states is constructed around broadly liberal principles of negative freedoms and reciprocal rights and obligations. All states have 'formal' equality in that all have sovereign rights over their own territories. Moreover, there is an assumption that under this system the status quo is natural, uncoerced, and good. Finally, it is presumed that there exists an impartial, unstated point of reference, variously understood to be the voice of the international community, international law, or even the United Nations. This contemporary system, unlike some previous international systems, 'condemns the assigned status of inequalities, and yet, in practice perpetuates them'. As the previous chapter sought to illustrate, difference, exclusion, and inequalities in the international system are reproduced in two central ways: first, through the exclusive ontology of the sovereign autonomy of states and the related construction of identity linked to citizenship and nationality; and second, through the structural and normative inequalities present in the global capitalist political economy.

As suggested earlier, the work of contemporary critical and postmodern theorists has begun to focus on the relationship between these institutions and processes of inclusion and exclusion in the international system and the creation of norms and values in an effort to construct emancipatory theories for social change. These theories are explicitly normative, although they do not accept the conventional distinction between normative and non-normative theory. Moreover, they differ from traditional ethical theories not only in their rejection of modernist assumptions about knowledge but also in their understandings of moral agency and the processes of moral, social, and political change. Critical theory and postmodern approaches reject assumptions about the autonomy of individual human judgement and the potential for moral progress based on individual agency. Instead, these approaches argue that moral action and moral and political change are inextricably linked to structures, institutions, and norms which are socially and historically determined. Thus, any reference to 'ethics' or 'morality' can have meaning only in the historically situated context of social structures and social relations.

These approaches have been useful in international relations theory insofar as they have begun to dispel the belief that ethics is somehow separate from politics and social relations. Moreover, they have helped to situate our moral concerns and give meaning to our strategies for the achievement of moral progress and political change. As argued in previous chapters, a useful approach to international ethics, including an ethics of care, must go beyond a focus on particular relationships and instances of individual moral responses towards the suffering and needs of other individuals; it must become aware of the wider structural and institutional causes of human suffering and find ways to integrate an interrogation of these causes into its ethical framework. Indeed, to be a truly global ethics, care ethics requires, as Jaggar clearly states in the chapter epigraph quotation, 'a kind of moral thinking that focuses not only on meeting immediate needs but on problematizing the structures that create those needs or keep them unfulfilled'.[16]

The following sections explore the approaches from Habermasian critical theory and Foucauldian ethics in order to determine whether they can contribute to the creation of a critical ethics for the global context. Importantly, it also examines what might be called 'feminist variants' on both Habermasian and Foucauldian ethics; both of these feminist variants are broadly sympathetic to the relational ontology and the concrete, situated focus of care ethics and attempt to integrate the insights of care with either discourse ethics or the ethics of self-creation. It is argued that while the strengths of all of these approaches must be recognized, their weaknesses are ultimately crippling, revealing them to be guilty of either lapsing into a spurious universalism or retreating into self-indulgent processes of individual re-creation. The final sections of this chapter elucidate an alternative approach—the critical ethics of care—derived from the social relations approach to the legal treatment of difference and from feminist approaches to global political economy. It is argued that a critical ethics of care avoids the pitfalls of the Habermasian and Foucauldian perspectives and their 'feminist variants', while helping us to reinvent the ethics of care as an ethics which is responsive to the wider structural and institutional causes of human suffering and critical in its treatment of relationships, difference, and processes of exclusion.

Critical Theory and Discourse Ethics

One of the most important developments in international relations theory in the last ten years has emerged out of the commitment of some theorists to 'incorporate the emancipatory method and aspirations of critical social theory' into the current debates. For various theorists, this effort has meant the application of critical theory methodology and epistemology to 'mainstream' IR concerns such as security and international political economy. One of the most influential theorists in demonstrating the influence of critical theory on normative questions in international relations is Andrew Linklater. Drawing heavily on the work of the Frankfurt School and, especially, Jürgen Habermas, Linklater has explored in depth the normative questions surrounding identity, inclusion, and exclusion in the international system. This section discusses Linklater's approach to these questions and his Habermasian solution to the problem of moral exclusion on a global scale. It argues that although Linklater's approach contributes many useful insights—not least of which is the argument taken from critical theory that knowledge and 'truth' (moral or otherwise) are socially constructed and thus cannot be judged by some impartial or metaphysical perspective—it is ultimately unconvincing. Linklater's reliance on the Habermasian notions of moral learning, ideal speech situation, and the force of the better argument ultimately represents a restatement of Kantian ideals of morality and justice. As such, it is a principled totalizing ethics which remains fixed on rational consensus and universal inclusion as the markers of moral progress.

In a 1992 paper, Linklater argues that 'questions of inclusion and exclusion are central to international relations, since states and the state system are, in themselves, systems of inclusion and exclusion'. He suggests that such questions have three dimensions: normative, concerning the philosophical justifications for excluding some persons from particular social arrangements while admitting others; sociological, concerning the workings and maintenance of systems of inclusion and exclusion; and praxeological, concerning the impact of systems of inclusion and exclusion on human action.[17] Specifically, Linklater contends that sovereign states are immersed in different layers of inclusion and exclusion: first, the state itself may be described as a system of inclusion and exclusion, with 'precise distinctions between citizens and aliens' and concepts of sovereignty and territoriality. Second, what Linklater calls 'societies of states', held together by international legal norms and moral principles, can be exclusionary by 'debarring those deemed unfit to belong'. Finally, he suggests, paradoxically, that the 'community of humankind'—ostensibly the only fully inclusive community—has been criticized for privileging a limited range of culturally specific powers and needs, usually those valued by the West, and devaluing or denigrating those which are cherished elsewhere.[18]

When considering what he calls 'the normative question of the state'—what justifications exist for excluding any human being from any social arrangement—Linklater invokes Habermas's claim that 'advanced moral codes are committed to granting every human being an equal right to participate in open dialogue about the configuration of society and politics'. Thus, unless the constitutive principles of a system of exclusion can command the consent of all (particularly those to be excluded from the social arrangement in question), it cannot be considered legitimate. Linklater likens this emphasis on consent to seventeenth-century contractarian approaches, relayed to later social and political thought by Rousseau and Kant, and eventually to Rawls. Most important, however, he sees this notion of 'answerability to others in the context of a universal dialogue' as central to the immanent critique used by the members of the Frankfurt School:

> Instead of appealing to an ethical standard which is external to the state, this approach turns the state's own universal moral discourse against its questionable particularistic practices. In modern times, it presses the anti-exclusionary dynamic in the evolution of modern citizenship further by considering its ramifications for the domain of world politics. The anti-exclusionary dynamic is the trend of lowering the barriers which prevent excluded groups, such as subordinate classes, racial and national minorities and women from enjoying the social and political rights monopolised by more powerful groups. To press this further is to recognise that the nation-state is one of the few bastions of exclusion which has not had its rights and claims against the rest of the world seriously questioned.[19]

Linklater insists that the ethical universalism which underpins this moral and social commitment is 'not a form of universalism with an inbuilt hostility to cultural diversity and difference'. Its goal, he claims, is not to bring 'aliens or outsiders' within a homogeneous moral association, but rather to recognize the 'rights of groups' which 'suffer exclusion from full participation in the national community'.[20]

The question of reform focuses on what Linklater calls 'praxeology'—the interplay of systems and structures with human action. Here, Linklater invokes Kant's belief that international moral progress is inherent in the character of 'the modern state and its emphasis on universal human rights'. States which have contested various forms of exclusion within their boundaries are obliged to question exclusion in international affairs. Thus, in accordance with the method of critique described earlier, Linklater's critical theory focuses on *the potential for internationalism which exists in most modern states* and aims to explore ways in which this potential can be realized in international conventions which enshrine the moral principles of an alternative world order.[21]

Linklater's approach should be welcomed for a number of reasons. First, and perhaps most importantly, the epistemology and methodology of critical theory reject the positivist orthodoxy of international relations theory. The critical theorists' central epistemological claim—that all knowledge is socially constructed—dissolves both the conventional separation of normative and non-normative theory and the implicit positivist belief that the 'norm need not be stated'. From a critical theory perspective, normative questions of inclusion and exclusion are not a 'subfield' but are intrinsic to what the study of international relations should be about. Moreover, such an approach demonstrates that the epistemological and normative 'starting points' cannot be taken for granted; any 'status quo', then, cannot be seen as necessarily good, uncoerced, or natural, given the role of ideology and power in preventing agents from knowing their true interests.

In spite of these advancements, this Habermasian critical theory approach remains flawed. While critical theory is clearly influenced, methodologically and epistemologically, by Marx, the ethics of this approach remains decidedly Kantian in origin. To argue that the existence of a conflict between citizenship and humanity reveals that the force of the better argument no longer favours the primacy of the state, and that 'insiders' and 'outsiders' alike must be included as 'moral equals' in 'political communities which supersede the nation-state', raises a number of serious questions, not only about moral motivation but also about moral motivation and political will.[22] The claim that it is possible to develop empirical accounts of the way in which methods of excluding the other have broken down historically because of the evolution of more sophisticated forms of moral argument begs the question: From whose perspective do these forms of moral argument actually appear to be 'more sophisticated'?[23] Although Linklater admits that it is only with certain states and civilizations that the logic of moral universalism has developed, he appears to find this unproblematic—even useful.[24] But surely, in order to arrive at a consensus, it is crucial to ask in what kind of societies we find people who are committed to living together in conditions of 'communicative competence'. The answer must be that it is a society of the kind that *we,* as distinct from the medieval English or the citizens of modern Zaire, inhabit.[25] Indeed, Geoffrey Hawthorn has made this point clearly in his comments on the return to Kantianism evident in both Habermas and Rawls, and on social theory itself; such theory, he concludes, 'in the course of trying to define a more general, even universal "we", has in the anthropological, sociological and political reflection that it has encouraged, succeeded only in reinforcing the conviction that the interesting "we" are many'.[26]

The work of Seyla Benhabib, like that of Linklater, is clearly influenced by Habermas's discourse ethics; what sets her work apart from Linklater's, however, is her attempt to integrate Habermas's communicative ethics with the feminist ethics of care. Briefly, Benhabib argues that a universalistic moral theory restricted to the standpoint of the 'generalized other' falls into epistemic incoherencies; moreover, such theories reflect a subject that is disembedded and disembodied.[27] Instead, Benhabib argues that moral theories can, and indeed must, retain their universalism, but that they must also be understood from the standpoint of the 'concrete' rather than the 'generalized' other; this standpoint requires us to view each and every rational being as an individual with a concrete history, identity, and affective-emotional constitution.[28]

From this starting point, Benhabib develops her theory of 'interactive universalism', which acknowledges the plurality of modes of being human, and differences among humans, without endorsing all these pluralities and differences as morally and politically valid.

> While agreeing that normative disputes can be settled rationally, and that fairness, reciprocity and some procedure of universalizability are constituents, that is, necessary conditions of the moral standpoint, interactive universalism regards differences as a starting point for reflection and action. In this sense, 'universality' is a regulative ideal that does not deny our embodied and embedded identity, but aims at developing moral attitudes and encouraging political transformations that can yield a point of view acceptable to all.[29]

This dialogic, interactive universalism relies on a Habermasian model of communicative need interpretation that facilitates the generation of universally prescribable norms but also recognizes difference. Such dialogues would be actual rather than hypothetical, and agents would be able to introduce 'metaconsiderations' about the very conditions and constraints under which such dialogue takes place and to evaluate their fairness.[30]

Like Linklater's approach, Benhabib's theory is both convincing and useful. For example, Benhabib's 'relational-interactive theory of identity' is persuasive, as is her rejection of the Rawls-Kohlberg emphasis on the autonomous self, the recognition of the other as 'just like oneself', impartiality, fairness, rights, and duties. However, her effort to integrate this position with a strong, Kantian-Habermasian moral universalism is less convincing, and its effect is to dilute the strengths of the other aspects of her argument.

As Kimberly Hutchings points out, the problem that remains for Benhabib's version of critical theory is to explain how the imaginary or actual dialogues to which she refers really do bridge the gap between transcendental and empirical, abstract and concrete, which she traces in Habermas's as well as Kant's thought. Committed to a position of strong ethical universalism, she sets her own mode of theorizing against postmodernism; in doing so, however, Hutchings suggests that she risks reducing both positions back into the 'crude fight between speculation and scepticism; and to underestimate the extent to which her vocabulary is already shared by the "enemy"'.[31] Thus, in spite of her normative commitment to Kant, Benhabib's own position—'interactive universalism'—clearly 'unsettles' any objective, universal norms of judgement.

Benhabib's Habermasian approach, like that of Linklater, is certainly effective for all of the reasons noted earlier. Indeed, it is particularly important insofar as it recognizes the limitations inherent in the idea of the 'abstract other' accepts the concept of the 'relational self' as articulated by feminist theorists of the ethics of care. However, ultimately it is her commitment to moral universalism which overpowers her commitment to the recognition of difference. What does it mean, we must ask, to 'acknowledge the plurality of modes of being human', or to 'regard difference as a starting point for reflection and action', if, in the end, that difference must give way to a totalizing universalism? Ultimately, her view seeks to develop moral attitudes and to encourage political transformations that can yield a point of view acceptable to all. Thus, difference must give way—as these diverse, concrete selves develop their moral attitudes—and accept, or consent to, a solution. How that solution is arrived at—and indeed, whose solution it is—remains remarkably opaque.

Postmodern Ethics: Individual Self-Creation

In *Moral Voices, Moral Selves,* Susan Hekman seeks to articulate a concept of the subject that is appropriate to the task of a feminist reconceptualization of moral theory. Her 'discursive subject' relies on elements of feminist theories of subjectivity, the notion of the relational self, the postmodern subject, and theories of race and ethnicity. Her wider purpose in articulating this concept is to employ it in a reconceptualization of moral theory, focusing on identity, agency/creativity, and resistance.[32]

Hekman relies explicitly on Foucault in order to uncover a theory of the self and subjectivity which can provide a basis for feminist theory. Foucault, she argues, criticizes the Cartesian subject for its inability to move beyond the rigid boundaries that define it; by moving beyond the Cartesian subject, we are forced to see the self in a new way. Hekman quotes Foucault: 'From the idea that the self is not given to us I think there is only one possible consequence: we have to create ourselves as a work of art'.[33] Following Foucault, Hekman argues that this act of self-creation is accomplished through a kind of 'discursive mix'. The act of self-creation is likened to the writing of a 'script' for life; by piecing together a different script from discourses other than those which we are expected to follow, the creation of identity is not only an aesthetic practice but, potentially, an act of resistance.[34]

It is this idea of resistance which links the idea of self-creativity to power, domination, and responsibility. The resistant subject, according to Hekman, is one that refuses to be scripted by the dominant discourse and turns instead to subjugated knowledge to fashion alternative discourses of subjectivity. Rejecting the common claim that this postmodern approach to subjectivity fosters nihilism, Hekman argues that it is precisely because we cannot assume that subjectivity is a given that we must take moral responsibility for the construction of ourselves as subjects. Ethics, in the Foucault/Hekman account, is a practice of self which would allow the games of power to be played with a minimum of domination.[35]

Hekman links this idea of the creative self and the discursive morality with feminist ethics and politics. By drawing these elements together, she argues that we emerge with a politicized ethics which listens to a plurality of different moral voices of equal standing; such an ethics allows us to live in a world of 'multiple truths and multiple discourses of knowledge' by recognizing the self as embodied, historical, cultural, and discursively constituted. Finally, this reconstructed moral theory provides the theoretical ground, Hekman argues, for a 'politics of difference' which is local, contextual, and resistant, a politics that defines the specific nature of particular instances of repression and attacks them as such.[36]

William Connolly, like Hekman, relies on Foucault, but also on Nietzsche, using the works of the two philosophers as a 'complement and corrective to the other'. In response to 'hegemonic claims about identity', Connolly argues, Nietzsche and Foucault devise strategies for cultivating care for identity and difference in their relations of discordant interdependence. Together they search not for an epistemic foundation for ethics, but for more and more ways to cultivate care for identity and difference in a world already permeated by ethical proclivities and predispositions to identity.[37]

Like Hekman, Connolly relies on Foucault in arguing that a recognition of the contingency of identity goes hand in hand with the responsibility to 'work on the self'; this 'work' involves coming to terms with the difficulties in negotiating relations between antagonistic formations; this, in turn, may take the form of an effort to strive to convert an antagonism of identity into an agonism of difference:

> An antagonism in which each aims initially at conquest or conversion of the other can now (given other supporting conditions) become an agonism in which each treats the other as crucial to itself in the strife and interdependence of identity/difference. . . . Each cultivates an appreciation of contingency and disjunction in the experience of identity so that the agonism of difference will not always have to be rolled back into the strategies of conquest, conversion, community, or tolerance.[38]

The idea is that when one construes one's identity as being laced with contingencies, one is in a better position to question and resist the drive to convert difference into otherness to be defeated, converted, or marginalized. Like Hekman, Connolly uses the term 'politics of difference'. Although he admits that the recognition of contingency cannot completely cure us of the tendencies to conceal, sublimate, restrain, or revise that which does not synchronize with our own ideals, he argues that in living one's own identity in a more 'ironic, humorous way, laughing occasionally at one's more ridiculous predispositions and laughing too at the predisposition to universalize an impulse simply because it is one's own', our responses to others will be motivated less by the belief that our particular identity is intrinsically true and more because 'one's reflective experience of contingency and relationality in identity elicits a reverence for life responsive to the politics of difference'.[39]

Connolly addresses the importance of these ideas for the problem of 'distance' or, in other words, for the context of international relations. He argues that contemporary international relations theory dissolves issues of identity and difference into its categories of theory, evidence, rationality, sovereignty, and utility. Focusing briefly on the work of Kenneth Waltz, Connolly argues that Waltz's emphasis on 'the useful' and the domain of 'problem-solving' becomes fixed through the categories of sovereignty, rationality, anarchy, and utility that organize both the theorists' representation of international relations and the major actors' own interpretation of those relations.[40] 'The sovereignty of sovereignty' is a phrase that encapsulates Connolly's critique of the exclusionary ontology of the states system: a collective politics of transcendental egoism flows from the role of the state as the sovereign institution of final accountability; in the territorial state, the politics of collective identity tends to organize the idealisms and egoisms of its legitimate members into a collective egoism, which becomes most intense whenever the state is faced with internal or external affronts to its self-assurance.[41]

While Connolly admits that it is 'not so easy to broaden one's "reflective experience of contingency and relationality in identity"', it could be argued that neither he nor Hekman recognize the scope or intensity of the structural and psychological obstacles which prevent individuals from taking on the responsibility to create and re-create themselves. As Hanna Papanek has argued, the extent to which individuals can choose their identity—perhaps by deciding on a particular kind of life or by giving or withholding their loyalty to a particular group—is also a measure of the freedom of action they have within the larger society. When states or other powerful institutions (such as political movements, social groups like castes or clans, or domestic groups) can effectively limit identity choices by enforcing conformity to norms or ideals, individual freedom of action declines.[42]

This is because, as Papanek points out, identities represent entitlements to shares of a group's or society's resources. An individual's sense of identity, then, can be shaped and reshaped—often very powerfully—by external forces bent on their own agendas of building new solidarities, new group boundaries, and new political alliances. Obedience to the norms of the group is one of the goals of leaders who seek strongly bounded and powerful groups of followers, especially if individuals are to be mobilized to act in ways that violate existing social norms.[43]

Thus, Foucault's ethics has been accused of advocating a retreat into an amoral aesthetics of existence which can only be indulged in by a privileged elite who do not have to face the harsh political and material realities of life.[44] It has been argued that understanding ethics in this way places primary moral value on the act of choosing itself, rather than on the actual choices that are made or, indeed, the justification of action in relation to wider political aims. Richard Wolin describes this as a kind of 'decisionist ethics' which privileges form over action, so that the adoption of any nonconventional subject position is endorsed, rather than an attempt to specify what subject positions should be adopted.[45]

Moreover, despite the fact that Foucault is careful to guard against privileging any one form of identity as inherently radical through an insistence on understanding personal identity as constituted by the myriad social relationships and practices in which the individual is engaged, his ethics is still open to the accusation that it privileges a notion of the self which establishes a relation with the self, rather than understanding the self as embedded in and formed through types of social interaction.

Postmodernists, and postmodern feminists, then, strive to develop a 'de-centred' and 'fractured' concept of the self, rather than a 'connected' or 'relational' self of an ethics of care.[46] The problem, then, with Foucault's work is not the notion of aesthetics per se, but rather the emphasis on the idea of an isolated process of self-stylization as the basis for a modern ethics of existence.[47]

A truly transformatory ethics cannot afford to limit its focus to the reinvention of the self or to the nurturance of individual relationships. While both of these activities do indeed possess moral value, they are ultimately inadequate if our goal is progressive social and political change. As McNay argues,

> Without an interactional notion of the self—that is, without making the analytical links between one's own actions and the social context—the individual cannot distinguish between what constitutes a radical exploration of identity and what is simply an arbitrary stylization of life. Without an understanding of how the individual's actions are constantly mediated through interaction with other individuals, Foucault cannot explain how the potential uncovered in the exploration of identity can be communicated to others in order to initiate progressive change at the level of the group, community or class. Foucault cannot produce a satisfactory answer to the dilemmas he himself poses because his theory of the self prioritizes an isolated individuality, rather than demonstrating how the construction of the self is inextricably bound up in various processes of social interaction.[48]

In spite of Hekman's conviction that Foucault's ethics is 'appropriate to the political requirements of feminism', it fails to answer questions about how an ethics of self-actualization can avoid lapsing inevitably into introversion and instead contribute to wider forms of progressive social change.[49] Moreover, the priority placed on the 'care of the self' in Foucauldian ethics stands in opposition to the feminist notion of care and the relational self: caring for others and the promotion of good, caring personal and social relations, both within and among groups, take moral priority. As demonstrated later in this chapter, it is the notion of the relational self which ultimately holds the key not only to the ethics of care but to an ethics which can rethink both the structural and psychological constructions of difference.

History gives us countless reasons—from the 'conquest of America' to the genocide of World War II—to know the answer to Connolly's poignant question: 'Is this fugitive and endless quest for surety of identity really worth the sacrifices it entails'?[50] But knowing that it is not worth it is not the same thing as finding a way to convince people it is not worth seeking. This requires the institutionalization of a framework for recognizing difference which can overcome the drive to universalize and at the same time take us closer to a real moral solution than we can find in the idea of self-creativity.

The Social Relations Approach

In her analysis of American society and law, Martha Minow isolates a number of different areas in the social sciences, and social thought more generally, which have come to recognize the importance of relationships, thus rejecting the standard assumption that objects are isolated and individuals are separate. Instead, proponents of this general view argue that connections, between persons and groups of persons as well as between knowledge and the objects of that knowledge, should be central to study and to prescription. Thus, Minow argues, 'perhaps the most significant assertion of the new theorists is that the relationships between the world and what people think about it must be part of any claims to understand the world'.[51] In the development of her approach, Minow is concerned both with ontology—'what exists'—and epistemology—'how knowledge is created and reproduced'. Relationships are crucial for Minow on *both* levels—things and especially people in the social world *exist in relationships,* and knowledge must be understood *in relation to* who makes the knowledge claims and from what vantage point, what material circumstances, and what degree of power.[52] In order to demonstrate the breadth and scope of 'relational' thinking, Minow explores a number of different disciplines which, in the twentieth century, have embraced relational approaches.

In philosophy, she cites the American pragmatists, including Dewey—'the most broad-gauged and influential thinking in this vein'—who argued that efforts should be made to understand the connections between self and other, that individuals are formed in social interaction, and that therefore ideas ultimately must be tested in light of social experience.[53] In social psychology and psychoanalytic theory, she cites the object-relations theories (discussed in chapter 2), which argue that a 'self' is a symbolic construct that depends on and emerges through relationships with others. In political theory, she cites communitarian and republican theories which articulate the importance of group membership, public values, and moral duties, thereby suggesting a departure from the assumptions that the individual is the focus for political theory and that the self has meaning apart from context and commitments.[54] But interestingly, it is feminist scholarship, including the work of Gilligan and other theorists of care, feminist historians, and feminist literary and legal theorists, that Minow finds most 'accessible and congenial' to her project.[55]

Minow argues that many feminists find relational insights crucial to any effort to recover women's experiences; in their view, the exclusion, degradation, or devaluation of women by political theorists, historians, social scientists, and literary theorists implies and imposes a reference point based on male experience. She points out that, besides criticizing as artificial the denigration of women, feminists argue that the experience of relative powerlessness has helped women to shape alternative ways of thinking about the world which accentuate an awareness of human interdependence. Referring to Sara Ruddick's *Maternal Thinking,* Minow states: 'Women's traditional roles as wives and mothers have cultivated the ability to provide daily care and a responsiveness to the experiences and needs of others'.[56]

Citing a wide range of feminist literature, including Gilligan and the ethics of care, feminist histories, literary theory, and psychological and moral theories, Minow argues that these feminist understandings capture what is crucial about relational thinking. Relational approaches, unlike rights analysis, enquire into the institutional practices that determine a norm against which some people seem different, or deviant. They encourage more debate and highlight as human choices—rather than as acts of discovery—the ways we treat people, the traits we call 'different', and the social institutions that embody and reinforce those assumptions. To address relationships, Minow argues, is to resist abstraction and to demand context.[57]

Minow advocates a shift in the paradigm we use to conceive of difference, a shift from a focus on the distinctions between people to a focus on the relationships within which we notice and draw distinctions.[58] What she calls the social relations approach to difference 'assumes that there is a basic connectedness between people, instead of assuming that autonomy is the prior and essential dimension of personhood'.[59] A concern with relationships, she argues, should alert a decision-maker to the power expressed in the process of categorizing people, or problems. Moreover, although relational concerns do not, as she points out, 'tell us what to do' in times of conflict and difficulty—that is, they do not provide principles which can be applied to typical moral situations—they do not necessarily lead to relativism.[60] On the contrary, she argues, following a relational approach, we can and do make judgements about right and wrong, but we do so in context and in light of particularized assessments of the patterns of power and meaning.[61] In this way, the study of difference could provide us with 'clues to broader problems of social policy and human responsibility'.[62]

Among her strategies for 'remaking difference' she includes 'challenging and transforming the unstated norm used for comparisons, taking the perspective of the traditionally excluded group, disentangling equality from its attachment to a norm that has the effect of unthinking exclusion, and treating everyone as though he or she were different'.[63] Thus, her imperatives to engage an observer in the problems of difference include,

> *Notice* the mutual dependence of people. *Investigate* the construction of difference in light of the norms and patterns of interpersonal and institutional relationships which make some traits matter. *Question* the relationship between the observer and the observed in order to situate judgements in the perspective of the actual judge. *Seek out* and consider competing perspectives, especially those of people defined as the problem. *Locate* theory within context; *criticize* practice in the light of theoretical commitments; and challenge abstract theories in light of their practical effects. *Connect* the parts and the whole of a situation; *see* how the frame of analysis influences what is assumed to be given.[64]

The importance of the social relations approach, in contrast to 'communicative ethics' in Habermasian critical theory, is that it represents a clear ontological and epistemological break with Kantianism and the consent-based reasoning behind theories of justice as impartiality. However, as Minow points out, the challenge presented by feminist strategies is not just to deepen an interest in 'responsibility' or 'care', contrasted with 'fairness' or 'rights'. The challenge, she claims, is to maintain a steady enquiry into the interpersonal and political relationships between the known and the knower; a concern for the relations between wholes and parts; a suspicion of abstractions, which are likely to hide under claims to universality what is in fact the particular point of view and experience of those in power; and a respect for particularity, concreteness, reflection on experience, and dialogue. Many feminists, she adds, urge recasting issues of difference as problems of dominance or subordination in order to disclose the social relationships of power within which difference is named and enforced. 'In sum', she concludes, 'feminist strategies question the assignment of difference to the "different person" by locating difference within relationships of differential power'. [65]

Minow's approach is intimately linked to, yet builds upon, the insights of care ethics. Interestingly, however, Minow does not advocate a wholesale rejection of rights, but rather a renewed conception of 'relational rights' which cannot be understood apart from the notion of responsibilities. Relational rights and responsibilities, then, draw attention to the claims that arise out of relationships of human interdependence; thus, such a view encompasses not only individual freedoms but also rights to enter into and sustain intimate associations consistent with the responsibilities those associations entail, underscoring connection between families and intimates and the larger community.[66]

Margaret Urban Walker's expressive-collaborative view of ethics, discussed in chapter 5, focuses on the social relations of power and difference, and the importance of criticism, in a way that is similar to Minow's approach. She argues that the job of moral criticism is to examine human social arrangements rather than to put forward universally valid standards of conduct or judgement. Moral relations are not 'simply' moral, but also social—the 'complex skein of roles, relations or statuses', she insists, must not be made to look incidental to what morality is really about, or really like. It is at our peril that we avert our eyes from the 'shabby spectacles' of real, everyday moral systems, most of which are 'imbalanced, one-eyed, mystifying, rigged'. Her vision of critical practice bears many similarities to that advocated by Minow:

> If it is characteristic of human societies (including our own) that moral standards, statuses, and distributions of responsibility work through social differences, rather than in spite of them, then to understand morality—what it is—is to see how morality works, and works better or worse, in just this way. If it is commonplace that the most obvious moral failings of human societies—cruelty, injustice, exploitation, oppression—are effected through their systems of social difference, then to mount effective moral criticism of these arrangements requires finding out precisely how relations of trust and responsibility can be manipulated and deformed into something ugly and dangerous, in just this way.[67]

A feminist response to inclusion and exclusion in the global context, then, must begin with an account of the social relations of difference. It regards social exclusion as an intensely moral question, yet one which cannot be separated from the social, political, and economic structures and relations in which it is embedded. An ethics of care values human relations and attachments and regards the promotion of good social relations within and among groups as a moral priority. It recognizes the need to focus on the permanent background to 'moral decisions'—the everyday relations which give meaning and context to so-called moral problems. However, at the same time, it acknowledges that all relations are infused with power, and that within every relationship there exists the potential for exploitation and domination. Thus, it advocates *attention to relationships*—among states and non-state actors in transnational social, political, and economic contexts—as a critical tool for uncovering and remaking the processes leading to the naming of 'difference' and the legitimation of patterns of exclusion.

Thus, while a critical ethics of care concentrates on particular persons and their relations with others, it does not ignore the structural conditions in which those relations are situated. Such an ethics is about attention to the *relationships between a problem and its context and particularities,* rather than preoccupation with abstracting a problem away from its context. As Minow argues, the relational turn (in feminist ethics) thus represents not a denial of or lack of interest in conflict and disunity, but *'a focus on the interpersonal and social contexts in which these and all other human relations occur.'*[68]

Insights from Feminist Global Political Economy

This final section explores briefly my hunch that there is a potentially fruitful relationship between these arguments in feminist ethics and social theory and the arguments of feminists theorists in GPE (global political economy). Recently, feminist theorists of global political economy have taken up the critical project, focusing their work on aspects of gender relations within the global political economy. Sandra Whitworth has argued that in the light of the recent movement in IPE (international political economy) to go well beyond simply adding actors and issues and to include a far more profound ontological and epistemological challenge to the discipline, the 'suggestion that women and gender may figure in international relations may not be as unwelcome a notion as it once was'. Indeed, she points out that many feminist critiques of mainstream IR have adopted epistemological strategies similar to those of the IPE scholars who preceded them.[69]

Jan Jindy Pettman argues that the dominant liberal and nationalist models in IPE rest on particular notions of the nature of man, states, and markets which are class-, culture-, and gender-specific, informed by masculinist models of human nature. Both models are profoundly gendered in their notions of power, wealth, and the state. Most important, however, both ignore the vast amount of women's labour—in domestic and subsistence production, in reproduction and community care—motivated not by competition and the profit motive, but by family, local responsibility, and 'care'.[70]

Indeed, liberal perspectives in particular are subject to criticism from feminist theorists of international political economy. J. Ann Tickner cites Sandra Harding and Alison Jaggar, who argue that liberalism's individual portrayal of human nature ignores the extent to which individuals exist in relationships with others. They conclude that if the need for interdependence were taken as a starting point, community and co-operation would not be seen as puzzling and unproblematic.[71]

Tickner goes on to argue that a feminist perspective on international political economy must be wary of discourses that generalize and universalize from theories based on assumptions taken from characteristics associated with Western men. For example, the lived experiences of many women have been closely bound to caretaking and child-rearing; these women would define rationality as contextual and personal rather than abstract. A feminist definition of rationality, therefore, would be tied to an ethic of care and responsibility, rather than to profit maximization. Finally, she argues that a feminist perspective would assume a connected, interdependent individual whose behaviour includes activities related to reproduction as well as production. This would require the breaking down of the artificial boundaries between the world of rational economic man in the public sphere of production and the activities that women perform 'outside' the economy as mothers, caretakers, and subsistence producers. Valuing child-bearing and child-rearing could help to reduce the excessive focus on the productive efficiency of an ever-expanding commodity production—a focus whose utility in a world of shrinking resources, vast inequalities, and increasing environmental damage is becoming questionable. A perspective that takes this redefined individual as its basic unit of analysis could help to create an alternative model of political economy that respects human relationships as well as their relation to nature.[72]

As Sandra Whitworth argues, as well as seeking to transcend male-gendered notions about human nature and rationality, feminist theorists of GPE are concerned with exploring how knowledge about sexual difference is sustained, reproduced, and manipulated by international institutions. Understood in this way, meanings about gender are maintained and contested through the practices and struggles *of actors engaged in relationships* with each other and the institutions in which they are involved. The content of what the relations of gender look like is arrived at, not in any static way, but through the activities of *real, living human beings* operating within real historical circumstances.[73]

The emphasis on uncovering ideas and perceptions about difference, the belief that actors are engaged, at a fundamental level, in relationships with each other and with institutions, and the stress on real, living, concrete human beings, as opposed to static, abstract subjects, reveals the affinities between feminist approaches to GPE and the ethics of care. By its very nature, however, feminist IPE also recognizes that the activities of human subjects take place within particular economic structures and material conditions within which women's lives are located. Thus, while it maintains a concern with the structured inequalities within which agents operate, at the same time it documents the actual experiences of particular women within the global political economy.[74]

Clearly, many feminist theorists of global political economy share an epistemological position regarding the socially constructed nature of knowledge, and a normative commitment to uncovering the ideas, ideologies, and social and economic structures which create different and unequal power relations.[75] For this reason, they can provide useful insights towards the construction of an extended account of relational ethics which takes account of the wider institutional and structural forces which obstruct the development of caring relations between persons.

Conclusion

This chapter has sought to elucidate the arguments made in earlier chapters which suggested that an approach to ethics in an era of globalization must pay attention to exclusionary social practices and structures in the contemporary global system: how boundaries are constructed, how 'difference' is assigned, and how moral and social exclusion is legitimated. In chapter 5, it was argued that exclusionary practices—inherent in both the system of territorially bounded, sovereign nation-states and the norms and structures of an increasingly globalized political economy—must be problematized if we are to understand how our perceptions of distant others are constructed and reconstructed. Understanding obstacles to moral responsiveness among distant strangers simply in terms of ignorance, egoism, or individual prejudice obscures the 'institutionalization of exclusion' which occurs not only within political communities but between them.[76]

In spite of the advances made in exploring these questions by critical theorists and postmodernists in international relations theory, it is feminist theory—including work in ethics, legal theory, and international political economy—which can help us to construct the most useful approach to inclusion and exclusion on a global scale. A relational perspective relies on the feminist ethics of care but is also committed to paying attention to exclusionary social practices and structures in the contemporary global system. A social relations approach to the legal construction of difference, and a critical approach to exclusionary institutions and structures in the global political economy, are uniquely compatible with the epistemology and ontology of care ethics. By integrating these approaches, it becomes possible to develop what might be called a *critical* ethics of care; this approach recognizes the inadequacy of abstract, universalizing moral theories and instead locates moral motivation and moral responsiveness in the particular relations among concrete persons. However, it also is acutely aware of the arguments against orthodox versions of the ethics of care—that this sort of ethics focuses exclusively on 'micro' moral situations, among intimates in the home or 'private sphere', to the exclusion of the wider social causes of suffering and need.

Critics have pointed out that relational ideas carry risks for vulnerable people if the underlying patterns of power remain unchanged.[77] Many moral and social theorists—feminist and nonfeminist—have expressed reservations about relational or interpersonal ethics; they fear that acknowledging people's mutual need for one another may exacerbate the dependence of those who have historically been more dependent without remaking the underlying social arrangements that produced that pattern.[78] Feminists have pointed to the specific dangers this poses to women: regarding women as existing and identifying themselves in relation to others—specifically, to men—perpetuates perceptions of women as dependent and relegates them to the private sphere, or, at best, to so-called caring professions, which continue to be undervalued in society. Indeed, this is a potential problem not only for women but for all vulnerable or historically dependent groups: impoverished peoples of the South, dispossessed or stateless persons, migrants, and refugees.

As a corrective to this potential limitation, this chapter has demonstrated the relevance of two other modes of relational thinking: in the social theory and legal analysis of feminist legal theory, and in feminist approaches to international political economy. These theoretical perspectives recognize the potential of relational thinking not only in understanding moral relations but in problematizing the norms and structures that underwrite and sustain exclusionary structures. Their critical epistemology is relational, in that it is based upon a recognition of the relationship between knowledge and the knower; moreover, their social and moral ontology is relational, in that there is a recognition that persons, institutions, states, and even worldviews exist in relation to one another. Thus, there is an explicit rejection of the idea of a 'norm' by which all others can be judged. Instead, a relational approach enquires into the institutional practices that determine a norm against which some people seem different, or deviant.[79]

A relational approach to care ethics is able to address moral problems of human suffering first, by recognizing that an understanding of the nature and patterns of personal and social relationships must be the starting point for any serious moral enquiry. Second, although this approach places a high moral value on the existence and maintenance of relationships characterized by continuous attention, responsiveness, and care, it also recognizes that there exists, within all relationships, the potential for exploitation and coercion. Thus, the approach is committed to the promotion of healthy, caring relations among individuals and groups, not through the application of some minimal, abstract principles of what justice demands, but according to the demands of the given situation, where real social relations among concrete persons need to be created or restored.

Using arguments from the social relations approach to the legal treatment of difference, and from critical/feminist approaches to global political economy, a critical-relational ethics of care responds to difference and exclusion by examining 'the *relationships between people* who have and people who lack the *power* to assign the label of difference', leading to the recognition that 'the name of difference is produced by those with the power to name and the power to treat themselves as the norm'. So-called consensus approaches, then, may be seen as expressing the perspectives of those in positions to enforce their points of view in the structure and governance of society.[80] A relational approach, by contrast, would enable us to think of difference not as 'empirically discoverable, consisting of traits inherent in the "different person"', but rather as something which grows from the ways in which 'societies assign individuals to categories and, on that basis, determine whom to include and who to exclude from political, social and economic activities'. While retaining the commitment to moral attention and responsiveness that is motivated by and located in concrete individuals and their particular relationships and attachments, this approach pays attention to the broader institutional and structural relations in which relations of care are located. The perspectives from feminist international political economy complement the epistemology and ontology of an ethics of care; such approaches accept that relationships among real, not abstract, persons must be the starting point of any enquiry, but they also problematize and critique the very structures within which those relations are located. Ultimately they work towards an emancipatory vision of a more humane world order.

Notes

1. Martha Minow, *Making All the Difference: Inclusion, Exclusion, and American Law,* Ithaca, NY: Cornell University Press, 1990, p. 111.
2. Jenny Edkins, 'Legality with a Vengeance: Famines and Humanitarian Relief in "Complex Emergencies"', in *Millennium: Journal of International Studies* 25, no. 3, Winter 1996: 563.
3. Minow, *Making All the Difference,* p. 20.
4. Ibid., p. 21.
5. R. B. J. Walker, *Inside/Outside: International Relations as Political Theory,* Cambridge: Cambridge University Press, 1993, pp. 50–51.
6. Andrew Linklater, *Men and Citizens in the Theory of International Relations,* 2nd ed., London: Macmillan, 1990, pp. 222–226. See also Andrew Linklater, *The Transformation of Political Community: Ethical Foundations of the Post-Westphalian Era,* Cambridge: Polity Press, 1998.
7. Seyla Benhabib, *Situating the Self: Gender, Community, and Postmodernism in Contemporary Ethics,* Cambridge: Polity Press, 1992.
8. Susan J. Hekman, *Moral Voices, Moral Selves: Carol Gilligan and Feminist Moral Theory,* Cambridge: Polity Press, 1995; William Connolly, *Identity/Difference: Democratic Negotiations of Political Paradox,* Ithaca, NY: Cornell University Press, 1991.
9. Minow, *Making All the Difference,* p. 15.

10. The phrase 'new cast for old models of socialism' is borrowed from Joan Tronto. Importantly, Tronto strongly denies that we can understand care ethics in this way. See Tronto, *Moral Boundaries*, p. 175.

11. Hekman, *Moral Voices*, p. 72.

12. Carol Gilligan, Ellen C. Dubois, Mary C. Dunlop, Catherine A. MacKinnon, and Carrie J. Menkel-Neadow, 'Feminist Discourse, Moral Values, and the Law—A Conversation', 1984 James McCormick Mitchell Lecture, *Buffalo Law Review* 34, no. 1 (Winter 1985): 73–74.

13. Ibid., pp. 20–21.

14. Ibid., pp. 50–70.

15. Ibid., p. 22.

16. Jaggar, 'Caring as a Feminist Practice', p. 197.

17. Andrew Linklater, 'The Question of the Next Stage in IR Theory: A Critical Theoretical Point of View', *Millennium: Journal of International Studies* 21, no. 1 (Spring 1992): 78.

18. Ibid., pp. 83–84.

19. Ibid., pp. 93.

20. Ibid.

21. Ibid., pp. 96–97.

22. Ibid., p. 218.

23. Ibid., p. 223.

24. Ibid., p. 224.

25. Geoffrey Hawthorn, *Enlightenment and Despair: A History of Social Theory*, 2nd ed., Cambridge: Cambridge University Press, 1987, p. 273.

26. Ibid., pp. 274–275.

27. Seyla Benhabib, 'The Generalised and the Concrete Other: The Kohlberg-Gilligan Controversy and Feminist Theory', in Seyla Benhabib and Drucilla Cornell, eds., *Feminism as Critique: Essays on the Politics of Gender in Late-Capitalist Societies*, Cambridge: Polity Press, 1987, p. 81. See also Benhabib, *Situating the Self*.

28. Ibid., p. 87.

29. Ibid., p. 81.

30. Ibid., p. 94.

31. Kimberly Hutchings, *Kant, Critique and Politics*, London: Routledge, 1996, pp. 172–174.

32. Hekman, *Moral Voices*, p. 109.

33. Foucault, quoted in Hubert Dreyfus and Paul Rabinow, *Michel Foucault: Beyond Structuralism and Hermeneutics*, Brighton: Harvester Wheatsheaf, 1982, p. 287.

34. Hekman, *Moral Voices*, p. 82.

35. Ibid., p. 84.

36. Ibid., pp. 159–160.

37. Connolly, *Identity/Difference*, p. 10.

38. Ibid., pp. 178–179.

39. Ibid., p. 180.

40. Ibid., p. 51.

41. Ibid., p. 205.

42. Hanna Papanek, 'The Ideal Woman and the Ideal Society: Control and Autonomy in the Construction of Identity', in Valentine M. Moghadem, ed., *Identity Politics and Women: Cultural Reassertions and Feminisms in International Perspective,* Boulder, CO: Westview Press 1994, p. 42.
43. Ibid., pp. 43–45.
44. Lois McNay, *Foucault and Feminism: Power, Gender, and the Self,* Cambridge: Polity Press, 1992, p. 159.
45. Ibid., p. 159. This section contains a useful summary and analysis of Wolin's critique of Foucault's ethics.
46. Benhabib, *Situating the Self,* pp. 195–196.
47. Ibid., pp. 109, 164.
48. Ibid., p. 165.
49. Ibid., p. 197.
50. Connolly, *Identity/Difference,* p. 210.
51. Minow, *Making All the Difference,* p. 178.
52. Ibid.
53. Ibid., p. 183. For an excellent analysis of the links between feminist philosophy and pragmatism, see Charlene Haddock Seigfried, *Pragmatism and Feminism: Reweaving the Social Fabric,* Chicago: University of Chicago Press, 1996.
54. Ibid., pp. 187, 192.
55. Ibid., p. 193.
56. Ibid., p. 194.
57. Ibid., p. 216.
58. Ibid., p. 15.
59. Ibid., p. 110.
60. Ibid., p. 222.
61. Ibid., p. 381.
62. Ibid., pp. 21–22.
63. Ibid., p. 16.
64. Ibid., p. 213.
65. Ibid., p. 217.
66. Martha Minow and Mary Lyndon Shanley, 'Revisioning the Family: Relational Rights and Responsibilities', in Mary Lyndon Shanley and Uma Narayan, eds., *Reconstructing Political Theory: Feminist Perspectives,* Cambridge: Polity Press, 1997, pp. 102–103.
67. Margaret Urban Walker, *Moral Understandings: A Feminist Study in Ethics,* New York: Routledge, 1998, pp. 211–212.
68. Minow, *Making All the Difference,* p. 198, my italics.
69. Sandra Whitworth, 'Theory as Exclusion: Gender and International Political Economy', in Richard Stubbs and Geoffrey Underhill, eds., *Political Economy and the Changing Global Order,* London: Macmillan, 1994, p. 119.
70. Jan Jindy Pettman, *Worlding Women: A Feminist International Politics,* London: Routledge, 1996, p. 158.
71. Alison Jaggar, cited in J. Ann Tickner, 'On the Fringes of the World Economy: A Feminist Perspective', in Craig Murphy and Roger Tooze, eds., *The New International Political Economy,* Boulder, CO: Lynne Rienner, 1991, p. 194.
72. Tickner, 'On the Fringes', pp. 203–204.

73. Sandra Whitworth, 'Theory as Exclusion', in Stubbs and Underhill, *Political Economy and the Changing Global Order*, p. 121.

74. Ibid., p. 122.

75. This is not to suggest that all feminist theorists of GPE approach their analyses from the same perspective. Just as there are differences in feminist theories in general, feminist theorists of GPE may adopt standpoint, critical feminist, or postmodern perspectives in their work. However, in spite of the obvious differences between these perspectives, they are united in their critique of orthodox realist and liberal approaches, and it is thus possible to point to similarities among these feminist theorists.

76. Diana T. Meyers, *Subjection and Subjectivity: Psychoanalytic Feminism and Moral Philosophy*, London: Routledge, 1994, p. 3.

77. Minow, *Making All the Difference*, p. 229.

78. Ibid.

79. Ibid., p. 216.

80. Ibid., p. 111.

7

A Critical Ethics of Care in the Context of International Relations

As much as a fifth of the world's 5.5 billion people live in the type of extreme poverty that makes them vulnerable to undernourishment and thereby prey to debilitating or life-destroying diseases. . . . It is important to carefully scrutinize, from the moral point of view, not only what, if anything, is to be done, but also how and why it is to be done.

William Aiken and Hugh LaFollette, *World Hunger and Morality*, 1996 (pp. 1–2)

The area of morals, and ergo of moral philosophy, can now be seen, not as a hole-and-corner matter of debts and promises, but as covering the whole of our mode of living, and the quality of our relations with the world.

Iris Murdoch, *Existentialists and Mystics*, 1997 (p. 380)

This chapter addresses what are often referred to as ethical issues in international relations. This is usually taken to mean the areas of practice, specific or general, to which ethical considerations apply. The idea of ethical 'issues' in international relations, however, assumes or implies a number of things: first, that the issues themselves are in some measure discrete, distinct, and separate from one another; second, that because there are *ethical* issues, there must also be some *non*-ethical issues in international relations; and finally, that the issues themselves may be regarded as distinct from the moral values and ethical ideas embedded in them. But as Roger Spegele points out, the separation of theory and practice which leads us to detach ourselves from our experience gives us a false view of the so-called nontheoretical side of life: 'A view of theory which stresses the inappropriateness of a detached and impersonal response to the way things are points up the fact that the nontheoretical side of life is not just activity or an event but a form of life'.[1]

In an attempt to avoid both of these implications, this chapter refers not to 'issues' but to 'contexts'. The aim is to present a more holistic picture of the world of global social relations—a world which cannot neatly be divided into issues, and where issues cannot be separated from our knowledge and understanding of them. Thus, while this chapter reinforces claims made earlier in the book—that all aspects of international relations are, by definition, ethical—it seeks to demonstrate how our understanding of certain aspects of global social, political, and economic relations may take on a new meaning and significance when viewed from the perspective of a critical ethics of care.

The first section discusses the dominant views on the central 'issues' in international ethics, analyzing critically the ways in which these issues have been explored. Specifically, it focuses on the ways in which questions regarding the moral authority of state sovereignty and the problem of intervention have been privileged within international ethics. This has contributed to the inability of moral reasoning in the context of international relations both to be critical in its approach and to motivate significant moral and political change. Neither the chosen topics and issues in international ethics—which focus predominantly on state autonomy and the wider claims of the global community and intervention—nor the styles of moral reasoning used to address them challenge the assumptions of orthodox international relations theory. The state centrism and the dichotomous, binary ontology used to explore these issues support and reproduce dominant statist approaches in international relations, while the abstract, formalized, rational forms of ethics used to address these so-called moral questions fits comfortably with the dominant positivist epistemology of prevailing international relations theory. The issues are framed within the dichotomy between communitarian values—articulated as the particularist rights of states, and cosmopolitan goals—and the universal obligations of the 'international community' to humanity as such. Thus, debates over sovereignty and intervention, for example, emerge as a logical puzzle, a problem to be solved through the construction and application of principles. But as Spegele points out, this view that all moral dilemmas are resolvable 'without remainder' is a false one; it is only after we accept the unresolvability—the untidy 'remainders'—of moral problems in international relations that we might actually embark on a type of moral thinking which works towards the achievement of real moral and political change.[2] The final part of this section explores this dilemma of sovereignty and intervention, focusing specifically on the problem of 'humanitarian intervention' and offering some reflections on how we might usefully rethink not only the answers but the questions surrounding intervention in the global political context.

The second section returns to the problem of social exclusion discussed in chapter 6. Specifically, the focus is on the ever-widening gap between rich and poor, and the extent to which our experience—not only in the form of economic policies, political strategies, and development projects but also in terms of our whole mode of living, the nature and quality of our attachments, and our objects of attention—may be shaped and moulded in order that consideration of widespread human suffering becomes a more central part of our everyday lives. This is not to say, however, that the proper role and value of sovereignty and the place of intervention are not central conceptual questions in international relations; certainly, questions about the nature of identity and community in the contemporary global order are a vital part of what international ethics must explore. As argued in chapter 4, we must recognize the limitations of an approach to ethics which concentrates on the source of moral value and the moral dilemmas which relate to that question; instead, moral reasoning in the global context must try to make sense of how personal and cultural attachments and social relations can lead to exclusion and domination, but also how they may be shaped and reconstructed in order to promote solidarity, strength, and well-being.

State Autonomy, Sovereignty, and Intervention

It has been argued that the most central question that normative international relations theory can pose is that of the moral status of the claim to autonomy made by all sovereign states. Specific questions, then, include:

> Do states have a *right* to be left to their own devices? If so, is this an *absolute right,* or is it conditional on their acceptance of self-imposed limits? Do all states have the *same kinds of rights* irrespective of their domestic circumstances? If states cannot be said to have a *right to be left alone,* who has the *right to intervene* in their affairs? Other states? Or the world community?[3]

Chris Brown divides the potential answers to these questions into two camps: cosmopolitan answers, which reject the state's right to autonomy when this autonomy could involve the violation of universally applicable standards of behaviour; and communitarian answers, which accept only those constraints on states' behaviour which grow out of the community itself.[4] Within international theory, he argues, this issue is set up in terms of intervention and non-intervention, thus linking a moral issue with a legal issue. Thus, he points out, the paradox of international relations emerges: in spite of the norm of non-intervention, it is generally acknowledged that there are circumstances in which this norm can and should be breached. The question is, which circumstances?[5]

Similarly, in *Ethics in International Relations,* Mervyn Frost lists thirteen ethical issues in international relations which he describes as 'crucial' and 'pressing'. The fifth issue on his list is: 'When is intervention by one state in the domestic affairs of another state justified?' This follows only questions relating to the causes and conduct of war, including nuclear weapons and individual obligations to participate in the use of force; the other issues on the list, moreover, include terrorism, wars of national liberation, the use and distribution of resources, problems of global ecology, the extent and nature of international organizations, and 'familiar' questions surrounding human rights.[6] Furthermore, he argues that *'all normative issues* in world politics today refer, either directly or indirectly, *to the state, inter-state relations* and *the role of individuals as citizens* of states'.[7] Thus, both of these writers give priority to the problem of the moral value of state autonomy, and they do so within an ontological framework which focuses on the state as moral agent in the international system of states and reduces the person to her role as citizen.

Chapter 4 explored the cosmopolitan/communitarian debate in international relations theory, arguing that this debate has become the central framework for discussing questions in normative international relations theory. The links between this framework of universal versus particular and the general question of the role of the state and state sovereignty in global society are not coincidental; indeed, the questions that are accepted as central or important and the frameworks used to analyze them are both interdependent and mutually constituting. If we regard states as autonomous actors within a global community, and if we regard persons as citizens within states and human beings within that global community, we emerge with a specific ontology which is both atomistic and dichotomous. Persons are divided by their role as citizen and their role as individual human being; states are torn between their political autonomy and territorial integrity and their role in the global community. Identity, community, and relationships become reduced to an intractable dilemma, focusing on the question of the source of moral value, in which the nature of our attachments and our identities are constrained by the ontology of the global system.

With this framework and this binary, atomistic ontology as a starting point, it is not surprising that questions surrounding state autonomy, intervention, and human rights assume priority on lists of ethical issues in international relations. States have rights to autonomy and sovereignty as well as duties to their citizens. They also, however, have some limited duties to the international community. States are autonomous agents; while they may have relations with other states, these relations are understood in legalistic, functional, or utilitarian terms. Individuals, too, are morally significant, but only insofar as they are defined either by the state, as citizens, or by their humanity. Individuals, moreover, are the bearers of rights; it is by virtue of their humanity that individuals possess rights, but it is only insofar as they are citizens of sovereign states that they have these rights guaranteed.

It is around this relationship between individual rights and state sovereignty that Michael Walzer builds his argument in *Just and Unjust Wars.*[8] Walzer makes much of the 'domestic analogy', which is based on the idea that states have rights in much the same way that individuals have rights. 'Every reference to aggression as the international equivalent of armed robbery or murder', he argues, 'and every comparison of home or country or of personal liberty and political independence, relies on what is called the domestic analogy'.[9] Like liberal theories of individual rights, states' rights are established through consent. The contract here, then, is a metaphor for a process of association and mutuality, 'the ongoing character of which the state claims to protect against external encroachment'. In Walzer's communitarian view, the individual's right to life and liberty makes little sense outside of the shared life and liberty of individuals in an independent community which they have made; the moral standing of any particular state, he claims, depends upon the reality of the common life it protects.[10] Thus, Walzer's 'legalist paradigm' is derived from the state's fundamental right to political sovereignty and territorial integrity—rights which are derived, in turn, from individual rights to life and liberty. From this position, Walzer argues strongly in favour of the principle that states should never intervene in the domestic affairs of another state, although he concedes that the very foundations of this principle require that we sometimes disregard it. Thus, while the practice of intervening often defends the territorial integrity and political independence of invaded states, it can sometimes be justified.[11]

One case where intervention can sometimes be justified, according to Walzer, is the case of humanitarian intervention. He explains:

> If the dominant forces within a state are engaged in massive violations of human rights, the appeal to self-determination in the Millian sense of self-help is not very attractive. That appeal has to do with the freedom of the community taken as a whole; it has no force when what is at stake is the bare survival or the minimal liberty of (some substantial number of) its members. Against the enslavement or massacre of political opponents, national minorities and religious sects, there may well be no help unless help comes from outside.[12]

Thus, while Walzer recognizes the need for humanitarian intervention when it is a response (with reasonable expectations of success) to acts 'that shock the moral conscience of mankind', he remains sceptical about the motives and practices of intervening states. 'States don't send their soldiers into other states, it seems, only in order to save lives'.[13]

Walzer's book is a classic example of a work in international ethics which starts from a fixed ontology and focuses on the moral dilemma of states' rights and international obligations. It also focuses on the moral aspects of war and violent conflict and relies on a liberal-contractualist moral reasoning, making use of moral concepts such as rights and duties. Walzer's is a broadly statist or communitarian argument which attempts to reconcile the rights of states with the rights of individuals by demonstrating how the latter are ultimately derived from the former. This work is paradigmatic of a whole body of literature which explores issues connected with sovereignty, intervention, and the 'just war' from the perspective of this dichotomy between individual rights and states' rights or, put another way, national rights and *inter*national obligations.

It has been a central argument of this book that moral reasoning about international relations must move beyond this fixed ontology, the principled, justificatory ethics, and the limited view of morality which currently characterizes international ethics, and towards a critical, relational ethics which refocuses attention on the permanent background to decisions rather than simply on the moral criteria for making decisions and the nature of subsequent moral action. The next section illustrates this argument by exploring in more detail the problem of humanitarian intervention, and how it has been—and might continue to be—explored in the context of international ethics.

Humanitarian Intervention

The agent, thin as a needle, appears in the quick flash of the choosing will. . . . The agent's freedom, indeed his moral quality, resides in his choices, and yet we are not told what prepares him for the choices.

Iris Murdoch, *Existentialists and Mystics*, 1997 (p. 343)

In essence, the story told here of humanitarianism during war and its various manifestations throughout history represents the eternal human struggle between compassion, based on recognition of a common humanity, and self-interest.

Thomas G. Weiss and Cindy Collins, *Humanitarian Challenges and Intervention*, 1996 (p. 197)

It has been argued that questions regarding the moral basis of state autonomy, state sovereignty, and its place within the international system have been the central focus of ethical debates in international relations. From this starting point, it is not surprising that intervention—and specifically, humanitarian intervention—has often been regarded as the quintessential moral issue in international relations. Indeed, it has been suggested that the very phrase 'humanitarian intervention' sounds 'moral' insofar as it may be contrasted with 'hard-headed considerations of national interest'.[14] But this, of course, is a narrow interpretation of what counts as moral; moreover, to equate 'moral' with 'cosmopolitan' is to refuse to recognize that even realist arguments in favour of non-intervention put forward a coherent ethical position.

This point is made by Nick Lewer and Oliver Ramsbotham in their paper '"Something Must Be Done": Towards an Ethical Framework for Humanitarian Intervention in International Social Conflict'. They break down the idea of humanitarian intervention into its two parts in an attempt to arrive at a definition. In order to count as humanitarian, they argue, intervention must be an attempt, carried out in the name of the international community, to remedy a situation in which fundamental human rights are being denied. In defining 'intervention', the authors rely on a broad definition of social intervention: 'any act . . . that alters the characteristics of another individual or the pattern of relationships between individuals'. Lewer and Ramsbotham qualify this definition with the caveat that their particular concern is only with intervention across state borders.[15]

The authors' central purpose in this paper is to set out an 'agreed ethic of humanitarian intervention to guide deliberation about what to do'.[16] They examine the debate over humanitarian intervention in international ethics, focusing on four positions: realism, utilitarianism, Kantian deontology, and natural law.[17] In summing up the debate, Lewer and Ramsbotham deliver this rather disappointing conclusion:

> [W]e may lump together all those who favour humanitarian intervention . . . whether we call them 'universalists', 'cosmopolitans', or 'solidarists', insofar as they acknowledge (a) universal rights and (b) concomitant universal obligations which both define an international or global community and determine how it ought to act. In contrast, arguments against humanitarian intervention tend to be of three kinds . . . realist . . . statist . . . relativist. Needless to say, many careful thinkers find themselves torn between the alternatives as they try to find a principled response to the challenges of international order and 'man's inhumanity to man'.[18]

In spite of their claim to take a broad view of what counts as a moral argument and to eschew the separation of politics and morality, the authors provide a framework for their debate which corresponds to the accepted ontology of orthodox international relations theory and the traditional modes of moral reasoning which focus on rights, obligations, and as they put it, 'choice, action and justification'.[19] Their own contribution to the debate on the ethics of humanitarian intervention takes the form of a set of *framework principles* which are, in fact, defining principles. In other words, the authors are suggesting that 'if there is such a thing as humanitarian intervention, then it is defined by framework principles of the sort set out here'. They argue that 'all those claiming to intervene . . .

on humanitarian grounds . . . must make their decisions in the light of this ethical framework. If they do not, they should not call their interventions "humanitarian"'.[20] The end result of their work is the formulation of ten ethical principles which are to act as a code to guide consistent and principled decision-making in this 'fraught area'.[21]

What appears, on the surface, to be a comprehensive analysis of the ethical 'dimensions' in humanitarian intervention is, however, partial and incomplete. The guiding principles and emergent analysis in this paper emanate from a specific set of assumptions about the nature of ethics and, specifically, of ethics in international relations. A very different picture would emerge, however, if we began from the perspective of a critical ethics of care in our moral consideration of humanitarian intervention.

First, we would question the validity of starting from the position that the morality of humanitarian intervention resides in 'choice, action and justification'—that is, in the moment of decision-making and hence in the criteria used to make a moral judgement and the principles applied to guide 'conduct' or 'action' once the decision has been taken. By contrast, a critical ethics of care refuses to reduce ethics to a moment of judgement but instead focuses our attention on the permanent background to those decisions which must be taken in times of crisis. From this perspective, ethics in international relations is concerned not only with specific issues, dilemmas, or conflicts but with the nature and quality of existing social relations. The focus is not simply on the moment when, for example, ethnic relations break down to a point where 'barbarous acts' finally 'outrage the conscience of mankind'.[22] Rather, it would interrogate the nature of 'normal' social relations in an attempt to understand the processes of exclusion and marginalization which themselves create the need for humanitarian intervention. These would include both relations within and between vulnerable communities, and between such communities and the powerful states and organizations of the North and West—the ostensive guardians of human rights and the leaders of the international community.

Second, from the perspective of a critical ethics of care, we would need to rethink both the moral concepts and the types of moral reasoning which are seen as relevant to humanitarian intervention. As Lewer and Ramsbotham's paper illustrates, it is most common to think in terms of principles that are universal and general and may be applied to any situation classifiable as humanitarian intervention. Within these principles, moreover, there is a focus on rights and duties: 'Where there is unacceptable denial or violation of human *rights*, actual or threatened, the international community has a *duty* to attempt redress and a prima facie *right* to intervene'.[23] There is an assumption, furthermore, that it is possible to arrive at principles that are universal—that is, 'endorsed by the international community'—and that the aim of 'impartial promotion of sustained human flourishing' is both possible and desirable. But if we are focusing not only on judgement and action but on our capacity to learn how to focus our sustained moral attention on others, on how to build strong attachments which encourage agents to be attentive and responsive and to recognize shared responsibilities, and on how to become more aware of the extent to which relationships can themselves act as a guide to the processes of naming 'difference' and thus of exclusion and marginalization, the goals of impartiality and universality recede into the background, and the idea of ethics as a set of principles outlining rights and duties seems not to take into account a whole range of moral concepts. This is not to concede to moral relativism, but simply to recognize that rules and principles which demand abstraction from real situations obscure the fact that we can only begin to make sense of morality and moral relations if we start with our contextual, situated experience.

Finally, it is important that we should question, and refuse to take as given, the ontology which reduces social attachments to the reciprocal relations of autonomous states in an anarchical system. This ontology reduces moral relations to the dichotomy between non-intervention—characterized by a commitment to state autonomy and sovereignty—and intervention, done in the name of individual human rights and the good of humanity as such. Morality becomes, as traditional Western ethics teaches us—and as articulated in the epigraph at the beginning of this section—'the eternal human struggle between compassion, based on recognition of a common humanity, and self-interest'. From the perspective of a critical ethics of care, however, this picture of morality as an 'eternal struggle' no longer seems relevant. If moral responses and the ability to act well emerge out of our personal and social attachments with others, then moral feeling and action are no longer separate from, but in fact part of, that which matters to moral agents.

Clearly, we cannot, nor should we, ignore the moral dilemmas and problems which arise out of the states system, including the difficulty of reconciling political sovereignty and the rule of non-intervention with the recognition that intervention may sometimes be justified. What should perhaps be questioned, however, is the extent to which what is seen as important or central to international ethics is predetermined by both a limited moral ontology—where states and citizens stand in opposition to the global community of humankind—and a particular style of moral reasoning that relies primarily on the moral concepts of rights and duties. Certainly, it is important that international relations theorists explore the moral basis of the apparently practical questions of sovereignty, intervention, and conflict. It is clear, moreover, that tensions do exist between the duties of states to their citizens and their responsibilities to act on the claims of those outside their own borders, as well as between our feelings of community and identity with our fellow citizens and our recognition of our own humanity.

However, this tidy dichotomy cannot even begin to capture the complexities of such notions as identity and community, nor does it adequately address the extent to which morality is present not just in the decisions of states at times of crisis ('Should we or should we not intervene?') but in the continuous background to these decisions. Thus, the moral question attached to the issue of 'complex emergencies', for example, becomes one of what duties or obligations states have to intervene to prevent human rights abuses and suffering. As Jenny Edkins argues, much of the literature on food aid and famine takes this approach, as do debates on humanitarianism more generally.[24] But moral consideration need not end with the question 'Should we intervene?'; instead, moral attention needs to be paid to developing an understanding of the moral relations which exist, and the moral decisions that are constantly being taken, both before and after the question of humanitarian intervention actually arises; this, in turn, demands a critical analysis of the social relations which exist within societies, and between societies in the global context.

From the perspective of a critical ethics of care, one of the central issues in international ethics—humanitarian intervention—may be understood not just as an ultimately intractable dichotomy between humanity and self-interest, between the global community and the state, or indeed, between ethics and politics. The 'states/citizens versus humanity' ontology which underwrites this moral dilemma leads to an unrealistic picture both of the nature of attachments and communities and of the nature and breadth of our moral experience. The moral content of this experience is reduced to the moment of moral judgement when faced with the question: 'Should the international community intervene in this humanitarian emergency?' Humanitarian intervention may present itself as the quintessential ethical issue in international relations; however, morality is embedded in the permanent background to that intervention, and in the nature and quality of the social relations which exist within and between communities. It is on this background, finally, that we must focus our moral attention.

Foregrounding Poverty and Exclusion

This section explores the continuous, ever-widening gap between rich and poor, particularly in the context of North-South relations, and the processes of exclusion and breakdown of social relations which lead to human suffering and, particularly, to poverty. Normative international relations theory has systematically obscured the extent to which the everyday processes, practices, and social relations in international relations often lead to devastating levels of human suffering. Many theorists would argue, of course, that suffering is their motivation for thinking about moral issues in international relations; 'just war' theorists, for example, would argue that setting out principles governing the conduct of war is aimed primarily at mitigating human suffering; human rights theorists, moreover, would claim that their approach is aimed directly at individual human suffering by relying on a conception of that to which all human beings are morally entitled, simply by virtue of their humanity. While this may indeed be the case, serious ethical consideration of human suffering must not be limited to trying to answer the question: 'Should any action be taken to relieve this suffering, and if so, what reason can we give to justify the taking of that action?' Answering this question marks the beginning, not the end, of ethical reflection.

To argue that we should focus our attention on world poverty is not to suggest that it has hitherto been ignored by normative theorists in international relations. Indeed, Chris Brown cites authors such as Rawls, Beitz, Barry, Singer, and O'Neill as those who, in the two decades since the problem of rich-poor relations came to be defined as such, have made 'quite impressive' philosophical progress. Yet, it is interesting to note that Brown also concedes that 'two decades of genuine philosophical progress have also been two decades of substantive political failure'.[25] This remarkable statement clearly illustrates the widely accepted separation between moral philosophy, on the one hand, and politics and international relations on the other. Virtually all of this progress has been in the form of debate on the question of 'international distributive justice'—a debate which, once more, relies on the cosmopolitan/communitarian framework, uses the language of rights and obligations, and attempts to formulate rules or principles of right action which may be universally applied. By and large, this debate has concentrated on the question of whether theories of justice for the domestic realm can be adapted to fit the international context, and on the related question of the scope of our obligations to redistribute wealth. In the context of these debates there is, interestingly, very little mention of poverty on a global scale—a subject which has only recently become the object of serious attention in international relations.[26]

In spite of the marginalization of questions of poverty in international relations, there has been significant analysis by philosophers of the ethics of world poverty.[27] The next section briefly examines the dominant approaches to poverty on a global scale—the rights-based approach and the Kantian, obligations-centred approach. It argues that neither of these approaches can take us any closer to mitigating the actual suffering of real people caused by continuing poverty. Poverty in the South is ongoing and part of the everyday lives of those whom it affects. What ethics must do is begin to make this poverty a part of the everyday lives of those who are, at present, unaware of the way they may be affected by it.

Leading Ethical Approaches to Poverty and Development

Rights-Based Approaches to Poverty

As argued in chapter 4, analysis of the ethical dimension of international relations is dominated overwhelmingly by the liberal-contractualist language of rights. Interestingly, rights-based ethics is preeminent not only in the academic research of philosophers and theorists of politics, international relations, and development studies but also in the 'practical' circles of policy-makers and analysts. As I have argued elsewhere, the remarkable influence of rights language in international politics today can be attributed to a number of factors.[28] In spite of the fact that today rights language is accessible and virtually universal, it emerged from and must be located within a particular tradition of political and economic organization that has seen a remarkable rise in the late twentieth century and is increasingly used as a standard for international legitimacy. This tradition—liberalism—emphasizes the primacy of the individual, specifically the individual's capacity to make rational decisions. Rights-based ethics exalts the moral value of individual autonomy; rights exist to protect the self from the undue interference of others and the state. Human rights are, moreover, a great leveller—to be recognized as human is to be recognized as equal to other human beings. To have human rights is, apparently, to have the dignity and the formal equality to which all human beings are entitled.

While we most readily associate human rights with those civil and political freedoms first articulated by the early liberals—freedom of speech, thought, conscience, and movement—contemporary advocates of rights are quick to point out that human rights have evolved considerably since the eighteenth and nineteenth centuries. Today there are two international covenants on rights—one on civil and political rights, and one on economic, social, and cultural rights. The latter covenant details the so-called welfare rights—to food, health care, education, and so on. Most advocates of rights today argue that these rights are as important, if not more important, than those which aim to secure people's legal and political freedom. Indeed, much contemporary analysis of rights regards these two sets of rights as indivisible and nonhierarchical. Thus, positive welfare rights are treated as the same in kind as negative political rights.

A right is an entitlement; to have a right is to be accorded the necessary freedom to pursue some chosen end. Thus, rights are not ends in themselves; they institutionalize and legalize restrictions on the ability of the state to obstruct our ability to pursue the ends that we choose for ourselves. Rights in the liberal-democratic tradition ensure not only negative liberty and formal equality but also pluralism, embodied in the idea of the separation of the right—which is universal and primary—from the good.

> The idea of the good remains indefinable and empty so that human choice may fill it. The sovereign moral concept is freedom, or possibly courage in a sense which identifies with freedom, will, power. This concept inhabits a quite separate top level of human activity since it is the guarantor of the secondary values created by choice.[29]

Interestingly, article 11 of the International Covenant of Economic, Social, and Cultural Rights refers not only to a right to 'adequate food' but also to a 'right of everyone to be free from hunger.' This second right not only places the emphasis on the agency of the individual rights-holder but describes the value of being properly nourished in terms of a negative freedom, rather than a positive good. If we wish, however, to articulate a moral claim regarding the evil of poverty, or hunger, is it really useful to describe that claim in terms of the right to be free from something? Certainly, poverty is a condition from which we all want to be 'free', but is it not perverse to focus on *freedom from* poverty? Even when we try to express the unacceptability of poverty as a right *to* something, the idea of right seems not to capture the scale of the activities and the experience—not only the political and economic decisions but the transformations of people's entire modes of life and connections with one another and with the world—that would be required in order to bring groups of people from a state of impoverishment to a state in which they could live healthy lives.

This is not to say that the moral language of rights is not useful. Today rights language is almost universally accessible; it acts as a rallying cry for social change by providing a vocabulary through which to articulate the values of empowerment and self-esteem. But we must be aware of the limits of rights language, and the extent to which this language is inseparable from the individualist ontology and freedom-based morality of liberal political and economic theory. A rights-based ethics is a contractualist ethics which either takes for granted, or proceeds as if, all parties were equal. It is based on the assumption that if moral subjects are given the right—the freedom—to live their 'own lives', they will be able to seek, claim, and enjoy the 'good life'. But not all goods of moral significance can be *claimed* by those who need or value them; not all those things we need or value make sense in the context of a contractual ethics of rights and correlative obligations. Again, this is not to say that what we clumsily call positive rights are not important; indeed, it is because they are so important that we must find a way of articulating the moral significance of human well-being that actually works towards its achievement.

It is perhaps telling that ultimately advocates of rights often abandon rights language in their attempts to defend it. For example, James Nickel argues that the right to food is not meaningful if it doesn't yield guidance as to who has the responsibility for ensuring that adequate food is available. He also admits that 'people are often perplexed by the right to adequate food because they are not sure what it means for them. Does it mean that they have an obligation to feed some particular hungry person, or to feed some fair share of the world's hungry?' Thus, when the need for moral action is considered, we seem to find it necessary to make sense of the *obligations* which may correspond to rights, rather than considering the rights themselves.[30] Similarly, Henry Shue argues that seriousness about rights leads to seriousness about duties, and that, moreover, seriousness about duties opens up the underlying social character of rights. Ignoring the positive duties correlative to a right, he argues, is like saying: 'We believe people have a "right not to be flooded", but we don't want to talk about dams, which are expensive economic projects'. What would a 'right not to be flooded' mean if nothing were done to block the flow of water?[31] Both writers seem to be suggesting that rights become meaningful only when we turn our attention to the nature of the duties or responsibilities which are necessary to ensure that rights are fulfilled. Moreover, as Shue suggests, we then realize that such duties and responsibilities must, inevitably, reflect social relations—attachments and communities, rather than individuals. It is only when we begin from social relations, recognizing them as both a moral and an ontological starting point, that we can think usefully about appropriate moral responses to world poverty. Before elucidating this argument, however, the next section explores the Kantian, obligations-centred approach in an attempt to uncover whether a focus on duties, rather than rights, can overcome the apparent limitations of rights-based ethics.

Duties and Obligations

At first glance, a Kantian approach to the moral question of poverty on a global scale appears to respond to the shortcomings of the rights-based approach. Because it is a theory of obligations rather than of human rights, it relies not on those who are impoverished but on those who, being free from want or hardship, are relatively powerful to act. Interestingly, however, despite the fact that Kantian philosophers are at pains to point out the differences between rights-based and duty-based ethics, it is worth remembering that both are examples of deontological, universal-prescriptive moral theories. Of course, it is important to explore the specific nature of Kantian ethics and avoid what has been described as its frequent and misleading assimilation to theories of human rights.[32] But as argued later in this chapter, the shortcomings of this approach result not from the way it diverges from rights theory but rather from the fact that it does not move far enough from the universalism and the abstraction found in rights-based ethics.

In its barest form, Kant's account of ethics requires moral agents to act only on principles that can be acted on by all. Justice, then, demands that we neither adopt nor condone institutions or policies which cannot be acted on by all. This is not to say, as Onora O'Neill points out, that justice demands that we have institutions and policies that receive either actual consent from all affected or the hypothetical consent of beings with enhanced, idealized rationality or knowledge. It is simply to claim that, for example, because principles which are committed to the injury of others will always represent a commitment that is possible for perpetrators but not for victims, they cannot be enacted by all and so are unjust. Thus, because poverty is clearly an enormous source of vulnerability and dependence of many sorts, it is unjust to leave in place the institutional structures which produce and perpetuate poverty.[33]

As proponents are quick to admit, Kant's strategy is rather minimal; it represents a certain attitude to *justification*—what types of principles can we demonstrate to be just. It represents a test for principles rather than a method for generating them, or a plan of action for implementing them. Moreover, it is an essentially negative strategy: it does not seek to show what constitutes a flourishing life or which lives are the most flourishing; it simply seeks to establish constraints that must be observed for any life to flourish. Kantian ethics is concerned, then, with the outline or limits rather than the target.[34] It is also very much concerned with justice and, hence, with the problem of *competing* claims—the fact that people want to act in different ways and simply want to be different. It does not, however, like some liberal theories of justice, confine justice to the availability of sufficient freedom to pursue subjective goods or preferences. Such accounts may give us a reasonable argument about motivation, but as O'Neill argues, they have some difficulty in providing a convincing account of justice.[35] Kant's formula, by contrast, is about laying down a minimal condition for achieving mutual consistency in the actions of a plurality of rational beings.[36] Thus, it does not just define or characterize the good human life, nor does it simply list those entitlements which may be claimed against others.

Certainly, a Kantian approach overcomes the problem of indeterminate agency found in rights-based ethics. However, it still does not offer us a satisfactory ethical approach to the problem of world poverty. As suggested earlier, in Kantian deontological ethics, claims about morality and justice neither reflect nor are generated by people's actual behaviour. It is this characteristic of the theory which has been at once its strength and its weakness. It has been a strength because it provides an answer to those critics who ask, 'Why tell us that justice demands that no one act with cruelty or deception when it is evident that people do, and that they will continue to do so?' The Kantian response is that the purpose of moral theory is to offer a moral justification for action, to tell us what the demands of morality are; this is more rather than less important, Kantians argue, as people continue to act in ways which transgress those demands. To the critics, however, these arguments are unconvincing. In spite of the claim that Kant's ethics is primarily concerned with establishing a strategy to ensure that the application of reason leads to the adoption of universal moral principles, critics insist that the powerful have no need and probably no desire to act according to the categorical imperative; thus, a strategy which is built around the notion of universalizability ends up faltering on the question of motivation.

This problem of motivation is linked to the Kantian theory of judgement and the reliance on rules-based forms of ethics. As Roger Spegele argues, Kant's account of judgement proceeds from the dubious assumption that the rules defining any concept suffice by themselves to determine whether something falls under that concept. But, he asks, is it always true that judgement has no other task than simply to see that such rules suffice to identify the things on which the concept may be predicated?[37] Indeed, even if all moral responses could be governed by rules (which is certainly doubtful), there is clearly a significant gap between the knowledge of rules and the ability of moral agents to determine, in real contexts, what moral action should be taken.

It could be argued, then, that Kant's ethics leaves unanswered large questions about motivation and how acts of pure will can necessarily bring about real social change. These are not the only weaknesses of Kant's ethics—one might also question the overwhelming focus on the concept of *obligation,* or the feasibility of constructing universal principles of justice which are both free from cultural and moral imperialism and not so abstract and minimal that they become meaningless. But these shortcomings are not of central importance here. What is of importance is the validity of a system of ethics which is concerned only with whether people *should* act morally, not with whether they *will.* Also under consideration is the view that we, as moral theorists, can be responsible only for providing justifications of moral action—that is answering the question 'Is this act morally justified?' rather than the questions 'What will motivate people to act morally?' and 'What form should our moral responses take?' or quite simply, 'How can we help?' An approach to ethics which is concerned only with the construction of an elegant and rigorous theoretical test for whether principles 'count' as 'moral' may deserve our intellectual respect, but it does not help us to get any closer to the deeply social and political problems surrounding the human suffering and deprivation brought on by world poverty.

The Permanent Background to Moral Action

If we are to reject approaches to poverty which focus exclusively on rights and obligations, then we must ask what it would mean, by contrast, to adopt a critical ethic of care in the context of world poverty. First, perhaps, we should ask what it would not mean. It would not mean that 'caring' would take the form of the wealthy and the powerful 'caring about' the weak and impoverished in a manner which is both paternalistic and dangerously close to robbing those moral 'subjects' of their own agency and self-esteem. This is a potential danger of an ethics of care which must be addressed. While care ethics, in a global context, *may* involve the creation of new social and even personal relations between groups and individuals from very different socioeconomic levels and territorial locations, and such new relations might, in turn, motivate moral attention and caring, it would also require that the powerful—states, NGOs (non-governmental organizations)—adopt strategies which pay attention to the relationships and attachments, both within existing communities and between members of organizations in the North and peoples in the South, and explore how those relations might perpetuate, or lead to solutions concerning, levels of poverty and well-being. This would be seen as an intensely moral task, but also one which is not separate from the goal of political and socioeconomic change to mitigate poverty, but indeed embodies that goal.

Furthermore, a relational approach to world poverty based on caring would not be one which argues that the appropriate moral response is one of individual-to-individual care, such as might be achieved through sponsoring a child in a developing country. Such an approach is not only limited, because it focuses attention on only a few rather than on the many who are suffering, but misguided, in that it either ignores or misunderstands the wider, structural causes of poverty. Indeed, it could even be argued that such an approach is potentially dangerous, because it is a paternalistic strategy based on the idea of charity, which encourages the reproduction of patterns of inequality and relations of dependence. While the approach suggested here does not advocate this one-to-one strategy, it does argue that the evident success of such an approach may teach us an effective lesson about the nature of moral motivation and responsiveness. Sponsoring a child is a meaningful moral response insofar as it is directed towards a concrete rather than a generalized other; the child, through photographs and letters, is 'known' by the moral agent as a real human being with a name, a face, and a history. Tied to this, of course, is the fact that the very act of 'sponsorship' creates a relationship, one which is akin to parenting and motivates moral responsiveness and feelings of care.

The approach advocated here does not mock or belittle such feelings and relationships, and it does not brand them as 'personal' and therefore beyond the scope of morality. But should we seek to translate these moral impulses into political action? As argued earlier, moral and political action aimed at reducing global poverty cannot be confined to one-to-one, personal relationships; such an approach would be neither realistic nor effective. What is required instead is a restructuring of political action in such a way that enduring relationships can flourish and agents can focus their moral attention and, ultimately, act with the virtues of care—attentiveness, responsiveness, and responsibility. If, then, the methods and activities of organizations involved in development and the eradication of poverty are structured in such a way that the growth of sustained, long-term connections between members from both the North and the South is encouraged—rather than ignored or actively discouraged—the development of genuine moral concern would be more likely to emerge.

Thus, instead of seeking to find wealthy and powerful parent-figures to provide material support and 'care about' impoverished children, attention must be paid to the ways in which parents themselves may be empowered to care adequately for their own children. But a strategy of empowerment need not rely on an ethos of individualism; achieving empowerment must involve not just a declaration of individual rights, or an articulation of 'our' moral obligations, but the creation of projects which help to promote healthy, strengthening social and personal ties within communities, and which are run on the basis of mutual attention and mutual learning between actors.

Jenny Edkins has discussed the implications of such an approach in the context of famine. She argues that, in our understanding of famine, we should move towards an approach based on an analysis of the relationships between people. This implies a movement from the abstract, logical, analytical approach implied by the question 'Should we intervene to stop exploitation and domination?' to the more practical, specific question 'How can we best act to promote good relations?' This approach suggests a different way of looking at, and responding to, famine:

> Famines can be seen . . . as processes where relationships between people have produced unacceptable results and transgressed limits of inhumanity.

> The web of relationships is more complex and extensive than the simple separations into 'winners' and 'losers', developed and underdeveloped, rich and poor can account for. Living with the inevitable antagonism—undecidability—at the heart of the social relations is arguably what we must learn to do.[38]

This is not an approach which seeks to valorize or romanticize existing and potential social relations. Rather, it is one which 'recognizes the potential for violent domination and inequalities in all social relationships'.[39] As argued in chapter 6, an ethics of care in the context of international relations—and specifically, in the context of world poverty—must be a critical approach which seeks to demonstrate that overcoming difference and exclusion demands sustained and continuous attention to the nature and functioning of social relations. Such an ethics can be useful in demonstrating that the existence of 'difference' which leads to processes of exclusion is neither natural nor objective, but that the act of naming difference can be understood only in the context of a relationship. Viewed in this way, no individual or group can be seen as objectively different and therefore deserving of social exclusion. Thus, while a critical-relational ethics of care places moral value on the sustained, continuous attention which characterizes stable, caring relations, it also seeks to situate social and personal relations in their wider sociopolitical and structural context of potentially exploitative social relations. From this perspective, poverty in the South would be regarded, in part, as a breakdown of global social relations: inequalities in power and influence have resulted in the legitimation of existing patterns of exclusion and domination. Patterns of local relations—familial attachments, gender relations, social hierarchies, and so on—would be explored in order to uncover the extent to which they may also perpetuate the impoverishment of certain groups within societies. An approach to ethics which values caring must examine these relations in an effort to create, or restore, a situation in which relations are characterized by mutual and self-respect. Certainly, in the case of global poverty the route to the creation of such relations is at least partially located in the structures of the global political economy, the workings of which may be reinterpreted from a critical-relational perspective, forcing us to rethink the apparently objective processes of capitalism.

Finally, it must be made clear that this approach to ethics is concerned not only with relationships but with the persons themselves whose lives are caught up in these intricate social and personal webs. An ethics of care takes seriously the identity and particularity of moral agents and subjects; it focuses not on the abstract other—the individual human being, who is thought to have a presocial identity—but on the concrete other, whose quality of life can be understood only through some basic knowledge of that person's particularity. This is not to suggest that we must gain an intimate understanding of the details of every person's life before we can begin to respond morally to their suffering; it does mean, however, that we should see it as a priority to gain as much knowledge as possible of the context of particular cases of poverty and suffering in order to respond to them usefully and effectively.

Commitment to relationships and sensitivity to the particularity of persons is also an important aspect of moral motivation which, in an ethics of care, is a crucial part of thinking about morality and moral responses. Dominant rights or duty-based approaches to ethics often tell us very little about motivation, concentrating instead on principles of justice or right action. To the extent that they do address motivation, they focus on the idea of 'shared humanity'. Certainly, this may elicit a rational response, in that we recognize the shared traits of humanity and therefore bestow some special status on all those exhibiting those traits; we may even respond emotionally to the rhetoric that 'no human being should have to suffer in such a way, or be subjected to such treatment'. These, of course, are all valid responses. As Hugh LaFollette and Larry May argue, moral obligations to 'humanity as such' are viewed by most people as separate from, and indeed competing with, the priorities of their everyday lives.

> [M]oral obligations which require us to abandon what is important to us, especially in the absence of some connection with those in need, will rarely be met by many people—and thus, will make no moral difference. Some might argue, on more abstract philosophical grounds, that we should not need that link. Perhaps that is true. But, whether we should need to feel this connection, the fact is, most people do need it. Thus, we want to know what will *actually* motivate people to act.[40]

An approach to ethics based on the idea of care is committed to the idea that we can, and must, learn to care. To illustrate how this may be possible, Iris Murdoch uses the example of love, and the attention it consumes. 'Deliberately falling out of love is not a jump of the will', she argues, 'it is the acquiring of new objects of attention and thus new energies as a result of refocusing'. 'Human beings are naturally "attached" and when an attachment seems painful or bad it is most readily displaced by another attachment, which an attempt at attention can encourage'.[41] We need not be physically close to our objects of attachments, nor need we accept the way that social and political structures have determined to whom and what we are 'naturally' attached. A critical ethics of care questions both the nature and quality of apparently natural attachments and encourages the focusing of moral energy on the creation of new and healthy attachments to address moral and social problems.

From the perspective of an ethics of care, it is our personal and social relations—our feelings of connection and responsibility—which motivate us to focus our attention and respond morally to the suffering of others. Thus, the ability to care with commitment about another can emerge only through sustained connections among persons and groups of persons. Of course, there are many people in the wealthy countries of the North for whom no such connections with impoverished communities in the South exist; this is why, at the outset, the focus must be on those members of organizations already involved in project work or the making of policy concerning poverty and development. Building long-term relationships must be made an explicit strategy of NGOs, transnational social movements, and governments. The current use of functional, issue-specific, superficial relationships, designed to maintain distance, impartiality, and reciprocity, must give way to a strategy focused on long-term relationships characterized by mutual learning and a sense of attachment rather than disconnection. Thus, while the question of moral motivation is indeed prior to the question of moral action, it need not be prior to the making of connections. After all, it is the business of development agencies to intervene in, and thus to create relationships with, the lives of those who are dogged by poverty. This chapter argues that the nature of those relationships is crucial to the type of moral responses that will emerge from them; relationships must allow participants in these projects to connect, in a sustained and enduring way, with the real circumstances of others' lives. As transnational social movements, and global civil society in general, continue to expand in both size and importance, more and more people may find themselves involved in such relationships, and the distance, both physical and moral, which exists between North and South may begin to shrink. That which remains distant to moral agents will never assume moral priority, in spite of what Kantian ethics and theories of justice as impartiality may tell us. Making the suffering of impoverished persons important to those who are in a position to do something about it relies on building enduring connections into their policies and strategies.

New Ethical Strategies for Eradicating Poverty

Certainly, given the embeddedness of the moral language of rights and duties, it is difficult to imagine how, and in what contexts, the language and strategies of a critical ethics of care would be put into practice. Indeed, as has already been argued, this moral language does not exist independently; rather, it is inextricably linked to the political philosophy of liberalism—a philosophy which currently dominates our thinking about the global political economy, international legitimacy, and development. Thus, as I have suggested, the moral discourse of rights and duties—emphasizing individual freedom and autonomy, formal equality and reciprocity—is unlikely to disturb the asymmetries in power and levels of well-being which currently characterize the global order. The separation of the right and the good in neo-Kantian liberal philosophy maintains the sovereignty of the concept of individual autonomy—associated with negative liberty and the notion of the pure moral will—which, in turn, leads to an exalting of the moral notions of individual rights and rational duties.

Such a contractualist ethics of rights and duties lies at the base of the apparently progressive discourse of 'partnership' which currently characterizes the strategies of many non-governmental organizations in the field of international development. In an effort to correct earlier practices which were guided by a paternalistic, universalizing ethos and a missionary-like approach to development, many Canadian development NGOs have, more recently, been searching for ways to construct relationships between First and Third World peoples which are based on equality and reciprocity. As a result of this effort, the idea of 'partnership' has emerged as a hegemonic discourse in Canadian policy towards the Third World. The term implies the construction of a new, egalitarian relationship between actors from both North and South, as opposed to the paternalism and hierarchy of the past.[42] As early as 1969, the report of the World Bank Commission on International Development, *Partners in Development*, used the language of liberal contractualist ethics explicitly: 'This calls for a new partnership based on an informal understanding expressing the reciprocal rights and obligations of donors and recipients'. In 1987 the Canadian government strategy for official development assistance, *Sharing Our Future*, also used the language of partnership. 'Fostering partnership' was the rhetoric used to 'help Canadians build a more equal partnership for progress with the people of the developing countries'; the aim was to 'bring development thinking in Canada out of the shadow of old donor-recipient attitudes and into the new era of global interdependence'.[43]

As Laura Macdonald argues, however, the language of interdependence and partnership conceals the real power relations at work in development policy. She quotes Brian Murphy of the Canadian NGO Inter-Pares:

> Partnership is a dichotomy, and implies an objectification of relationships. . . . Partnership implies a division: a division of labour, of reward, of responsibility, of authority, of ownership. Partnership is a limited, negotiated relationship for mutually supportive, but separate action towards limited but (at least on the surface) mutually consistent goals. Partnership does not

challenge existing relations or disparities, for example, or power, resources or affluence. Partnership, based within disparity, can only work to maintain and increase the existing disparity and fundamental inequality between and among partners.[44]

As this critique implies, certain members of the NGO community have begun to recognize the inherent limitations in the discourse of partnership, and in the ethics of formal equality which underwrites it. Thus, Murphy suggests that those actors from the North and the South who are involved in development projects and processes should not be seen as partners but as colleagues and protagonists in a common political project. In line with this alternative ethos, new practices are being suggested, such as asking groups from the South to carry out evaluations of the programs of NGOs in the North, thus reversing the normal pattern. But perhaps most important, there is a growing recognition among members of the NGO community of the need to dismantle the prevailing ideology, 'its language, its syntax, its questions and its answers, and the possibilities it predicts, and prevents'.[45]

It is in this spirit that a new model for North-South relations has emerged among some northern NGOs. This model refers not to 'partnership' but to 'partnering' and ties this to the idea of 'accompanying' or 'accompaniment'. This model is based on respect for control by the local partner and an attempt to provide nonmonetary forms of support for the struggles of local groups and a deeper form of commitment to the processes of social change in the Third World.[46] Specifically, accompanying is described as a 'process of moving along side by side in dialogue and experimentation which creates organisational improvement and yields knowledge about change'. The principles and practices of this approach include 'a commitment to learning as an attitude and ethic' and 'seeing totalities and people at all levels, not just bits and pieces of each other'.[47] The accompaniment approach often includes development education and political advocacy work within the NGOs' home countries, both to support Third World struggles and to promote social change within the North.[48] As Macdonald points out,

> This type of work attempts to break down stereotypical images of the South, and to identify shared interests between individuals in both South and North. While this is certainly not the dominant pattern among NGO programs, it is a necessary model for constructing counter-hegemonic global identities.[49]

This kind of approach is also visible in the recommendations of the Swedish Ministry of Foreign Affairs document *Partnership with Africa:*

Proposals for a New Swedish Policy Towards Sub-Saharan Africa.[50] Although titled *Partnership with Africa,* the recommendations eschew the traditional view of partnership as limited, reciprocal interaction based on mutual gain in the context of a particular issue or project. Particularly notable in this document is the commitment to 'strengthen long-term contacts between Sweden and African nations and societies'; an awareness that real social and political progress requires attention to constructions of 'difference' and 'otherness' in the context of relations; and finally, a recognition that Sweden's relations with Africa should not be understood as seeking to yield 'merely humanitarian results at a distance' but as playing a part in 'moulding our own reality through global dependence'.[51] It advocates adopting long-term and enduring perspectives on relations with Africa, and strengthening mechanisms that institutionalizing the practice of 'listening' as an important element in Sweden's Africa policy.[52] Moreover, there is a commitment to acknowledging the existing inequality in the relationship between Sweden and Africa: the economically stronger party, it is proposed, while being open about its imposition of condition, must also assume particular responsibility for the nature of its own role.[53] The links between this strategy and a critical ethics of care are evident:

> Co-operation that forges alliances can take place in trade and other economic activity or in research, sport, the arts, municipal activity, etc. Friendship societies and the like can be an important resource in alliance-forging work. The purpose, time perspective and resource inputs must be broader than for an individual export deal or aid-financed project. . . . The parties cannot be expected to bind themselves in the long term without practical experience of the co-operation concerned.[54]

Certain grassroots strategies which target women also illustrate the potential significance of approaching development from the perspective of a critical ethics of care. What is important about these alternative, grassroots views is that they are 'based on close, face-to-face interaction between organizations and their constituencies so that ideas and policies are shaped in the crucible of everyday practice rather than in the upper echelons of remote and rule-bound bureaucracies'.[55] These are strategies of *closeness* rather than distance or *remoteness,* based on promoting *interaction* rather than following *rules.*

What is now widely known as the 'empowerment' approach is the latest in a long series of perspectives on the promotion of women and women's needs and interests in the development process. What is significant and qualitatively different about this approach is the theme of collective identity that underpins most empowerment strategies. This theme refers not only to the social basis of gender subordination and the related recognition that women experience subordination as 'inevitable and interpersonal', but to the fact that women's collective strength—through the quality of their attachments—is seen as the most important transformatory resource at their disposal.[56]

The Grameen Bank in Bangladesh is becoming well-known for its successes in providing credit to the poor and assetless—mainly women—based on the recognition that the major constraint on their well-being was the lack of access to financial institutions, rather than to the waged labour market. Starting out as a poverty eradication programme, what was a small credit operation in 1976 became an independent national bank in 1983, with women constituting over 90 percent of bank borrowers. Similarly, the less well-known Self Employed Women's Association (SEWA) in India also works with poor, self-employed women, but primarily in urban areas. This association emerged in response to the expressed needs of women workers in the unorganized sector who had largely been ignored by the male-dominated trade-union movement.[57]

As Naila Kabeer points out, the initial needs identified by both SEWA and the Grameen Bank were economic ones. But the great strength of these participatory methods is the recognition of other, non-economic needs and the realization that categories of needs are not discrete, but interdependent.[58] Most important, however, are the opportunities for women to uncover the socially constructed and socially shared basis of apparently individual problems.[59] The Grameen Bank, for example, focuses explicitly on building new collective identities for women through the process of group formation; they also emphasize the interpersonal dynamics involved in the process. It is not only the women themselves who have built attachments and solidarities; women borrowers have interacted with bank workers to agree on tangible and intangible aspects of social development.[60]

Group formation is critical to Grameen credit disbursement, insofar as the group is involved in making decisions about lending and also, significantly, in providing social collateral.[61] SEWA also has a model of joint action at the heart of its organizational strategy; through cooperatives and more conventional unions, SEWA provides a social connection to a section of the workforce whose members are either isolated within the home or in dispersed and shifting work locations. These strategies clearly value the quality of personal attachments for their potential to bring about social change, but they are also critical about the ability of 'normal ties' to act in a counterhegemonic and progressive manner:

> Access to these new and collective relationships, built around their shared needs and interests as workers and as women, has given SEWA's members an opportunity to think of themselves in terms other than those imposed by their traditional domestic, caste and community roles.[62]

Finally, a recognition of the value of attachments for social change is evident in the Bankura experiment, an association between the Centre for Women and Development Studies (CWDS), a research group, and *samitis* (groups) of poor women in West Bengal. CWDS was brought in initially to advise these groups of women who were expressing demands for wage labour. CWDS saw a role for a middle-class women's group in setting up the first channels of communication between poorer rural women's organizations and the wider decision-making structures within the development sphere. They stressed the value of such strategic coalitions as a way of overcoming some of the constraints that poorer women faced. CWDS promoted professional management training to enable the women to manage their enterprises. An analysis of the Bankura experiment argued that:

> women's subordination within rural social relations, their dependent positions within their households, and the drudgery that characterizes their existence had created a structural isolation which prevented the growth of collective forms of consciousness and action to transform their lives.[63]

As one woman involved in the experiment plainly states:

> We were like frogs in a dark well. No one had thought of extending our minds. Our idea of *we* meant the family, or at most, the village or the caste in the village. When we became members of a multivillage, multicaste organization, we suddenly expanded. Now it has become so much bigger—we are a part of a network of organizations.[64]

These new approaches to development suggest a clear role for a critical ethics of care in the context of North-South relations. First, they demonstrate that a purely economic interpretation of the strategies of states and non-state actors in development is inadequate to achieve a clear understanding of the motives, assumptions, and goals which inform policies and projects. These approaches are guided explicitly by *an ethics*, which is more than just a recognition of a problem that, for instance, 'it is morally wrong that people live in poverty'—a problem about which it is often assumed that we can address and solve using economic strategies. By contrast, these approaches reject the separation of economics, politics, and morality by recognizing the transformatory potential of so-called intangible resources such as 'social networks, organizational strength, solidarity and a sense of *not being alone*'.[65]

The nature of this ethics, however, is significant, insofar as it seeks to promote strong, healthy, caring attachments among members of existing communities, as well as to create new networks across communities and new alliances, which often break down or crosscut traditional personal and social ties. As the rhetoric of partnership, stressing rights and duties, individual autonomy, and formal equality, gives way to the strategy of accompaniment and long-term partnering, there is a growing recognition that moral problems, and their economic and political dimensions, must be addressed, and potential solutions found, at the level of social relations. These approaches, moreover, view relationships in a critical light, and with an awareness that all attachments contain the potential for paternalism, dependence, and even violence and exploitation. Thus, the participatory approaches of the NGOs discussed earlier teach them to really look at and listen to the women themselves, in order to understand which relationships and attachments are most conducive to the fostering of strength and solidarity.

This is not to say, however, that such strategies ignore the values of independent selfhood. Indeed, the language of empowerment, self-esteem, and self-determination is central to these grassroots, participatory approaches to development. But there is a recognition that self-esteem and autonomy exist only in the context of relationships; it is the quality of attachments which can both rob us of our self-esteem and restore it. Thus, the Women's Aid Organization in Malaysia, which was set up in 1982 to provide a range of support services to women with violent husbands, has as its primary concern the restoration of self-esteem and autonomy to women whose experience has badly damaged these resources. But there is a recognition that this goal can be achieved only by coming to terms with what has been happening to these women within the marital relationship, and crucially, attempts are made to provide women with interactions very different from the brutalizing and self-corrosive experiences they have been through. Finally, there is also an acceptance within the organization that this does not happen automatically or overnight, but through a slow and patient process.[66]

Conclusion

The purpose of this chapter has been to explore some concrete contexts in which a critical ethics of care may offer a useful starting point for achieving social and political change on a global scale. If international ethics confines itself to questions concerning sovereignty, intervention, and international distributive justice, it will never progress beyond the fixed ontology, the dichotomous analytical frameworks, and the narrow modes of moral reasoning by which it is currently characterized.

This chapter has focused explicitly on the problem of world poverty and, specifically, the ongoing and ever-widening gap between rich and poor in a North-South context. It has been suggested that a useful approach to poverty on a global scale must go beyond the articulation of the rights of the poor and/or 'our' duties to the poor; what is required, instead, is a focusing of moral attention on the networks of personal and social relations within which we may uncover, paradoxically, both the causes of and solutions to exclusion, marginalization, suffering, and poverty. Thus, an ethical approach to poverty in international relations must not be separate from, but inextricably linked to, economic and political approaches which are committed to the building of long-term attachments, but which are also critical of both existing and potential relations in terms of their capacity for domination, inequality, and even violence. Relationships, then, are regarded as a good in themselves, but also as a critical tool. Projects to mitigate poverty would concentrate on promoting strong, healthy relations both within and between local communities in the South, but also between such communities and NGOs, states, and organizations in the North.

There are those who will be dissatisfied with these arguments—those who would prefer to cling to the familiar language of rights and duties, justice and reciprocity, and the apparent certainty offered to us by the kind of ethics which 'tells us what to do' and give us universal standards by which to judge the justice or injustice of all forms of human activity. Those will be the same people who will continue to dismiss or to misunderstand the idea of 'care'—who will regard it as sentimental, nepotistic, relativistic, paternalistic, and even dangerous—and who will continue to champion a form of ethics which tells us only where we ought to be, rejecting the claim that we must start from where we are now.

Part of the purpose of this book, however, has been to dispel some of these misconceptions about the ethics of care—particularly the claim that the moral values upheld by an ethics of care are relevant only in the context of intimate, personal, already caring relations, such as those between parents and their children. It has been argued that to confine the ethics of care to the private sphere is fundamentally to leave in place the dichotomy between 'public' and 'private', as well as to leave undisturbed and unchallenged the traditional approaches to ethics—characterized by impartiality, rationality, and universalizability—which define our understandings of ethics and justice in the public sphere. It has been argued that an ethics of care can and must be seen as relevant to international relations or, quite simply, to social relations on a global scale. Understanding this relevance, however, relies on a broader understanding of the relational nature of the ethics of care; while healthy personal and social relations based on sustained, focused attention and mutual respect should be recognized as morally valuable and good, social relations may also be used as a critical device for uncovering patterns of exclusion and subordination. Thus, the ability to care about others involves not only learning how to be attentive and patient, how to listen and respond, but also how to rethink our own attitudes about difference and exclusion by locating that difference within relationships, thus dispelling the claim that any one person or group of persons is naturally and objectively 'different'.

These strategies are intensely moral; that does not suggest, however, that they can be separated from political and economic strategies in the context of international relations. Theorists of international relations or international political economy can no longer sustain the argument that ethics is marginal or irrelevant to international relations; although the contemporary world may still be characterized by discord, difference, and exclusion, it is undeniably a world of accelerating and intensifying social relations across borders. In such a world, the responsibility of international relations theorists to engage in ethical inquiry regarding the nature of those social relations is not necessarily greater than it ever was before, but it is more readily apparent. It is the responsibility of those who make it their business to think about ethics in the context of international relations, however, to ensure that the types of moral reasoning and moral responses about which they write actually connect with the real circumstances of international relations and, ultimately, with the real circumstances of people's lives. This book has suggested that this can be achieved best through a phenomenological approach to ethics, which values human connections but at the same time uses them as a starting point for critical analysis. Globalizing care demands not an uncritical extension of caring responses across borders to all of humankind; rather, it demands an awareness of social relations as a starting point for ethical inquiry and a commitment to using those relationships as a critical tool for uncovering, and beginning to address, the relations of oppression and subordination which exist at the global level.

Notes

1. Roger Spegele, *Political Realism in International Theory,* Cambridge: Cambridge University Press, 1996, p. 238.
2. Ibid., p. 202.
3. Chris Brown, *International Relations Theory: New Normative Approaches,* Hemel Hempstead: Harvester Wheatsheaf, 1992, p. 109.
4. Ibid., p. 110.
5. Ibid., p. 112.
6. Mervyn Frost, *Ethics in International Relations,* Cambridge: Cambridge University Press, 1996, pp. 76–77.
7. Ibid., p. 79, my italics.
8. Michael Walzer, *Just and Unjust Wars,* 2nd ed., New York: Basic Books, 1992.
9. Ibid., p. 58.

10. Ibid., p. 54.
11. Ibid., p. 86.
12. Ibid., p. 101.
13. Ibid., pp. 107, 101.
14. Nick Lewer and Oliver Ramsbotham, '"Something Must Be Done": Towards an Ethical Framework for Humanitarian Intervention in International Social Conflict', Peace Research Report 33, Bradford: University of Bradford, Department of Peace Studies, August 1993, p. 52.
15. Ibid., pp. 25–26.
16. Ibid., p. 54.
17. The section entitled 'Non-Western Ethical Traditions' seems to point out that although non-Western states may have differing views on intervention, human rights, and ethics in general, there must be, and indeed is, transcultural acknowledgement of the principle of humanitarian intervention (pp. 64–65).
18. Ibid., p. 64.
19. Ibid., p. 47.
20. Ibid., p. 106.
21. Ibid., p. 83.
22. Preamble to the Universal Declaration of Human Rights, quoted in Lewer and Ramsbotham, '"Something Must Be Done"', p. 12.
23. Ibid., p. 98.
24. Jenny Edkins, 'Legality with a Vengeance: Famines and Humanitarian Relief in "Complex Emergencies"', *Millennium: Journal of International Studies* 25, no. 3, Winter 1996: 573.
25. Brown, *International Relations Theory,* p. 183.
26. Onora O'Neill's excellent book *Faces of Hunger: An Essay on Poverty, Justice, and Development* (London: Allen & Unwin, 1986) is an exception to this. It could be said, however, that this work does not directly engage with debates in international relations theory—although this, of course, is no reason to suggest that it is not relevant to international relations theory. Also, it is important to note that although O'Neill is directly concerned with the problem of poverty and hunger on a global scale, the work remains firmly within the Kantian tradition and seeks to construct a principled account of justice based on the demands of duty emanating from rational principles of practical reason.
27. The growth of 'applied ethics' represented an attempt by certain moral and political philosophers to create a bridge between philosophical thinking and the 'realities' of social crises. In 1974 Peter Singer's article 'Philosophers Are Back on the Job' championed the philosophical turn to applied ethics, employing the ethics of famine relief as a leading example. See Peter Singer, 'Philosophers Are Back on the Job', *New York Times Magazine,* July 7, 1974, pp. 17–20. For a discussion of ethics and world hunger, see David A. Crocker, 'Hunger, Capability, and Development', in Aiken and LaFollette, *World Hunger and Morality.*
28. See Fiona Robinson, 'The Limits of a Rights-Based Approach to International Ethics', in Tony Evans, ed., *Human Rights Fifty Years On: A Reappraisal,* Manchester: Manchester University Press, 1998.
29. Iris Murdoch, *Existentialists and Mystics: Writings on Philosophy and Literature,* London: Chatto & Windus, 1997, p. 366.

30. James Nickel, 'A Human Rights Approach to World Hunger', in Aiken and LaFollette, *World Hunger and Morality*, p. 176.

31. Henry Shue, 'Solidarity Among Strangers and the Right to Food', in Aiken and LaFollette, *World Hunger and Morality*, p. 118.

32. Onora O'Neill, 'Ending World Hunger', in Aiken and LaFollette, *World Hunger and Morality*, p. 94.

33. Onora O'Neill, *Towards Justice and Virtue: A Constructive Account of Practical Reason*, Cambridge: Cambridge University Press, 1996, pp. 147–148.

34. Ibid., p. 146.

35. Ibid., p. 141.

36. O'Neill, 'Ending World Hunger', p. 105.

37. Spegele, *Political Realism*, p. 237.

38. Edkins, 'Legality with a Vengeance', p. 573.

39. Ibid., p. 563.

40. Hugh LaFollette and Larry May, 'Suffer the Little Children', in Aiken and LaFollette, *World Hunger and Morality*, p. 81.

41. Murdoch, *Existentialists and Mystics*, p. 345.

42. Laura Macdonald, 'Unequal Partnerships: The Politics of Canada's Relations with the Third World', *Studies in Political Economy*, no. 47, Summer 1995: 130–131.

43. Quoted in ibid., pp. 132–133.

44. Quoted in ibid., pp. 134–135.

45. Ibid., p. 135.

46. I am very grateful to Laura Macdonald for bringing to my attention the links between an ethics of care and the accompaniment approach to development.

47. Alan Fowler, *Striking a Balance: A Guide to Enhancing the Effectiveness of Non-governmental Organisations in International Development*, London: Earthscan, 1997, p. 207.

48. Laura Macdonald, 'Globalising Civil Society: Interpreting International NGOs in Central America', *Millennium: Journal of International Studies* 23, no. 2, Summer 1994: 284.

49. Ibid.

50. I am indebted to Sam Gibson for bringing this document to my attention. Indeed, I am grateful for the helpful feedback I received from the entire audience at the Faculty of Social and Political Sciences, University of Cambridge, where I presented a paper on this subject in December 1997, and from the seminar series organizer, Toni Erskine.

51. Swedish Ministry of Foreign Affairs, *Partnership with Africa: Proposals for a New Swedish Policy Towards Sub-Saharan Africa*, Stockholm: Ministry of Foreign Affairs, 1997, pp. 7–8, 16.

52. Ibid., pp. 17, 22.

53. Ibid., p. 20.

54. Ibid., p. 86.

55. Naila Kabeer, *Reversed Realities: Gender Hierarchies in Development Thought*, London: Verso, 1994, p. 223.

56. Ibid., p. 253.

57. Ibid., p. 231.
58. Ibid., pp. 232, 234.
59. Ibid., p. 245.
60. Ibid., pp. 247–248.
61. Ibid., p. 254.
62. Ibid., p. 255.
63. Ibid., p. 252.
64. Ibid., p. 253.
65. Ibid., p. 246, my italics.
66. Ibid.

Bibliography

Aiken, William, and Hugh LaFollette, eds. *World Hunger and Morality.* 2nd ed. Upper Saddle River, NJ: Prentice-Hall, 1996.

Anderson, Benedict. *Imagined Communities: Reflections on the Origin and Spread of Nationalism.* Rev. ed. London: Verso, 1991.

Baier, Annette. *Moral Prejudices: Essays on Ethics.* Cambridge, MA: Harvard University Press, 1994.

Barry, Brian. *The Liberal Theory of Justice.* London: Clarendon Press, 1973.

______. *Justice as Impartiality.* Oxford: Oxford University Press, 1995.

Beitz, Charles. *Political Theory and International Relations.* Princeton, NJ: Princeton University Press, 1979.

______. 'Cosmopolitan Ideals and National Sentiment'. *Journal of Philosophy* 80, no. 10, 1983: 591–600.

______. 'Sovereignty and Morality in International Affairs'. In David Held, ed., *Political Theory Today.* Cambridge: Polity Press, 1991.

Benhabib, Seyla. 'The Generalised and the Concrete Other: The Kohlberg-Gilligan Controversy and Feminist Theory'. In Seyla Benhabib and Drucilla Cornell, eds., *Feminism as Critique: Essays on the Politics of Gender in Late-Capitalist Societies.* Cambridge: Polity Press, 1987.

______. *Situating the Self: Gender, Community, and Postmodernism in Contemporary Ethics.* Cambridge: Polity Press, 1992.

______. 'Cultural Complexity, Moral Interdependence, and the Global Dialogical Community'. In Martha Nussbaum and Jonathan Glover, eds., *Women, Culture, and Development: A Study of Human Capabilities.* Oxford: Oxford University Press, 1995.

Berlin, Isaiah. 'Two Concepts of Liberty'. In *Four Essays on Liberty.* Oxford: Oxford University Press, 1969.

Blum, Lawrence A. 'Gilligan and Kohlberg: Implications for Moral Theory'. In Mary Jeanne Larrabee, ed., *An Ethic of Care: Feminist and Interdisciplinary Perspectives.* London: Routledge, 1993.

______. *Moral Perception and Particularity.* Cambridge: Cambridge University Press, 1994.

Brown, Chris. 'International Political Theory and the Idea of World Community'. In Ken Booth and Steve Smith, eds. *International Relations Theory Today.* Cambridge: Polity Press, 1995.

______. *International Relations Theory: New Normative Approaches.* Hemel Hempstead: Harvester Wheatsheaf, 1992.

Bunch, Charlotte. 'A Global Perspective on Feminist Ethics and Diversity'. In Eve Browning Cole and Susan Coultrap-McQuin, eds., *Explorations in Feminist Ethics: Theory and Practice.* Bloomington: Indiana University Press, 1992.

Card, Claudia, ed. *Feminist Ethics.* Lawrence: University of Kansas Press, 1991.

______. 'Gender and Moral Luck'. In Virginia Held, ed., *Justice and Care: Essential Readings in Feminist Ethics.* Boulder, CO: Westview Press, 1995.

Chodorow, Nancy. *The Reproduction of Mothering: Psychoanalysis and the Sociology of Gender.* Berkeley: University of California Press, 1978.

Clement, Grace. *Care, Autonomy, and Justice: Feminism and the Ethic of Care.* Boulder, CO: Westview Press, 1996.

Cole, Eve Browning, and Susan Coultrap-McQuin, eds. *Explorations in Feminist Ethics: Theory and Practice.* Bloomington: Indiana University Press, 1992.

Connolly, William. *Identity/Difference: Democratic Negotiations of Political Paradox.* Ithaca, NY: Cornell University Press, 1991.

Cox, Robert. 'Multilateralism and World Order'. In Robert Cox with Timothy J. Sinclair, *Approaches to World Order.* Cambridge: Cambridge University Press, 1996.

Crocker, David A. 'Hunger, Capability, and Development'. In William Aiken and Hugh LaFollette, eds., *World Hunger and Morality,* 2nd ed., Upper Saddle River, NJ: Prentice-Hall, 1996.

Dillon, Robin S. 'Care and Respect'. In Eve Browning Cole and Susan Coultrap-McQuin, eds., *Explorations in Feminist Ethics: Theory and Practice.* Bloomington: Indiana University Press, 1992.

Dreyfus, Hubert, and Paul Rabinow. *Michel Foucault: Beyond Structuralism and Hermeneutics.* Brighton: Harvester Wheatsheaf, 1982.

Dunn, John. *Western Political Theory in the Face of the Future.* Cambridge: Cambridge University Press, 1979.

Edkins, Jenny. 'Legality with a Vengeance: Famines and Humanitarian Relief in "Complex Emergencies". *Millennium: Journal of International Studies* 25, no. 3, Winter 1996.

Elshtain, Jean Bethke 'Sovereignty, Identity, and Sacrifice'. In V. Spike Peterson, ed., *Gendered States: Feminist (Re)visions of International Relations Theory.* London: Lynne Rienner, 1992.

______. 'International Politics and Political Theory'. In Ken Booth and Steve Smith, eds., *International Relations Theory Today.* Cambridge: Polity Press, 1995.

Ethics. Special issue—Symposium on Duties Beyond Borders. Vol. 98, no. 3, July 1988.

Forsyth, Murray. 'The Tradition of International Law'. In Terry Nardin and David Mapel, eds., *Traditions of International Ethics.* Cambridge: Cambridge University Press, 1992.

Fowler, Alan. *Striking a Balance: A Guide to Enhancing the Effectiveness of Non-Governmental Organisations in International Development.* London: Earthscan, 1997.

Friedman, Marilyn. *What Are Friends For? Feminist Perspectives on Personal Relationships and Moral Theory.* Ithaca, NY: Cornell University Press, 1993.

______. 'Beyond Caring: The De-Moralization of Gender'. In Virginia Held, ed., *Justice and Care: Essential Readings in Feminist Ethics.* Boulder, CO: Westview Press, 1995.

Frost, Mervyn. *Ethics and International Relations: A Constitutive Theory.* Cambridge: Cambridge University Press, 1996.

Fukuyama, Francis. *The End of History and the Last Man.* New York: Basic Books, 1992.

Gellner, Ernest. *Nations and Nationalism.* Oxford: Blackwell, 1983.

Giddens, Anthony. *The Consequences of Modernity.* Cambridge: Polity Press, 1990.
Gilligan, Carol. *In a Different Voice: Psychological Theory and Women's Development.* 2nd ed. Cambridge, MA: Harvard University Press, 1993.
______. 'Reply to Critics'. In Mary Jeanne Larrabee, ed., *An Ethic of Care: Feminist and Interdisciplinary Perspectives.* London: Routledge, 1993.
Gilligan, Carol, Ellen C. Dubois, Mary C. Dunlop, Catherine A. MacKinnon, and Carrie J. Menkel-Neadow, 'Feminist Discourse, Moral Values, and the Law—A Conversation', 1984 James McCormick Mitchell Lecture, *Buffalo Law Review* 34, no. 1 (Winter 1985): 73–74.
Harding, Sandra. 'The Instability of the Analytical Categories of Feminist Theory'. In Helen Crowley and Susan Himmelweit, eds., *Knowing Women: Feminism and Knowledge.* Cambridge: Polity Press, 1992.
Hawthorn, Geoffrey. *Enlightenment and Despair: A History of Social Theory.* 2nd ed. Cambridge: Cambridge University Press, 1987.
______. *Plausible Worlds: Possibility and Understanding in History and the Social Sciences.* Cambridge: Cambridge University Press, 1992.
Hekman, Susan. *Moral Voices, Moral Selves: Carol Gilligan and Feminist Moral Theory.* Cambridge: Polity Press, 1995.
Held, Virginia. *Feminist Morality: Transforming Culture, Society, and Politics.* Chicago: University of Chicago Press, 1993.
Held, Virginia, and Alison Jaggar, eds. *Justice and Care: Essential Readings in Feminist Ethics.* Boulder, CO: Westview Press, 1995.
Hirst, Paul, and Grahame Thompson. *Globalization in Question.* Cambridge: Polity Press, 1996.
Hoagland, Sarah Lucia. 'Some Thoughts About "Caring"'. In Claudia Card, ed., *Feminist Ethics.* Lawrence: University of Kansas Press, 1991.
Hobbes, Thomas. *Leviathan.* Edited by Richard Tuck. Cambridge: Cambridge University Press, 1991.
Hutchings, Kimberly. *Kant, Critique and Politics.* London: Routledge, 1996.
Ignatieff, Michael. *Blood and Belonging: Journeys into the New Nationalism.* London: Chatto & Windus, 1993.
Jackson, Robert. *Quasi-States: Sovereignty, International Relations, and the Third World.* Cambridge: Cambridge University Press, 1990.
Jaggar, Alison M. *Feminist Politics and Human Nature.* Totowa, NJ: Rowman, 1983.
Jaggar, Alison M. 'Caring as a Feminist Practice of Moral Reason'. In Virginia Held, ed., *Justice and Care: Essential Readings in Feminist Ethics.* Boulder, CO: Westview Press, 1995.
James, Allison. *Childhood Identities: Self and Social Relationships in the Experience of the Child.* Edinburgh: Edinburgh University Press, 1993.
James, Susan. 'The Good-Enough Citizen: Female Citizenship and Independence'. In Susan James and Gisela Bock, eds., *Beyond Equality and Difference.* London: Routledge, 1992.
Johansen, Robert C. 'Military Policies and the State System as Impediments to Democracy'. In David Held, ed., *Prospects for Democracy: North, South, East, West.* Cambridge: Polity Press, 1993.
Kabeer, Naila. *Reversed Realities: Gender Hierarchies in Development Thought.* London: Verso, 1994.

Kant, Immanuel. *The Groundwork of the Metaphysic of Morals.* Translated and analyzed by H. J. Paton. London: Routledge, 1991.

Kegley, Charles R., Jr. 'The Neoliberal Challenge to Realist Theories of World Politics: An Introduction'. In Charles R. Kegley, Jr., ed., *Controversies in International Relations Theory: Realism and the Neoliberal Challenge.* New York: St. Martin's Press, 1995.

Keohane, Robert. 'International Relations Theory: Contributions from a Feminist Standpoint'. In Rebecca Grant and Kathleen Newland, eds., *Gender in International Relations.* London: Macmillan, 1991.

______. 'International Liberalism Reconsidered'. In John Dunn, ed., *The Economic Limits to Modern Politics.* Cambridge: Cambridge University Press, 1992.

Keohane, Robert, and Joseph Nye. *Power and Interdependence: World Politics in Transition.* Boston: Little, Brown, 1977.

Krause, Jill. 'The International Dimension of Gender Inequality and Feminist Politics: A New "Direction" for International Political Economy?' In Andrew Linklater and John MacMillan, eds., *Boundaries in Question: New Directions in International Relations.* London: Pinter, 1995.

LaFollette, Hugh, and Larry May. 'Suffer the Little Children'. In William Aiken and Hugh LaFollette, eds., *World Hunger and Morality.* 2nd ed. Upper Saddle River, NJ: Prentice-Hall, 1996.

Lewer, Nick, and Oliver Ramsbotham. "Something Must Be Done": Towards an Ethical Framework for Humanitarian Intervention in International Social Conflict." Peace Research Report 33. Bradford, England: University of Bradford, Department of Peace Studies, August 1993.

Linklater, Andrew. *Men and Citizens in the Theory of International Relations,* 2nd ed. London: Macmillan, 1990.

______. 'The Question of the Next Stage in International Relations Theory: A Critical-Theoretical Point of View'. *Millennium: Journal of International Studies* 22, no. 1, 1992: 77–98.

______. *The Transformation of Political Community: Ethical Foundations of the Post-Westphalian Era.* Cambridge: Polity Press, 1998.

Long, David. 'The Harvard School of Liberal International Theory: A Case for Closure'. *Millennium: Journal of International Studies* 24, no. 3, 1995: 500.

Macdonald, Laura. 'Globalising Civil Society: Interpreting International NGOs in Central America'. *Millennium: Journal of International Studies* 23, no. 2, Summer 1994.

______. 'Unequal Partnerships: The Politics of Canada's Relations with the Third World'. *Studies in Political Economy,* no. 47, Summer 1995.

Maddock, Rowland. 'The Global Political Economy'. In John Baylis and N. J. Rengger, eds., *Dilemmas of World Politics: International Issues in a Changing World.* Oxford: Oxford University Press, 1992.

Mapel, David R. 'The Contractarian Tradition and International Ethics'. In Terry Nardin and David R. Mapel eds., *Traditions of International Ethics,* Cambridge: Cambridge University Press, 1992.

Mapel, David R., and Terry Nardin. 'Convergence and Divergence in International Ethics'. In Terry Nardin and David R. Mapel, eds., *Traditions of International Ethics,* Cambridge: Cambridge University Press, 1992.

Massey, Doreen. *Space, Place, and Gender.* Cambridge: Polity Press, 1992.

May, Larry, Marilyn Friedman, and Andy Clark, eds. *Mind and Morals: Essays on Ethics and Cognitive Science.* Cambridge, MA: MIT Press, 1996.

McNay, Lois. *Foucault and Feminism: Power, Gender, and the Self.* Cambridge: Polity Press, 1992.

Meyers, Diana T. *Subjection and Subjectivity: Psychoanalytic Feminism and Moral Philosophy.* London: Routledge, 1994.

Miller, David. 'The Ethical Significance of Nationality'. *Ethics* 98, no. 4, 1988: 705–722.

______. 'Bounded Citizenship'. Paper presented at the University of Sussex Seminars in Social and Political Thought, 10 October 1996.

Minow, Martha. *Making All the Difference: Inclusion, Exclusion, and American Law.* Ithaca, NY: Cornell University Press, 1990.

Minow, Martha, and Mary Lyndon Shanley. 'Revisioning the Family: Relational Rights and Responsibilities'. In Mary Lyndon Shanley and Uma Narayan, eds., *Reconstructing Political Theory: Feminist Perspectives.* Cambridge: Polity Press, 1997.

Murdoch, Iris. *Existentialists and Mystics: Writings on Philosophy and Literature.* London: Chatto & Windus, 1997.

Nagel, Thomas. *The View from Nowhere.* Oxford: Oxford University Press, 1986.

______. *Equality and Partiality.* Cambridge: Cambridge University Press, 1991.

Nardin, Terry. *Law, Morality, and the Relations of States.* Princeton, NJ: Princeton University Press, 1983.

Nardin, Terry, and David R. Mapel, eds. *Traditions of International Ethics.* Cambridge: Cambridge University Press, 1992.

Nicholson, Linda J. 'Women, Morality, and History'. In Mary Jeanne Larrabee, ed., *An Ethic of Care: Feminist and Interdisciplinary Perspectives.* London: Routledge, 1993.

Nickel, James. 'A Human Rights Approach to World Hunger'. In William Aiken and Hugh LaFollette, eds., *World Hunger and Morality.* 2nd ed. Upper Saddle River, NJ: Prentice-Hall, 1996.

Noddings, Nel. *Caring: A Feminine Approach to Ethics and Moral Education.* Berkeley: University of California Press, 1984.

______. 'The Alleged Parochialism of Caring'. *American Philosophical Association Newsletter on Feminism and Philosophy* 90, no. 2, Winter 1991: 97–98.

Norton, Anne. *Reflections on Political Identity.* Baltimore: Johns Hopkins University Press, 1988.

Nozick, Robert. *Anarchy, State, and Utopia.* Totowa, NJ: Rowman, 1974.

Nunner-Winkler, Gertrude. 'Two Moralities? A Critical Discussion of an Ethic of Care and Responsibility Versus an Ethic of Rights and Justice'. In Mary Jeanne Larrabee, ed., *An Ethic of Care: Feminist and Interdisciplinary Perspectives.* London: Routledge, 1993.

Okin, Susan Moller. 'Reason and Feeling in Thinking About Justice'. In Cass R. Sunstein, ed., *Feminism and Political Theory.* Chicago: University of Chicago Press, 1990.

______. 'Thinking Like a Woman'. In Deborah Rhode, ed., *Theoretical Perspectives on Sexual Difference.* New Haven, CT: Yale University Press, 1990.

O'Neill, Onora. *Faces of Hunger: An Essay on Poverty, Justice, and Development.* London: Allen and Unwin, 1986.

______. 'Justice, Gender, and International Boundaries', In Robin Attfield and Barry Wilkins, eds., *International Justice and the Third World.* London: Routledge, 1992.

______. 'Justice, Capabilities, and Vulnerabilities'. In Martha Nussbaum and Jonathan Glover, eds., *Women, Culture, and Development: A Study in Human Capabilities.* Oxford: Oxford University Press, 1995.

______. 'Moral Standing and State Boundaries'. Christopher Thorne Memorial Lecture, University of Sussex, 5 December 1995.

______. 'Ending World Hunger'. In William Aiken and Hugh LaFollette, eds., *World Hunger and Morality,* 2nd ed. Upper Saddle River, NJ: Prentice-Hall, 1996.

______. *Towards Justice and Virtue: A Constructive Account of Practical Reason.* Cambridge: Cambridge University Press, 1996.

Papanek, Hanna. 'The Ideal Woman and the Ideal Society: Control and Autonomy in the Construction of Identity'. In Valentine M. Moghadem, ed., *Identity Politics and Women: Cultural Reassertions and Feminism in International Perspective.* Boulder, CO: Westview Press, 1994.

Peterson, V. Spike, and Anne Sisson Runyan. *Global Gender Issues.* Boulder, CO: Westview Press, 1993.

Pettman, Jan Jindy. *Worlding Women: A Feminist International Politics.* London: Routledge, 1996.

Rigterink, Roger J. 'Warning: The Surgeon Moralist Has Determined That Claims of Rights Can Be Detrimental to Everyone's Health'. In Eve Browning Cole and Susan Coultrap-McQuin, eds., *Explorations in Feminist Ethics: Theory and Practice.* Bloomington: Indiana University Press, 1992.

Robinson, Fiona. 'Rethinking Ethics in an Era of Globalisation'. Sussex Papers in International Relations, no. 2. Brighton: University of Sussex, 1996.

______. 'The Limits of a Rights-Based Approach to International Ethics'. In Tony Evans, ed., *Human Rights Fifty Years On: A Reappraisal.* Manchester: Manchester University Press, 1998.

______. 'Beyond Rights and Duties: Building Attachments and Focusing Moral Attention on World Poverty'. In Paris Yeros and Sarah Owen, eds., *Poverty in World Politics.* London: Macmillan, forthcoming.

Rubin, Gayle. 'The Traffic in Women: Notes on the "Political Economy" of Sex'. In Reyna Reiter, ed. *Toward an Anthropology of Women.* New York: Monthly Review Press, 1976.

Ruddick, Sara. *Maternal Thinking: Towards a Politics of Peace.* New York: Women's Press, 1989.

Sandel, Michael. 'Justice and the Good'. In Michael Sandel, ed., *Liberalism and Its Critics.* Oxford: Blackwell, 1984.

Scholte, Jan Aarte. 'The Globalization of World Politics'. In John Baylis and Steve Smith, eds., *The Globalization of World Politics: An Introduction to International Relations.* Oxford: Oxford University Press, 1997.

Seigfried, Charlene Haddock. *Pragmatism and Feminism: Reweaving the Social Fabric.* Chicago: University of Chicago Press, 1996.

Shapiro, Ian. *The Evolution of Rights in Liberal Theory.* Cambridge: Cambridge University Press, 1986.

Shaw, Martin. *Global Society and International Relations.* Cambridge: Polity Press, 1994.

Shklar, Judith. *The Faces of Injustice.* New Haven, CT: Yale University Press, 1990.

Shue, Henry. 'Solidarity Among Strangers and the Right to Food'. In William Aiken and Hugh LaFollette, eds., *World Hunger and Morality.* 2nd ed. Upper Saddle River, NJ: Prentice-Hall, 1996.

Singer, Peter. 'Philosophers Are Back on the Job'. *New York Times Magazine,* 7 July 1974, pp. 17–20.

Skinner, Quentin. 'The Idea of Negative Liberty: Philosophical and Historical Perspectives'. In Richard Rorty, J. B. Schneewind, and Quentin Skinner, eds., *Philosophy in History.* Cambridge: Cambridge University Press, 1984.

______. 'The Paradoxes of Political Liberty'. In David Miller, ed., *Liberty.* Oxford: Oxford University Press, 1991.

Smith, Anthony. *National Identity.* London: Penguin, 1991.

Smith, Steve. 'The Forty Years' Detour: The Resurgence of Normative Theory in International Relations'. *Millennium: Journal of International Studies* 21, no.3, 1992: 489–508.

Spegele, Roger. *Political Realism and International Theory.* Cambridge: Cambridge University Press, 1996.

Spragens, Thomas A., Jr. 'Communitarian Liberalism'. In Amitai Etzioni, ed., *New Communitarian Thinking: Persons, Virtues, Institutions, and Communities.* Charlottesville: University of Virginia Press, 1995.

Swedish Ministry of Foreign Affairs. *Partnership with Africa: Proposals for a New Swedish Policy Towards Sub-Saharan Africa.* Stockholm: Swedish Ministry of Foreign Affairs, 1997.

Taylor, Charles. *Sources of the Self.* Cambridge: Cambridge University Press, 1989.

______. 'Atomism'. In Will Kymlicka, ed., *Justice in Political Philosophy.* Aldershot: Edward Elgar, 1992.

______. *Philosophical Arguments.* Cambridge, MA: Harvard University Press, 1995.

Thompson, Janna. *Justice and World Order: A Philosophical Inquiry.* London: Routledge, 1992.

Tickner, J. Anne. 'On the Fringes of the World Economy: A Feminist Perspective'. In Craig Murphy and Roger Tooze, eds., *The New International Political Economy.* Boulder, CO: Lynne Rienner, 1991.

Tronto, Joan. *Moral Boundaries: A Political Argument for an Ethic of Care.* London: Routledge, 1993.

______. 'Women and Caring: What Can Feminists Learn About Morality from Caring?' In Virginia Held, ed., *Justice and Care: Essential Readings in Feminist Ethics.* Boulder, CO: Westview, 1995.

Tuck, Richard. *Natural Rights Theories: Their Origin and Development.* Cambridge: Cambridge University Press, 1979.

Vincent, R. J. 'The Idea of Rights in International Ethics'. In Terry Nardin and David R. Mapel, eds., *Traditions of International Ethics.* Cambridge: Cambridge University Press, 1992.

Walker, Margaret Urban. 'Moral Particularity'. *Metaphilosophy* 18, nos. 3 and 4 (July-August 1987): 171–185.

______. 'Moral Understandings: Alternative "Epistemology" for a Feminist Ethics'. In Virginia Held, ed., *Justice and Care: Essential Readings in Feminist Ethics.* Boulder, CO: Westview Press, 1995.

______. *Moral Understandings: A Feminist Study in Ethics.* London: Routledge, 1998.

Walker, R. B. J. *Inside/Outside: International Relations as Political Theory.* Cambridge: Cambridge University Press, 1993.

Walzer, Michael. *Just and Unjust Wars,* 2nd ed. New York: Basic Books, 1992.

______. *Spheres of Justice: A Defence of Pluralism and Equality.* Oxford: Oxford University Press, 1983.

Weber, Cynthia. 'Good Girls, Little Girls, and Bad Girls: Male Paranoia in Robert Keohane's Critique of Feminist International Relations'. *Millennium: Journal of International Studies* 23, no. 2, 1993: 337–348.

Weiss, Thomas G., and Cindy Collins. *Humanitarian Challenges and Intervention: World Politics and the Dilemmas of Help.* Boulder, CO: Westview Press, 1996.

Whitworth, Sandra. 'Theory as Exclusion: Gender and International Political Economy'. In Richard Stubbs and Geoffrey Underhill, eds., *Political Economy and the Changing Global Order,* London: Macmillan, 1994.

Williams, Bernard. *Moral Luck.* Cambridge: Cambridge University Press, 1981.

______. *Ethics and the Limits of Philosophy.* 2nd ed. London: Fontana, 1993.

Williams, John. 'Nothing Succeeds Like Success? Legitimacy and International Relations'. In Barry Holden, ed., *The Ethical Dimensions of Global Change.* London: Macmillan, 1996.

Index